Ikenaga 2 Jos Leys

"A relatively simple formula can generate immensely complex images." – **Jos Leys**

Investigations

IN NUMBER, DATA, AND SPACE®

Student Activity Book

Common Core Edition

Glenview, Illinois • Boston, Massachusetts
Chandler, Arizona • Upper Saddle River, New Jersey

The Investigations curriculum was developed by TERC, Cambridge, MA.

This material is based on work supported by the National Science Foundation ("NSF") under Grant No.ESI-0095450. Any opinions, findings, and conclusions or recommendations expressed in this material are those of the author(s) and do not necessarily reflect the views of the National Science Foundation.

ISBN-13: 978-0-328-69754-0

ISBN-10: 0-328-69754-0

1 2 3 4 5 6 7 8 9 10 V011 15 14 13 12 11

Ikenaga 2 Jos Leys

"A relatively simple formula can generate immensely complex images." – Jos Leys

Investigations
IN NUMBER, DATA, AND SPACE®

Student Activity Book

Trading Stickers, Combining Coins

UNIT 1

Photographs

Every effort has been made to secure permission and provide appropriate credit for photographic material. The publisher deeply regrets any omission and pledges to correct errors called to its attention in subsequent editions.

Unless otherwise acknowledged, all photographs are the property of Scott Foresman, a division of Pearson Education.

Photo locators denoted as follows: Top (T), Center (C), Bottom (B), Left (L), Right (R), Background (Bkgd).

59 Getty Images

Trading Stickers, Combining Coins

Investigation 1

Investigation 2

Problems for Adding and Subtracting 10s (page 1 of 4)

1. Tori's stickers

Joel's stickers

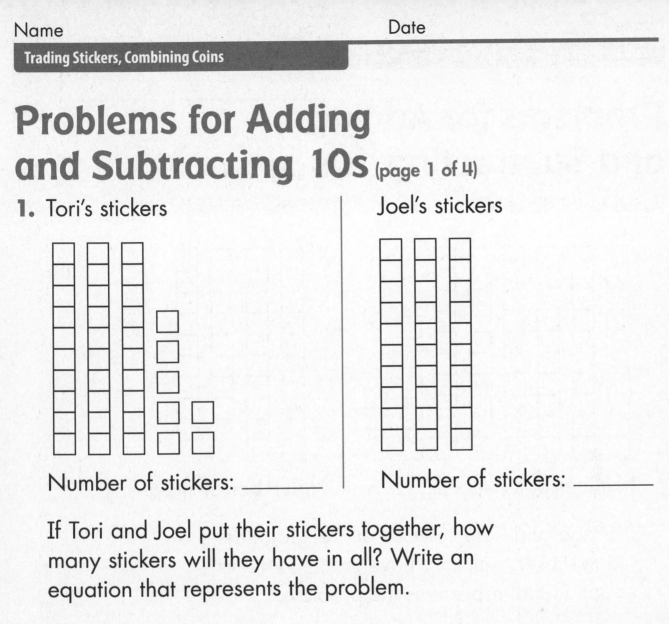

Number of stickers: _____

Number of stickers: _____

If Tori and Joel put their stickers together, how many stickers will they have in all? Write an equation that represents the problem.

Equation: _____

Trading Stickers, Combining Coins

Problems for Adding and Subtracting 10s (page 2 of 4)

2. Diego's stickers   Kate's stickers

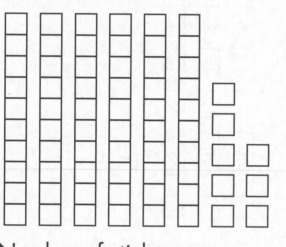

Number of stickers: _____   Number of stickers: _____

If Diego and Kate put their stickers together, how many stickers will they have in all? Write an equation that represents the problem.

Equation: _____

Problems for Adding and Subtracting 10s (page 3 of 4)

Solve the problems below, and show how you got your answers. Remember to write equations for each problem.

3. a. Jasmine went to Sticker Station and bought 62 soccer stickers and 10 dance stickers. How many stickers did she buy?

b. Jasmine went back the next day and bought 20 more stickers. How many stickers does she have now?

4. a. Victor had 82 stickers. He gave 10 to his best friend Noah. How many stickers did Victor have then?

b. Later, Victor gave 20 stickers to his brother and 20 stickers to his sister. How many stickers does Victor have now?

Problems for Adding and Subtracting 10s (page 4 of 4)

Solve the problems below, and show how you got your answers.

5. 27 + 10 = _____

    37 + 10 = _____

    47 + 20 = _____

6. 78 − 10 = _____

    68 − 10 = _____

    58 − 20 = _____

7. Tiana's stickers

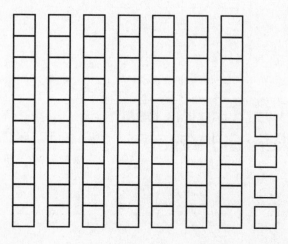

How many stickers does Tiana have? _____

If she gives 20 stickers to Lily and 20 stickers to Justin, how many stickers will she have? _____

How Many Stickers?

NOTE Students practice representing 2-digit numbers using the sticker context.

SMH 6, 7–8

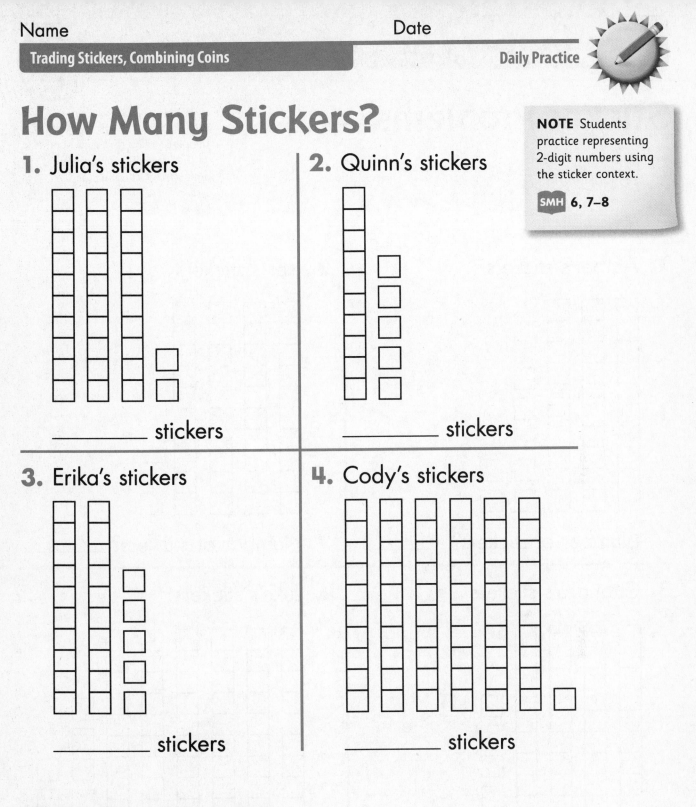

1. Julia's stickers

_____ stickers

2. Quinn's stickers

_____ stickers

3. Erika's stickers

_____ stickers

4. Cody's stickers

_____ stickers

Ongoing Review

5. Find the missing number: 160, 260, 360, 460, _____

A. 860   **B.** 560   **C.** 500   **D.** 480

Sticker Problems (page 1 of 2)

> **NOTE** Students are reviewing the place value of 2-digit numbers as they recognize and represent amounts by using 10s and 1s.
>
> **SMH** 6, 7–8

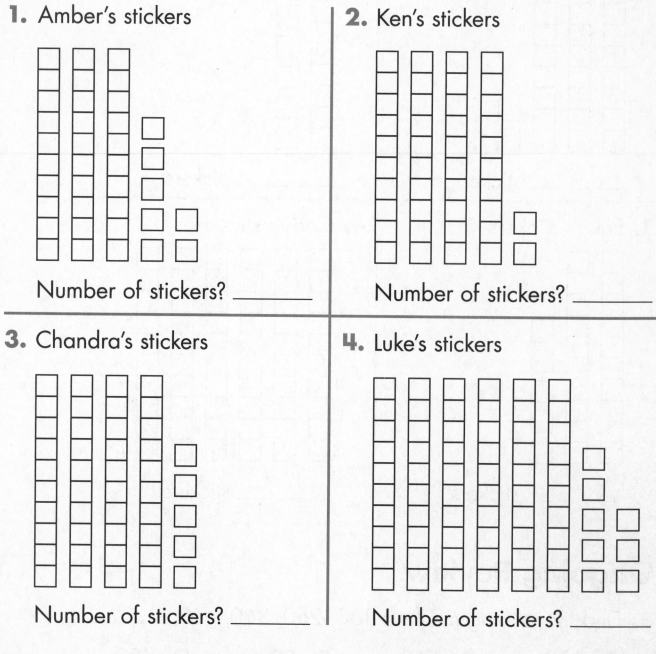

1. Amber's stickers

Number of stickers? _____

2. Ken's stickers

Number of stickers? _____

3. Chandra's stickers

Number of stickers? _____

4. Luke's stickers

Number of stickers? _____

Sticker Problems (page 2 of 2)

5. Show 37 stickers. Use strips of 10 and singles.

6. Show 51 stickers. Use strips of 10 and singles.

Story Problems 1 (page 1 of 2)

For each problem, write an equation that represents the problem. Then solve the problem, and show your work.

1. Maria had 46 stickers. She went to Sticker Station and bought 3 more strips of 10 and 2 singles. How many stickers does Maria have now?

2. Danny had 87 stickers. He gave 35 stickers to his little brother. How many stickers does Danny have now?

3. Ari had 63 baseball cards. His mother gave him her collection of 26 cards. How many baseball cards does he have now?

Story Problems 1 (page 2 of 2)

4. Ms. Ruiz's students baked 75 muffins for the bake sale. They sold 53. How many muffins did they have left?

5. Alex had 72 stickers. He went to Sticker Station and bought 4 strips of 10 and 7 singles. How many stickers does he have now?

6. Deonte counted 47 squirrels on Saturday at the park. He went back on Sunday and counted 42 more. How many squirrels did he count in all?

Adding and Subtracting 10s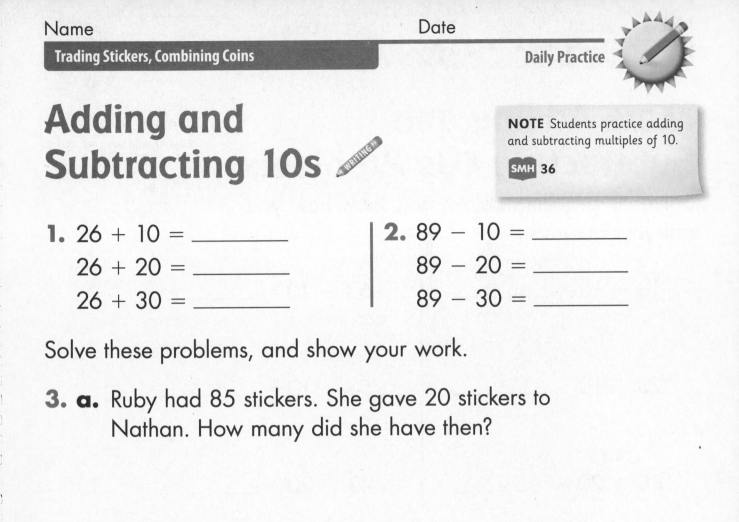

NOTE Students practice adding and subtracting multiples of 10.

SMH 36

1. 26 + 10 = _____

26 + 20 = _____

26 + 30 = _____

2. 89 − 10 = _____

89 − 20 = _____

89 − 30 = _____

Solve these problems, and show your work.

3. a. Ruby had 85 stickers. She gave 20 stickers to Nathan. How many did she have then?

b. Ruby's mother gave her 20 more stickers. How many does Ruby have now?

How did you figure this out?

_____

_____

_____

Ongoing Review

4. 45 + 20 + 10 = _____

A. 65   **B.** 75   **C.** 55   **D.** 30

More Adding and Subtracting 10s Problems

NOTE Students practice adding and subtracting 10 and 20.

SMH 36

Solve the problems below, and show how you got your answers.

1. 18 + 10 = _____

28 + 10 = _____

38 + 20 = _____

2. 63 – 10 = _____

53 – 10 = _____

43 – 20 = _____

3. a. Ashley had 36 stickers. Her father gave her 10 more. How many stickers did she have then?

b. Ashley's mother gave her 20 more stickers. How many does she have now?

Story Problems 2

For each problem, write an equation that represents the problem. Then solve the problem, and show your work.

1. Vanessa went to Sticker Station and bought 6 strips of 10 and 3 single star stickers, and 2 strips of 10 and 9 single moon stickers. How many stickers did Vanessa buy in all?

2. The third and fourth grade students from Lincoln School went to see a mask exhibit at the local art museum. They saw 54 masks from Africa and 32 masks from South America. How many masks did they see in all?

3. Carlos had 58 basketball cards. His friend Marcus gave him 36 more. How many basketball cards does he have now?

Sticker Equations

Figure out how many stickers are shown. Write an equation that represents each group of stickers.

NOTE Students review the place value of 2-digit numbers as they recognize and represent amounts by using 10s and 1s.

SMH 6, 7–8

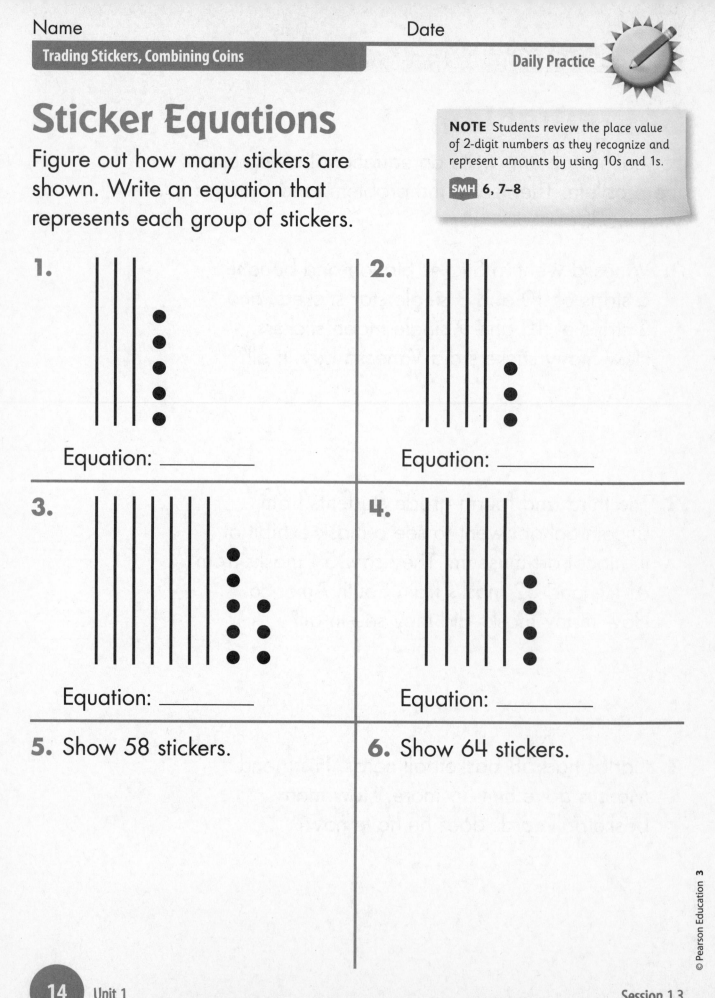

1.

Equation: _____

2.

Equation: _____

3.

Equation: _____

4.

Equation: _____

5. Show 58 stickers.

6. Show 64 stickers.

How Many More Stickers to Get 100? (page 1 of 2)

Solve each problem below, and record your strategy by using equations. If you used 100 grids, the 100 chart, or the class number line, show how you used those tools.

1. Misaki went to Sticker Station. She bought 28 animal stickers. How many more does she need to have 100 animal stickers?

2. Ryan bought 43 flower stickers at Sticker Station. How many more does he need to have 100 flower stickers?

How Many More Stickers to Get 100? (page 2 of 2)

3a. Ana went to Sticker Station on Tuesday and bought 37 airplane stickers. On Friday, she bought 42 more. How many does she have now?

3b. How many more stickers does Ana need to have 100 airplane stickers?

4a. Derek has 24 baseball stickers. He went to Sticker Station and bought 35 more baseball stickers. How many does he have now?

4b. How many more stickers does Derek need to have 100 baseball stickers?

Addition Problems

Solve these problems, and show your work.

NOTE Students solve addition problems in which the sum of the ones digits is greater than 10.

1. Kayla bought 25 animal stickers and 27 star stickers. How many stickers did she buy?

2. Cesar has 19 guppies. His friend Sara moved away and gave him her 26 guppies. How many guppies does he have now?

3. 33 + 27 = _____

4. 33 + 28 = _____

Ongoing Review

5. 27 + 27 = _____

    A. 54   **B.** 56   **C.** 44   **D.** 414

Story Problems 3

Write an equation that represents the problem. Then solve the problem, and show your work.

> **NOTE** These problems provide practice adding and subtracting 2-digit numbers. Ask your child to explain how he or she solved each problem.

1. Seth went to Sticker Station. He bought 3 strips of 10 and 6 single soccer stickers, and 8 strips of 10 and 3 single animal stickers. How many stickers did Seth buy?

2. Janelle collected bottles to bring to the recycling center. She collected 64 bottles on Saturday and 55 on Sunday. How many bottles did she bring to the recycling center?

3. James had 67 marbles. He gave 30 of the marbles to his sister. How many marbles does he have now?

Trading Stickers, Combining Coins

Capture 5 Recording Sheet

Record your starting number, the changes you use,
and your ending number for each move, like this:

16 + 10 + 10 − 2 = 34

_____

_____

_____

_____

_____

_____

_____

_____

_____

Dimes and Pennies

NOTE Students practice breaking up 2-digit numbers into 10s and 1s as they find combinations of dimes and pennies that equal a given amount.

SMH 9, 37–38

1. Show three ways to make 41¢, using dimes and pennies.

2. Show three ways to make 87¢, using dimes and pennies.

Collect $2.00 Recording Sheet

Play *Collect $2.00*. On each turn, write down the
amount you collect and the total you have.

	How much did you collect?	How much money do you have now?		How much did you collect?	How much money do you have now?
Turn 1			Turn 16		
Turn 2			Turn 17		
Turn 3			Turn 18		
Turn 4			Turn 19		
Turn 5			Turn 20		
Turn 6			Turn 21		
Turn 7			Turn 22		
Turn 8			Turn 23		
Turn 9			Turn 24		
Turn 10			Turn 25		
Turn 11			Turn 26		
Turn 12			Turn 27		
Turn 13			Turn 28		
Turn 14			Turn 29		
Turn 15			Turn 30		

Trading Stickers, Combining Coins

How Many More to 100?
How Much More to $1.00? (page 1 of 2)

Use a number line to solve these two problems.
Write equations to represent each step.

1. Lexi has 37¢. She wants to buy a comic book
that costs $1.00. How much more money does
she need?

2. Matt is reading a book with 100 pages. He has
read 56 pages so far. How many more pages
must he read to finish the book?

Trading Stickers, Combining Coins

How Many More to 100?
How Much More to $1.00? (page 2 of 2)

Solve these two problems. Use a number line to
show your strategy for the second part of each one.
Write equations that represent your work.

3. a. The third-grade students in Mr. Fisher's
   class want to read 100 chapter books by
   Thanksgiving. In September, they read
   26 books. In October, they read 37.
   How many books have they read so far? _____

b. How many books do they need to read in
   November to reach their goal of 100?

$$\longleftrightarrow$$

4. a. Kevin's little sister had 33 cents in her
   piggy bank. Kevin gave her 25 cents
   more. How much money does she have now? _____

b. How much more does she need to have $1.00?

$$\longleftrightarrow$$

Problems for *Capture 5*

Ava and Leo are playing *Capture 5*.

NOTE Students solve problems that involve adding and subtracting multiples of 10.

SMH 20–24, 36

1. Ava's game piece is on 36. She wants to capture a chip that is on 72.

| −10 | +30 | −1 | +1 | −2 |

Can she do it with these Change Cards? If so, how? If not, explain why not.

2. Leo's game piece is on 50. There are three chips left on 6, 39, and 73.

| +20 | −30 | +2 | −1 | −3 |

Can Leo capture any of the chips with these Change Cards? If so, how? If not, explain why not.

Writing Equations for *Capture 5*

NOTE This homework is based on a math game that students have been playing in which they practice adding and subtracting 10s and 1s and writing equations.

SMH 20–24, 36

1. Michelle's game piece was on 58. She used these cards to capture a chip:

| +2 | +30 | +2 |

Where did she land? Write an equation to show her moves.

Equation: _____

2. Jamal's game piece was on 19. He used these cards to capture a chip:

| +30 | −10 | −2 |

Where did he land? Write an equation to show his moves.

Equation: _____

How Many More?
How Much More? (page 1 of 3)

Solve each problem, and record your strategies by using equations. If you use 100 grids or number lines to solve the problems, show how you used those tools.

1. a. Diana bought 28 balloon stickers at the Sticker Station. Her sister gave her 23 more. How many does she have now?

b. How many more does she need to have 100?

2. a. Lily and Andre want to collect 100 cans for a food drive for people without homes. Lily collected 47, and Andre collected 31. How many cans have they collected so far?

b. How many more do they need to have 100 cans?

How Many More?
How Much More? (page 2 of 3)

3. Taylor has 47¢. She wants to buy a notebook that costs $1.00. How much more money does she need?

4. a. Jack's mother gave him 75¢ on Monday. His father gave him 50¢ on Tuesday. How much money does he have now?

b. Jack wants to buy a ticket for the magic show at the science museum. The ticket costs $2.00. How much more money does he need?

How Many More?
How Much More? (page 3 of 3)

5. Sue and Alondra are planning a children's art show. They want to have 100 pieces of art in the show. So far, children have given them 68 pieces of art. How many more do they need to have 100 pieces for their art show?

6. a. Luis has collected 88 basketball stickers. Tomorrow he plans to buy 30 more. How many basketball stickers will he have then?

b. How many more would Luis need to have 200 basketball stickers?

How Many More to 50?

Solve each problem, and show your work.

NOTE Students practice finding combinations of numbers that equal 50.

SMH 32–35

1. 14 + _____ = 50

2. 32 + _____ = 50

3. 8 + _____ = 50

4. 26 + _____ = 50

5. 41 + _____ = 50

6. 12 + _____ = 50

137 Stickers (page 1 of 2)

Show all of the ways you can think of to make the number 137 with stickers.

Sheets of 100	Strips of 10	Singles

137 Stickers (page 2 of 2)

Sheets of 100	Strips of 10	Singles

Flag Stickers

NOTE Students practice making representations of numbers using 100s, 10s, and 1s.

SMH 7–8, 9

1. Leslie bought 158 flag stickers. They come in sheets of 100, strips of 10, and singles. Sketch at least five different combinations for 158. Write an equation for each combination.

Ongoing Review

2. How many stickers are represented by this sketch?

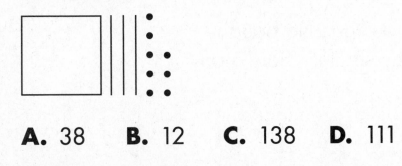

A. 38   **B.** 12   **C.** 138   **D.** 111

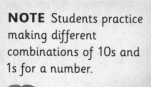

Problems for 78 Stickers

Solve the problems below, and show your work.
Write an equation for each combination of
strips and singles.

> **NOTE** Students practice
> making different
> combinations of 10s and
> 1s for a number.
>
> **SMH** 9

1. Emma bought 78 stickers at Sticker Station.
She bought 7 strips of 10 and some singles.
How many singles did she buy?

70 + _____ = 78

2. Kiara bought 78 stickers as well. She bought
6 strips of 10 and some singles. How many
singles did she buy?

3. Joshua bought 78 stickers, too. He bought
4 strips of 10 and some singles. How many
singles did he buy?

4. David also bought 78 stickers. He bought
2 strips of 10 and many singles. How many
singles did he buy?

Adding Multiples of 10

Solve these problems. Fill in each sum on the 100 chart below.

NOTE Students review adding multiples of 10 and locating numbers on the 100 chart.

SMH 14, 36

1. 66 + 10 = _____   **2.** 31 + 40 = _____

3. 16 + 20 = _____   **4.** 24 + 40 = _____

5. 13 + 10 = _____   **6.** 28 + 30 = _____

7. 53 + 20 = _____   **8.** 50 + 40 = _____

9. 15 + 30 = _____   **10.** 9 + 20 = _____

11. 22 + 60 = _____   **12.** 27 + 20 = _____

		3			6				
								19	
21									
		33							40
	42								
	52								
		63					68		
									80
			84						
91						97			

Addition Card Categories

After sorting your addition cards into categories, write each combination in the correct space below.

For example, 9 + 1 = _____ will go in the space labeled *Make 10 Combinations*.

Make 10 Combinations	Doubles
Near Doubles (Doubles Plus or Minus 1)	**Plus 10 Combinations**
Plus 9 Combinations	**Remaining Combinations**

Using the Number Line

Use a number line to solve these problems.
Write an equation to represent each step.

NOTE Students solve missing addend problems and represent their solutions on number lines and with equations.

SMH 26–28, 32–34

1. Marisa has 63¢. She wants to buy a book for $1.00. How much more money does she need?

⟵————————————————————⟶

2. Amir is reading a book with 100 pages. He has read 13 pages so far. How many more pages must he read to finish the book?

⟵————————————————————⟶

Ongoing Review

3. 22 + _____ = 100

   A. 88   **B.** 122   **C.** 76   **D.** 78

Practice with Addition Combinations

NOTE Students are reviewing the addition combinations (addition "facts") they worked on in Grade 2 and practicing those they don't yet know. Ask your child to explain how the clues help with these combinations.

 SMH 16–19

1. Which addition combinations are you practicing?

_____   _____

_____   _____

_____   _____

2. Write two addition combinations that are hard for you, and explain what helps you remember them.

Addition combination: _____

What helps me:

_____

_____

Addition combination: _____

What helps me:

_____

_____

3. How did you practice your addition combinations? Who helped you?

_____

_____

_____

_____

Trading Stickers, Combining Coins

Close to 100 Recording Sheet

Game 1   Score

Round 1: _____ + _____ = _____   _____

Round 2: _____ + _____ = _____   _____

Round 3: _____ + _____ = _____   _____

Round 4: _____ + _____ = _____   _____

Round 5: _____ + _____ = _____   _____

TOTAL SCORE _____

Game 1   Score

Round 1: _____ + _____ = _____   _____

Round 2: _____ + _____ = _____   _____

Round 3: _____ + _____ = _____   _____

Round 4: _____ + _____ = _____   _____

Round 5: _____ + _____ = _____   _____

TOTAL SCORE _____

Related Problem Sets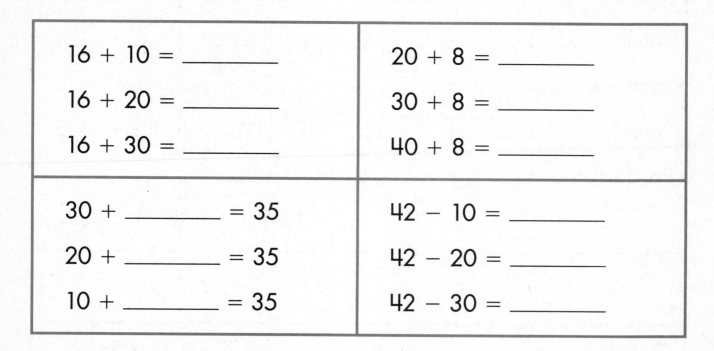

Solve the following sets of related problems.
Think about how you would use one problem
to solve the next one in the set.

NOTE Students solve
related addition and
subtraction problems.

SMH 31

16 + 10 = _____	20 + 8 = _____
16 + 20 = _____	30 + 8 = _____
16 + 30 = _____	40 + 8 = _____
30 + _____ = 35	42 − 10 = _____
20 + _____ = 35	42 − 20 = _____
10 + _____ = 35	42 − 30 = _____

Do you notice any patterns in the answers
in each set? Choose one set and describe
the pattern you see. Explain why
you think that pattern is happening.

Problems for *Close to 100* (page 1 of 2)

1. Tom and Shanice are playing *Close to 100*.

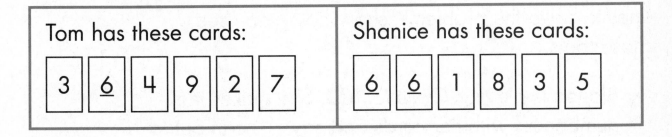

Tom has these cards:

| 3 | 6̲ | 4 | 9 | 2 | 7 |

Shanice has these cards:

| 6̲ | 6̲ | 1 | 8 | 3 | 5 |

Find the 4 cards that will get each player as close to 100 as possible.

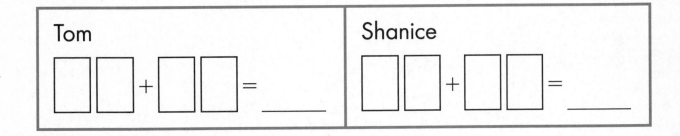

Tom

☐☐ + ☐☐ = ____

Shanice

☐☐ + ☐☐ = ____

2. Who is closer to 100? _____

3. Choose either Tom's or Shanice's hand. Explain how you chose which cards to use to get as close to 100 as possible.

Problems for *Close to 100* (page 2 of 2)

Solve each problem, and record your strategy by using equations. If you use 100 grids or number lines to solve the problems, show how you used those tools.

4. Bianca is playing *Close to 100*. She makes the number 57 with her cards and says, "I can get to 100 exactly." What 2-digit number will she make to get to 100 exactly? Explain how you know.

5. Caleb is playing *Close to 100*. He makes the number 31 with his cards and says, "I can get to 100, too." What 2-digit number will he make to get to 100 exactly? Explain how you know.

Sums That Equal 100

Solve these problems and show your work.

NOTE Students practice finding sums that equal 100.

SMH 32, G5

1. _____ + 37 = 100

2. 27 + _____ = 100

3. _____ + 63 = 100

4. 53 + _____ = 100

5. 25 + 15 + 25 + _____ = 100

More Problems for *Close to 100*

NOTE Students practice finding pairs of 2-digit numbers that add to 100. Ask your child to explain how he or she chose which cards to use.

SMH G5

Suppose that you are dealt these hands in the game *Close to 100*. Which numbers would you make to get sums as close to 100 as possible?

1.

| 8 | 5 | 2 | 7 | 1 | 3 |

Score

_____ _____ + _____ _____ = _____

2.

| 1 | 7 | 0 | 8 | 2 | 9 |

Score

_____ _____ + _____ _____ = _____

3.

| 4 | 3 | 6 | 1 | 2 | 7 |

Score

_____ _____ + _____ _____ = _____

Make a Dollar Recording Sheet

Write an equation for each pair of cards that you
find that add to $1.00.

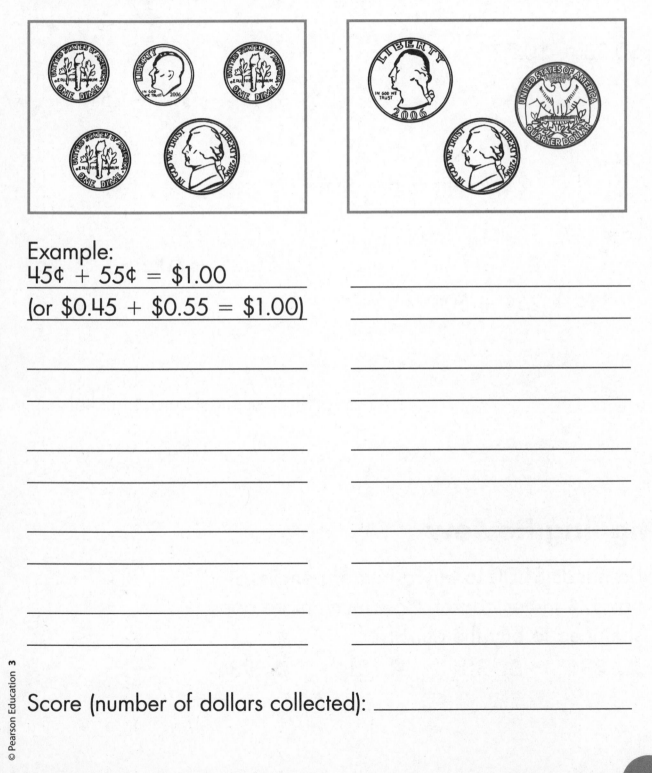

Example:
45¢ + 55¢ = $1.00
(or $0.45 + $0.55 = $1.00)

Score (number of dollars collected): _____

Adding to Make $1.00

1. Circle the combinations that equal $1.00.

NOTE Students practice finding combinations of amounts of money with sums of $1.00.

SMH 25, 37–38

62¢ + 38¢

$0.33 + $0.77

25¢ + 19¢ + 31¢ + 25¢

2 quarters and 4 dimes

$0.25 + $0.25 + $0.25

35¢ + 25¢ + 50¢

1 quarter, 7 dimes, and 1 nickel

Ongoing Review

2. Lia needs $1.00 to buy a box of pencils. She has 17¢ in her pocket. How much more does she need to buy the pencils?

A. 83¢   **B.** 30¢   **C.** 31¢   **D.** 93¢

dding Up Coins (page 2 of 2)

Savanna is trying to make a dollar.
She chooses the following card:

a. How much money is
shown on Savanna's card? _____

b. How much more does
she need to make $1.00? _____

c. Draw coins on the blank card below that
equal the amount she needs to make $1.00.
Draw circles, and write the amount of each coin.

© Pearson Education 3

Adding Up Coins (page 1 of 2)

1. What is the total value of these coins?
Show how you figured it out.

NOTE Stude
adding money
different com
to equal the s

SMH 25, 37-

2. Show two different ways to make 96¢
with coins.

Story Problems 4

Solve each problem, show your work, and write an equation.

1. 67 third graders and 53 fourth graders went on a field trip to the art museum. How many students went on the field trip in all?

2. Tasha had $2.00. At the store, she bought a notebook that cost 68¢. How much money does she have now?

3. Robby brought bottles and cans to the recycling center. He got $1.25 for the cans and $0.55 for the bottles. How much money did he get in all?

At the Corner Store

Solve the problems, and show your work.

NOTE Students add and subtract amounts of money.

SMH 20–24, 32–34

Here are some things that are for sale at the corner store.

Notebook	$0.68	Calendar	$1.10
Pen	$0.47	Magnet	$0.52
Ruler	$0.43	Buttons	$0.80

1. Grace has $2.00. What could she buy that would cost exactly $2.00? Show how you know.

2. Juan bought a notebook and a pen. How much change would he get from $2.00?

Ongoing Review

3. 10 + _____ = 20 + 110

   A. 100   **B.** 120   **C.** 140   **D.** 30

Trading Stickers, Combining Coins

Sheets, Strips, and Singles

1. Tyrell bought 163 stickers at Sticker Station. Show at least two combinations of sheets, strips, and singles that he could have bought to equal 163 stickers. Use at least one sheet, one strip, and one single in each combination.

Sheets of 100	Strips of 10	Singles

2. Show at least two ways that Tyrell could have bought 163 stickers if he bought only strips of 10 and singles.

Strips of 10	Singles

Twice as Nice

Think about doubles as you solve
each problem.

NOTE Students practice solving story
problems by using addition.

SMH 20–24

1. There are 36 crayons in one box of crayons.
How many crayons are in two boxes?

2. There are 15 fish in one tank and the same
number in another tank. How many fish are in
the two tanks?

3. Faith has two rows of tomato plants. Each row
has 43 plants. How many tomato plants are in
the two rows?

4. There are 12 eggs in one dozen. How many
eggs are in two dozen?

5. There are 30 books on each shelf in Mr. Woo's
classroom. How many books are on two shelves?

Practice with Addition Combinations 2

1. Which addition combinations are you practicing?

NOTE Students are reviewing the addition combinations (addition "facts") they worked on in Grade 2 and practicing those they don't yet know. Ask your child to explain how the clues help with these combinations.

SMH 16–19

_____   _____

_____   _____

_____   _____

2. Write two addition combinations that are hard for you, and explain what helps you remember them.

Addition combination: _____

What helps me:

_____

_____

Addition combination: _____

What helps me:

_____

_____

3. How did you practice your addition combinations? Who helped you?

_____

_____

_____

_____

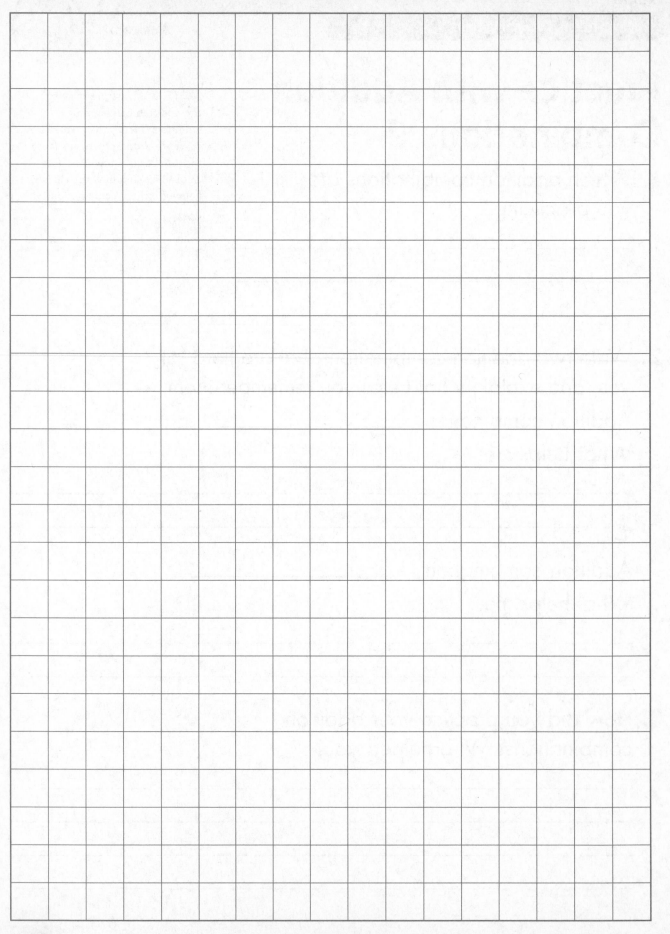

Hundreds, Tens, and Ones Problems ✏️ WRITING

Solve each problem, show your work, and write an equation.

1. a. Oops! Jake is playing *Collect $2.00*, but he keeps forgetting to trade his coins. He has 14 dimes and 37 pennies. How much money does he have? _____

b. How much more money does Jake need to get to $2.00? _____

2. Colette wants to put stickers in her sticker book. She has 15 strips of 10 and 3 singles. How many pages of 100 can she fill? How many stickers will she have left over for the next page? _____

Explain how you know.

3. Abby's mother needs dimes for the parking meter near her work. She has a one-dollar bill and 28 pennies in her wallet. How many dimes can she trade the dollar and 28 pennies for? _____ How many pennies will she have left over? _____

NOTE Students add and subtract amounts of money.

Going Shopping

Solve the problems, and show your work.

Here are some things that are on sale at the market this week.

Apple	$0.38	Can of peaches	$1.11
Berries	$0.99	Vegetable soup	$0.89
Raisins	$0.62	Carrots	$1.01

1. Tyler bought an apple and some berries. How much change did he get from $2.00?

2. Celia bought two of these items. She spent exactly $2.00. What could the two items be?

How do you know?

Practice with Addition Combinations 3

NOTE Students are reviewing the addition combinations (addition "facts") they worked on in Grade 2 and practicing those they don't yet know. Ask your child to explain how the clues help with these combinations.

SMH 16–19

1. Which addition combinations are you practicing?

_____   _____

_____   _____

_____   _____

2. Write two addition combinations that are hard for you, and explain what helps you remember them.

Addition combination: _____

What helps me:

_____

_____

Addition combination: _____

What helps me:

_____

_____

3. How did you practice your addition combinations? Who helped you?

_____

_____

_____

_____

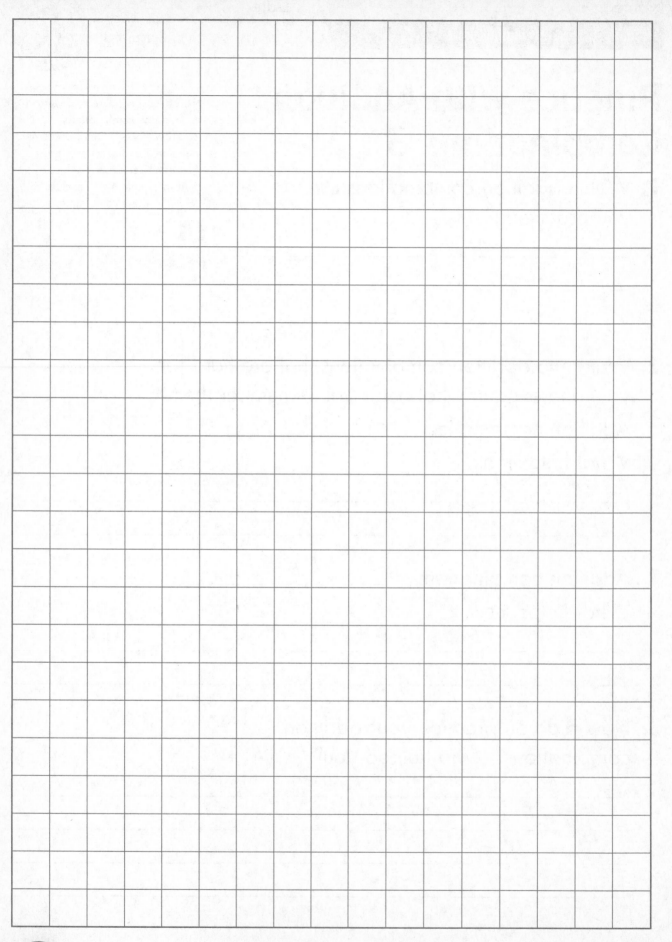

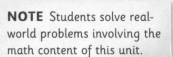

Selling Lemonade

Solve the problems, and show your work.

Kim, Gina, and Adam sell cups of lemonade to collect money for their school fund. Here are the prices.

⬭	small	$0.10
⬭	medium	$0.15
⬭	large	$0.20

1. In one hour, they sold 2 small cups, 3 medium cups, and 1 large cup. How much money did they make? _____

2. In another hour, they made $1.00 altogether. What could they have sold? _____

3. In a third hour, they made $2.00 altogether. What could they have sold? _____

Ikenaga 2 Jos Leys

"A relatively simple formula can generate immensely complex images." – **Jos Leys**

Investigations

IN NUMBER, DATA, AND SPACE®

Surveys and Line Plots

Investigation 3

What Did You Find Out About Ms. Cutter's Grade 3 Class? ✎

1. What is your question about Ms. Cutter's class?

_____

_____

_____

_____

2. List three things you found out from the data.

a. _____

_____

_____

b. _____

_____

_____

c. _____

_____

_____

Related Problem Sets

Solve the following sets of related problems. How can you use one problem to solve the next one?

NOTE Students practice solving addition and subtraction problems in related sets.

SMH **36**

1. $78 - 10 =$ _____

$78 - 20 =$ _____

$78 - 30 =$ _____

$78 - 40 =$ _____

2. $80 + $ _____ $= 84$

$70 + $ _____ $= 84$

$40 + $ _____ $= 84$

$20 + $ _____ $= 84$

3. $50 + 36 =$ _____

$60 + 36 =$ _____

$70 + 36 =$ _____

$80 + 36 =$ _____

4. $95 - 20 =$ _____

$95 - 40 =$ _____

$95 - 60 =$ _____

$95 - 80 =$ _____

Popular Pets

Here are data from Mr. Garcia's third-grade
class about the pets that students have at home.

NOTE Students organize
data and list what they
know from the data.

SMH 90–91

dog	cat	hamster	dog	lizard	cat
hamster	fish	bird	dog	fish	hamster
cat	bird	cat	cat	lizard	dog
dog	fish	dog	bird	hamster	dog

1. Organize the data above in a way that makes
sense to you.

2. What can you say about the pets that students in
Mr. Garcia's class have?

3. How many students gave "cat" as their answer
to the question?

Subtraction and the 100 Chart

NOTE Students practice subtracting 10 and multiples of 10 from any number, and then they fill in the missing numbers on the 100 Chart.

SMH 36

Solve these problems. Fill in the totals on the 100 Chart.

$63 - 10 =$ _____ $85 - 30 =$ _____ $52 - 50 =$ _____

$96 - 30 =$ _____ $74 - 40 =$ _____ $41 - 30 =$ _____

$76 - 50 =$ _____ $18 - 10 =$ _____ $89 - 60 =$ _____

$66 - 20 =$ _____ $98 - 40 =$ _____ $57 - 30 =$ _____

		3			6				10
								19	
21				25					
		33					38		
	42		44						50
						57			
			64				68		
71				75					80
		83						89	
91					96				

© Pearson Education 3

What Is the Rule?

How do the things in the first group go together? Write the rule.

NOTE Students determine the rule by which objects have been sorted.

SMH 90–91

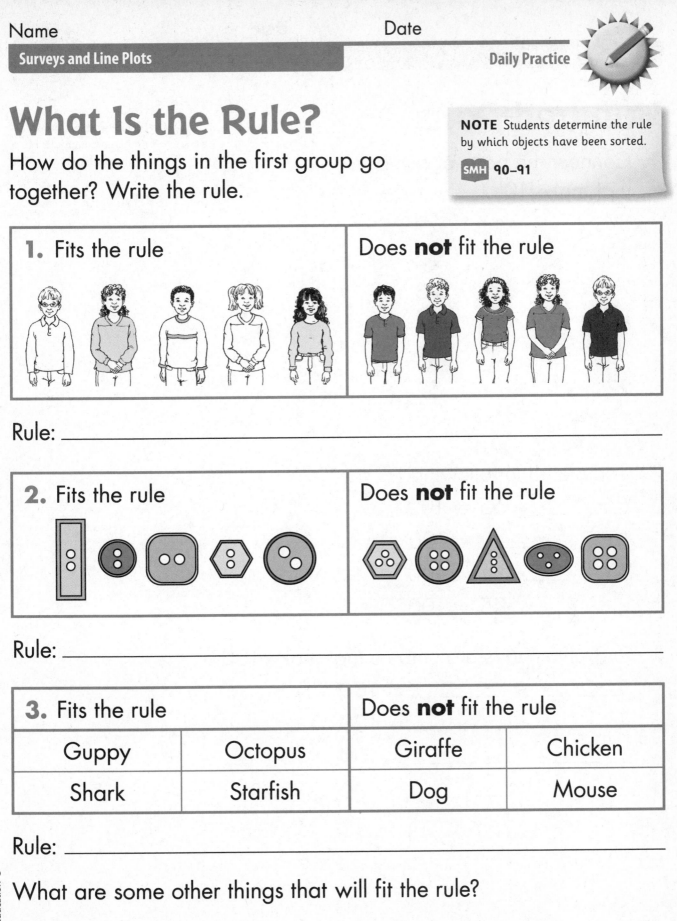

1. Fits the rule — Does **not** fit the rule

Rule: _____

2. Fits the rule — Does **not** fit the rule

Rule: _____

3. Fits the rule		Does **not** fit the rule	
Guppy	Octopus	Giraffe	Chicken
Shark	Starfish	Dog	Mouse

Rule: _____

What are some other things that will fit the rule?

_____

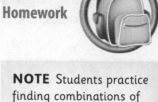

Hundred Pairs

1. Connect the pairs of numbers that make 100.

37	29
48	32
71	73
81	96
68	63
27	52
	19

2. Complete the following.

_____ + 55 = 100

15 + _____ = 100

30 + _____ = 100

_____ + 45 = 100

3. Find other pairs of numbers that make 100.

_____ + _____ = 100

_____ + _____ = 100

_____ + _____ = 100

_____ + _____ = 100

How Do You Get to School? (page 1 of 3)

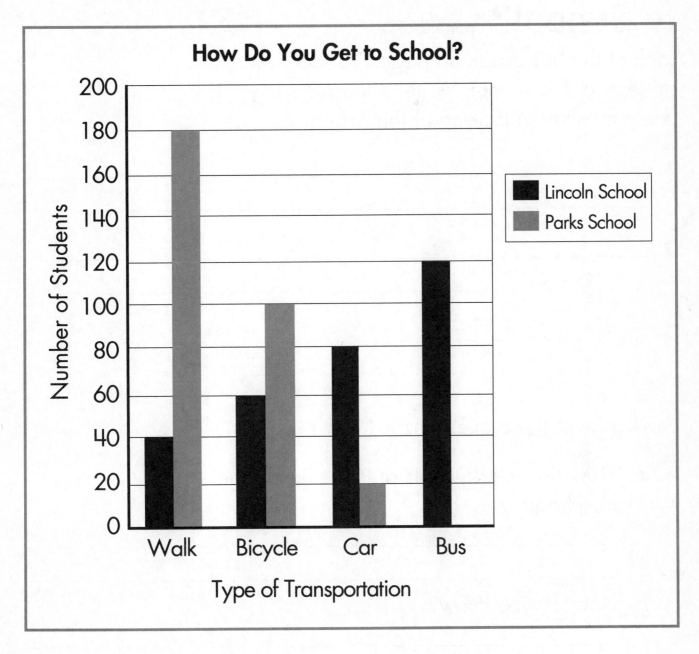

How Do You Get to School?

Number of Students (y-axis: 0, 20, 40, 60, 80, 100, 120, 140, 160, 180, 200)

Type of Transportation (x-axis: Walk, Bicycle, Car, Bus)

Legend: Lincoln School, Parks School

How Do You Get to School? (page 2 of 3)

Look at the bar graph on page 7 about how students get to school. Write at least 3 things you can tell from looking at this graph.

1. _____

   _____

2. _____

   _____

3. _____

   _____

Now answer these questions:

4. **a.** How do most students at Parks School get to school?

   _____

   _____

   b. How do you know?

   _____

   _____

How Do You Get to School? (page 3 of 3)

5. At Lincoln School, how many students take the bus?

_____

6. At Lincoln School, how many students either walk or ride a bike?

_____

7. a. How many students at Parks School do **not** walk to school?

_____

b. How do you know?

_____

_____

8. Compare how students travel to school at Lincoln School and Parks School. Are the ways the same or different? What might be some reasons for the similarities or differences?

_____

_____

_____

_____

How Many More to 100?

Solve the following problems and show your solutions on the number lines provided.

NOTE Students practice finding combinations of 2-digit numbers that add up to 100.

SMH 15, 27, 29

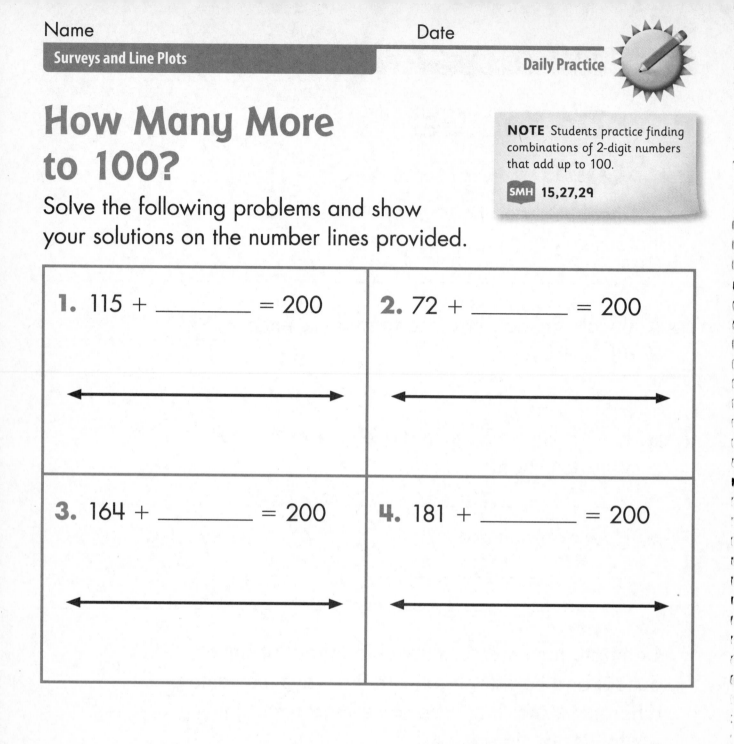

1. $115 + \underline{\hspace{2cm}} = 200$

2. $72 + \underline{\hspace{2cm}} = 200$

3. $164 + \underline{\hspace{2cm}} = 200$

4. $181 + \underline{\hspace{2cm}} = 200$

What Is Your Favorite Season?

NOTE Students read and interpret data from a bar graph.

SMH 92

Use the bar graph to answer the questions below.

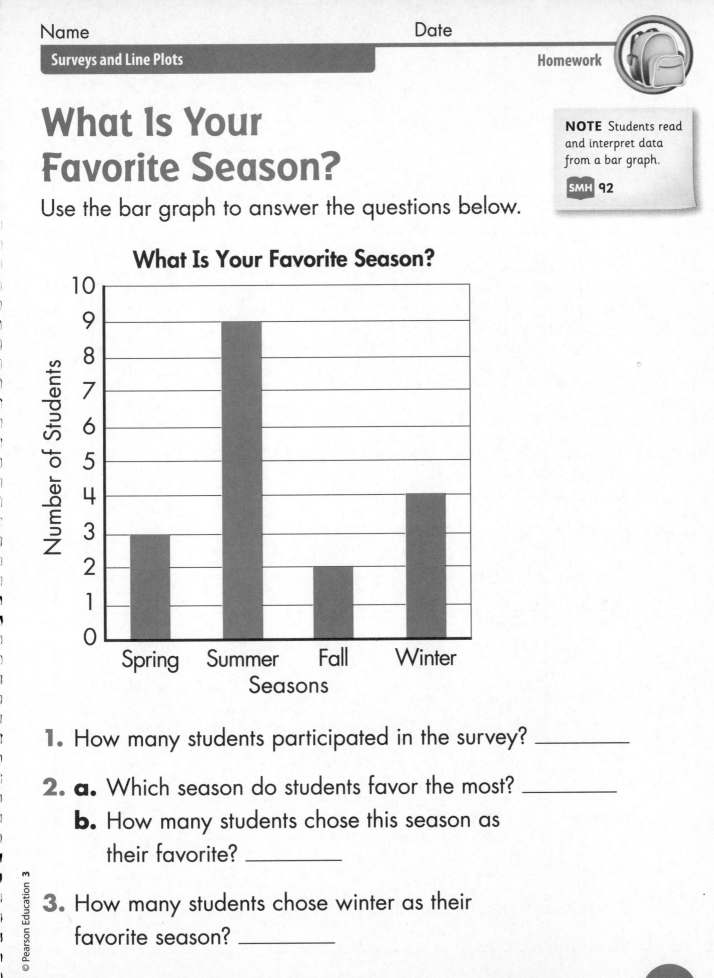

What Is Your Favorite Season?

1. How many students participated in the survey? _____

2. **a.** Which season do students favor the most? _____

   b. How many students chose this season as their favorite? _____

3. How many students chose winter as their favorite season? _____

12 Unit 2

What Is Your Favorite Mealtime? (page 1 of 2)

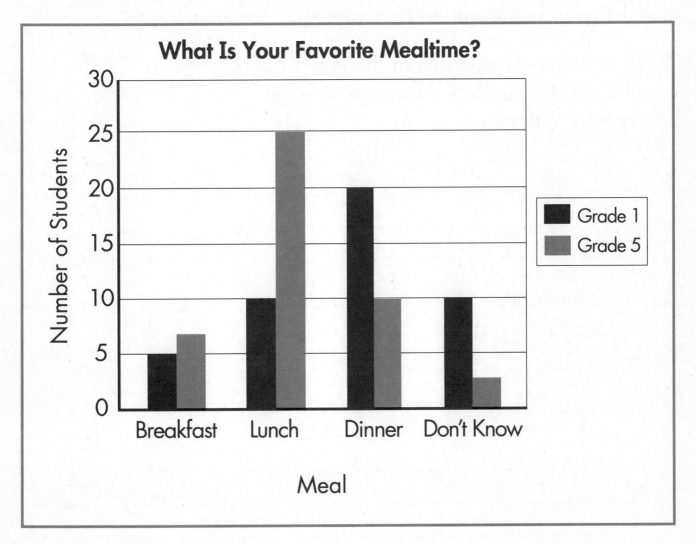

What Is Your Favorite Mealtime? (page 2 of 2) ✎ WRITING

Use the graph on page 13 to answer the questions.

1. Compare the responses of the first graders and the fifth graders. How are they the same or different?

_____

_____

_____

_____

2. Write three other things you can tell from looking at the graph.

a. _____

_____

_____

_____

b. _____

_____

_____

_____

c. _____

_____

_____

_____

What Is the Missing Number?

NOTE Students review addition combinations up to 10 + 10.

SMH 16–19

Fill in the missing numbers for each addition combination in the chart.

8 + 5 = _____	_____ + 7 = 11	3 + _____ = 12
_____ + 9 = 16	4 + _____ = 8	6 + 4 = _____
3 + _____ = 9	9 + 4 = _____	7 + _____ = 11
8 + _____ = 18	8 + 7 = _____	5 + 7 = _____
10 + _____ = 19	_____ + 6 = 12	9 + _____ = 18
5 + 6 = _____	10 + 6 = _____	_____ + 3 = 9
8 + _____ = 17	3 + _____ = 11	_____ + 4 = 9
5 + 8 = _____	_____ + 6 = 14	9 + _____ = 14
3 + 7 = _____	7 + _____ = 15	10 + 7 = _____

Coin Combinations

How many of each coin would
you use to make the total amount?

NOTE Students practice finding combinations
of coins that equal a given amount.

SMH 37–38

Total Amount	(quarter)	(dime)	(nickel)	(penny)
41¢				
67¢				
33¢				
99¢				
84¢				
22¢				
Find several different ways to make 55¢.				

Displaying Data

NOTE Students group a given set of data.

SMH 90–91

1. How could you group these students?
   Make a graph to represent your data.

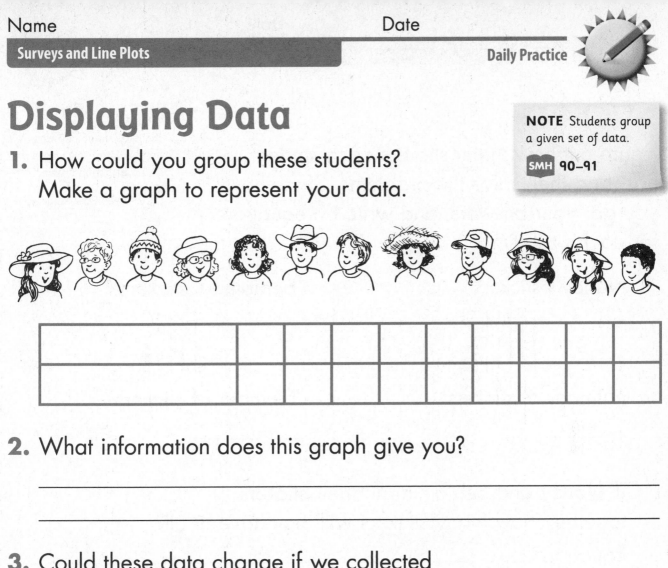

2. What information does this graph give you?

   _____

   _____

3. Could these data change if we collected
   information from a different group of students?
   Why or why not?

   _____

   _____

Ongoing Review

4. Leo, Mai, and Louis have a total of 15 pockets.
   Which shows a way the children could be
   wearing 15 pockets altogether?

   A. 10 + 8 + 1   **B.** 9 + 2 + 5

   C. 7 + 3 + 5   **D.** 6 + 5 + 2

Stickers

Figure out how many stickers each student has, and then solve the problems. Show how you got your answers, and write an equation for each problem.

NOTE Students review the place value of 2-digit numbers and solve addition and subtraction problems.

SMH **7–8, 20–24, 32–35**

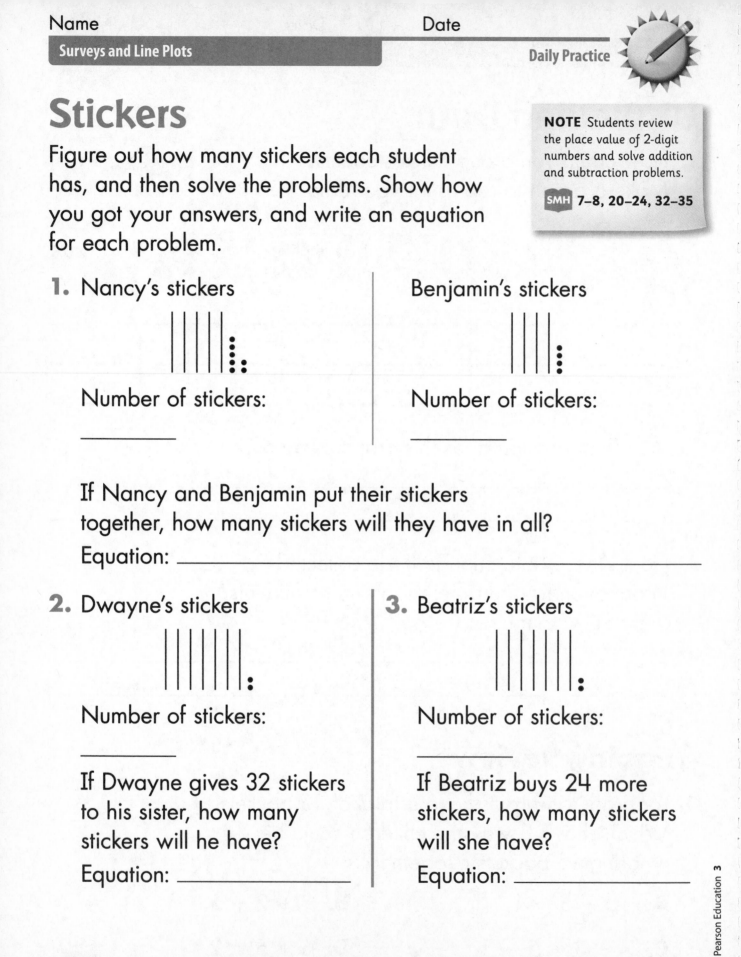

1. Nancy's stickers

Number of stickers:

_____

Benjamin's stickers

Number of stickers:

_____

If Nancy and Benjamin put their stickers together, how many stickers will they have in all?

Equation: _____

2. Dwayne's stickers

Number of stickers:

_____

If Dwayne gives 32 stickers to his sister, how many stickers will he have?

Equation: _____

3. Beatriz's stickers

Number of stickers:

_____

If Beatriz buys 24 more stickers, how many stickers will she have?

Equation: _____

What Is Your Favorite Fruit?

NOTE Students compare two sets of data on a bar graph.

SMH 93–94

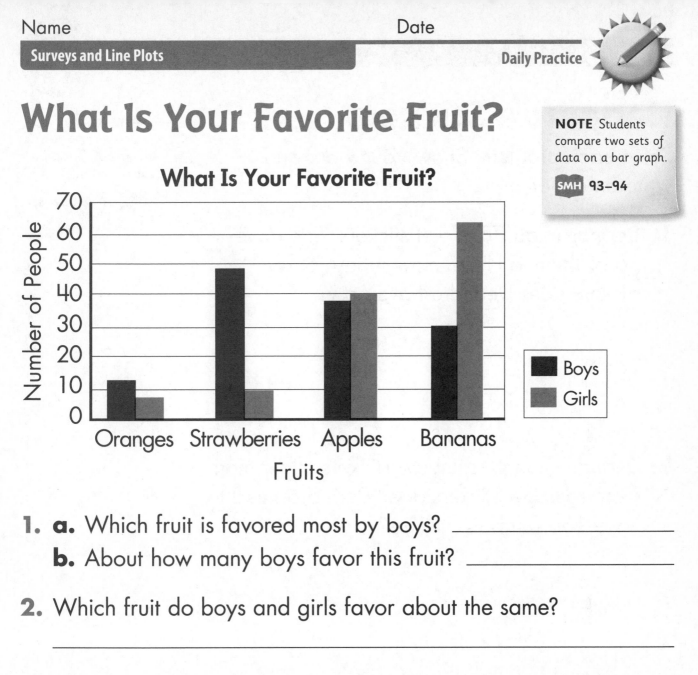

What Is Your Favorite Fruit?

1. **a.** Which fruit is favored most by boys? _____

   b. About how many boys favor this fruit? _____

2. Which fruit do boys and girls favor about the same?

   _____

3. What are 2 things that you see from looking at this graph? Use words such as *about half, more/less than half, very few,* or *almost all* to describe the data.

   _____

   _____

Ongoing Review

4. Which fruit is favored most by girls?

   A. Oranges   **B.** Strawberries   **C.** Apples   **D.** Bananas

Deondra's Stickers

Solve each problem. Show your work and write an equation.

NOTE Students solve 2-digit addition and subtraction problems about stickers.

SMH 20–24, 32–35

1. Deondra had 78 rocket stickers. She gave 36 of them to Philip. How many rocket stickers does Deondra have now?

2. Deondra has 47 rainbow stickers. How many more rainbow stickers does Deondra need to have 100 rainbow stickers?

3. On Monday, Deondra bought 45 planet stickers. On Tuesday, her mother gave her 58 more. How many planet stickers does Deondra have now?

How Many Years in This School? (page 1 of 2)

Ms. G's Grade 5 class in King School took a survey about how many years they have been in their school. Here is the list of the students in the class and how many years each student has been in the school.

Name	Years	Name	Years	Name	Years	Name	Years
Jane	1	Greg	2	Kari	5	Frank	3
Elisa	6	Phil	1	Holly	2	Keith	1
Rob	4	Linnea	5	Sam	1	Alice	2
Ann	2	Marie	4	Pete	1	Susan	6
Steve	2	Mel	5	Jeff	3	David	4
Deb	1	Jesse	2	Liza	2		

1. Draw a line plot of the data in the space below or on grid paper.

How Many Years in This School? (page 2 of 2)

2. What can you say about the number of years the students in Ms. G's class have been in King School? Write at least 3 things you can say about the data.

a. _____

_____

_____

_____

b. _____

_____

_____

_____

c. _____

_____

_____

_____

Questions About Us

Make a list of 5 questions that you might be interested in collecting data about for our class and another class. The questions should be about something you can count. The answer to your question should be a number, as in the question we used today: "How many years have you been in this school?"

1. _____

_____

_____

2. _____

_____

_____

3. _____

_____

_____

4. _____

_____

_____

5. _____

_____

_____

Sticker Story Problems

For each problem, write an equation that represents what the problem is asking. Then solve the problem and show your work.

NOTE Students solve addition and subtraction problems with 2-digit numbers.

SMH 20–24, 32–35

1. Adam went to Sticker Station on Monday and bought 47 train stickers and 20 baseball stickers.

   a. How many stickers did he buy?

   b. Adam went back to Sticker Station the next day and bought 36 more stickers. How many does he have now?

2. Pilar had 78 stickers. She gave 35 to her best friend, Kim. How many stickers does Pilar have now?

3. Edwin had 64 stickers. He went to Sticker Station and bought 45 more stickers. How many stickers does Edwin have now?

Sal and Joe's Apples (page 1 of 2)

Sal and Joe's Apple Farm sells its apples in baskets. Apples are not all the same size, so there can be different numbers of apples in different baskets.

One day, Mr. Ruiz came to the farm to buy some apples for his party. He wanted to make sure that he had enough apples for everyone, but he did not want to have to count the apples in a basket.

The next day, Ms. Warren came to buy apples to make some pies. She knows how many apples she needs for each pie. If she is going to make 30 pies, she wants to know how many baskets of apples to buy.

Sal and Joe want to get an idea of how many apples are typically in a basket so that they can answer their customers' questions. What do you think they should do to get an idea of how many apples are typically in a basket?

Sal and Joe's Apples (page 2 of 2)

Sal and Joe decide to do an experiment. They will take 20 baskets of apples and count how many apples are in each basket. They think this will help them figure out about how many apples are in one basket. Here are the data they collect:

Basket	Number of Apples	Basket	Number of Apples	Basket	Number of Apples
A	11	H	13	O	12
B	10	I	12	P	10
C	12	J	11	Q	11
D	12	K	10	R	11
E	10	L	9	S	13
F	10	M	16	T	10
G	9	N	12		

1. Make a line plot for Sal and Joe's data about how many apples are in a basket.

About How Many Apples Are in a Basket? ✏️

1. Write three things you notice about the data.

a. _____

_____

_____

b. _____

_____

_____

c. _____

_____

_____

2. What do you think Sal and Joe should say when someone asks them, "About how many apples are in a basket?" Give your reasons, according to the data.

_____

_____

_____

_____

A Fine Line

This line plot shows the number of cubes students in Ms. Martin's class can hold in their hands.

NOTE Students describe a set of data on a line plot.

SMH 96–98

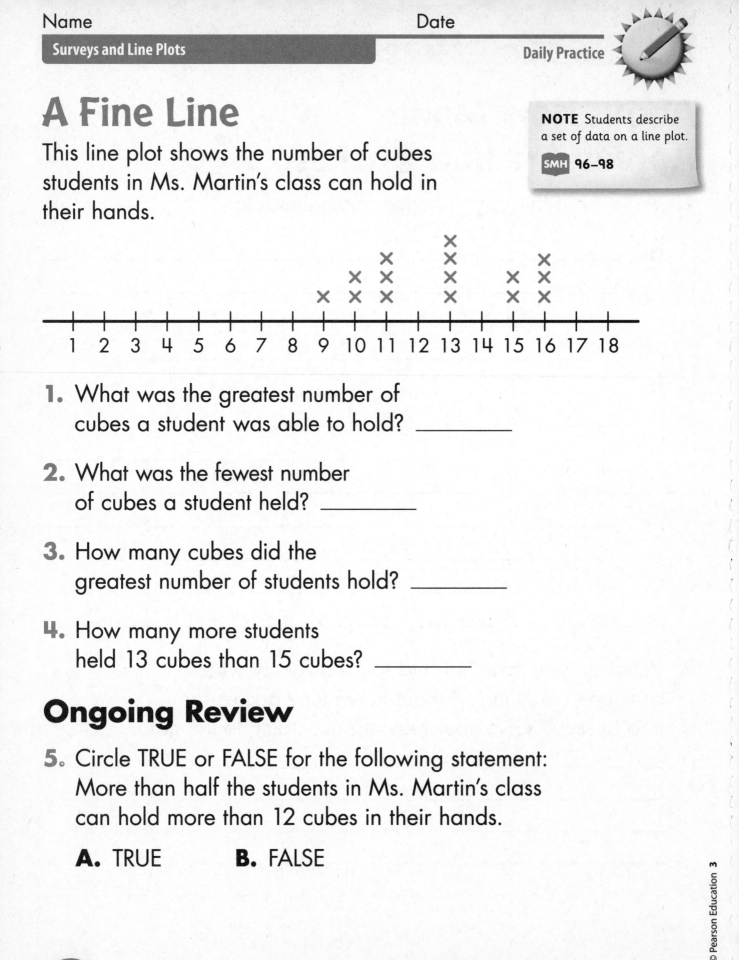

1. What was the greatest number of cubes a student was able to hold? _____

2. What was the fewest number of cubes a student held? _____

3. How many cubes did the greatest number of students hold? _____

4. How many more students held 13 cubes than 15 cubes? _____

Ongoing Review

5. Circle TRUE or FALSE for the following statement: More than half the students in Ms. Martin's class can hold more than 12 cubes in their hands.

   A. TRUE   **B.** FALSE

Picking Strawberries

Solve each problem. Show your work and write an equation.

NOTE Students solve 2-digit addition and subtraction problems.

SMH **20–24, 32–35**

1. While Pilar was at the farm, she picked 52 strawberries in the morning and 36 strawberries in the afternoon. How many strawberries did Pilar pick?

2. Adam picked 46 strawberries in the morning and 37 strawberries in the afternoon. How many strawberries did Adam pick?

3. Airani picked 98 strawberries at the farm. When she got home, she and her mother ate a total of 26 strawberries. How many strawberries were left?

30 Unit 2

Making and Interpreting Pictographs (page 1 of 2)

Use the data to make a pictograph.

Favorite Sports Chosen by Students	
Sport Chosen	**Number of Students**
Baseball	8
Basketball	4
Football	12
Soccer	6

Title: _____

Key: Each _____ = _____

Making and Interpreting Pictographs (page 2 of 2)

Use your pictograph to answer the questions.

1. Which sport was chosen by the greatest number of students?

2. Which sport was chosen by the fewest number of students?

3. How many more students chose football than basketball?

4. Suppose you added another sport to your graph. How many pictures would you draw if you wanted to show that 10 students chose hockey?

© Pearson Education 3

Pictographs

Use the pictograph below to answer
the problems.

NOTE Students interpret a pictograph.

Paper Airplane Contest	
Keisha	✈ ✈ ✈
Chris	✈ ✈ ✈ ✈ ✈ ✈ ✈ ✈ ✈
Cameron	✈ ✈ ✈ ✈ ✈ ✈ ✈
Jane	✈ ✈ ✈ ✈
Murphy	✈ ✈

Each ✈ = 4 feet

1. Whose airplane traveled the shortest distance?

_____

2. How far did Jane's airplane travel?

_____ feet

3. How far did Chris's airplane travel?

_____ feet

4. How much farther did Cameron's airplane travel
than Keisha's airplane?

_____ feet

31D Unit 2

A Survey Question

1. What do you want to find out? Decide on a question your group will use for your survey. Write your question.

   _____

   _____

   _____

2. Think about how you and others would answer your question. Do you need to make it clearer? Do you need to make it easier to understand? If you decide to revise your question, write the new question here.

   _____

   _____

   _____

3. Try your question with another group. Talk with them and with your own group about whether you need to make any more changes to your question. Write your revised question here.

   _____

   _____

   _____

4. If you have time, try your question with one more group and revise it again, if necessary.

   _____

   _____

86 Stickers

Solve the problems below and show your work.
Write an equation for each combination of strips
and singles.

NOTE Students solve
sticker problems.

SMH 7–8, 9

1. Elena bought 86 stickers at Sticker Station.
   She bought 8 strips of 10s and some singles.
   How many singles did she buy?

   $$80 + \underline{\hspace{2cm}} = 86$$

2. Oscar bought 86 stickers as well. He bought
   7 strips of 10s and some singles. How many
   singles did he buy?

3. Edwin also bought 86 stickers. He bought
   2 strips of 10s and many singles. How many
   singles did he buy?

4. Jung bought 86 stickers, too. He bought some
   strips of 10s and 36 singles. How many strips of
   10 did he buy?

Push-Up Contest

Students in Ms. Ramirez's class held a contest to see how many push-ups they can do in 1 minute. Here are the data:

NOTE Students read and interpret data from a line plot.

SMH 97–98

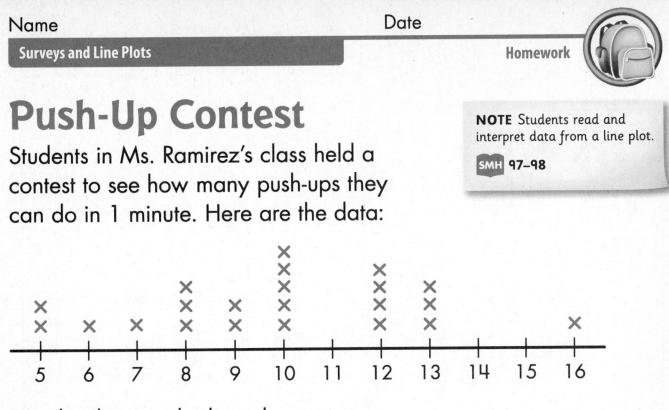

Use the data on the line plot to answer the questions.

1. What are 2 things you see from looking at this line plot? Use *about half*, *more/less than half*, *very few*, or *almost all* to describe the data.

   _____

   _____

2. How many students did 12 push-ups? _____

3. What is the typical number of push-ups a student can do in 1 minute? _____

4. Is there an outlier in the data? If so, what is it? _____

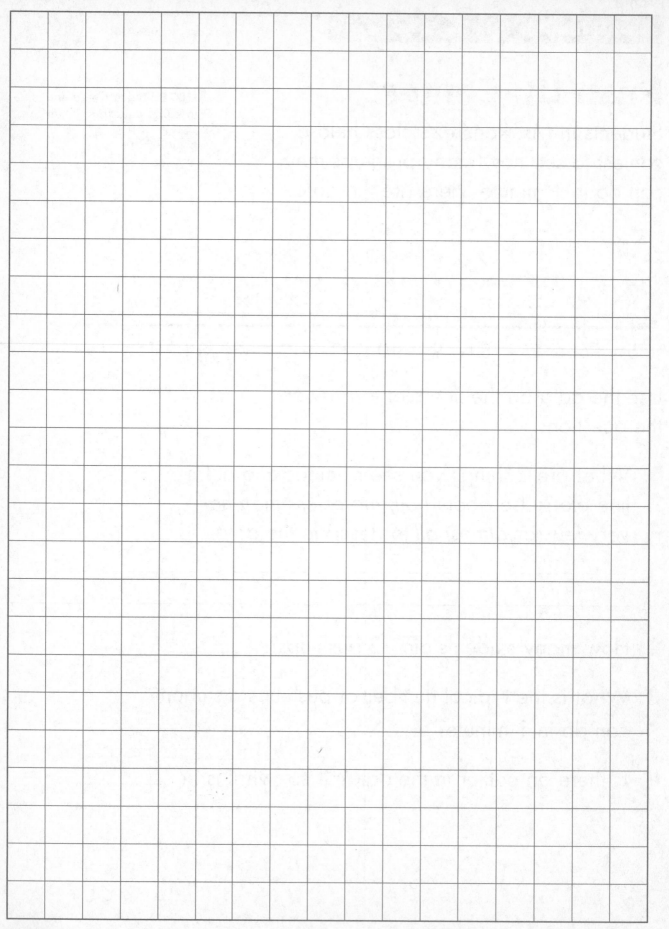

Marbles

For each problem, write an equation that represents what the problem is asking. Then solve the problem and show your work.

NOTE Students practice writing addition and subtraction equations.

SMH 25, 32–35

1. Philip has 37 red marbles and 64 yellow marbles. How many marbles does he have in all?

2. Ines had 47 marbles. Her mother gave her 20 marbles, and her brother gave her 30 marbles. How many marbles does Ines have now?

3. Kathryn had 66 marbles. She gave 32 marbles to her cousin. How many marbles does she have now?

4. Pilar had 52 marbles. Her mother gave her 15 marbles. Her grandfather gave her 25 marbles. How many marbles does she have now?

5. Nancy had 75 marbles. On her way home, she lost 32 of them. How many marbles does Nancy have now?

6. Denzel has 42 blue marbles, 28 green marbles, and 35 orange marbles. How many marbles does he have in all?

Giant Steps

This line plot shows how many giant steps students in Room 222 took to walk the length of their classroom.

NOTE Students describe data on a line plot.

SMH 97–98

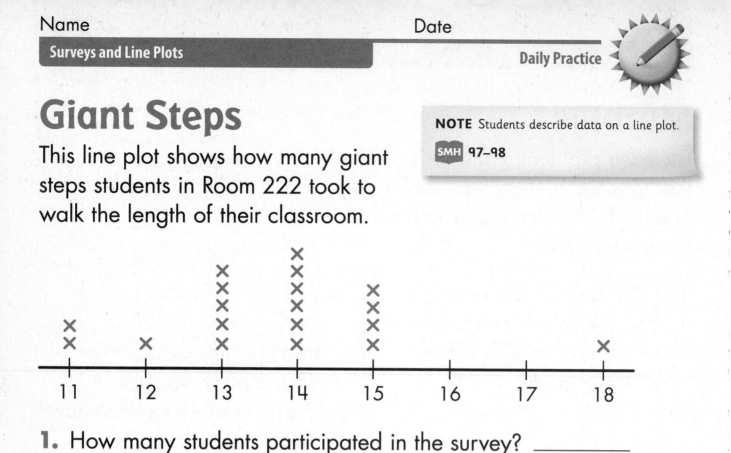

1. How many students participated in the survey? _____

2. What number of giant steps were taken by more students than any other number of steps? _____

3. What were the fewest giant steps taken to walk the length of the classroom? _____

4. What were the most giant steps taken to walk the length of the classroom? _____

Ongoing Review

5. What is the outlier in the line plot data?

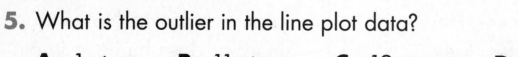

A. 1 step   **B.** 11 steps   **C.** 12 steps   **D.** 18 steps

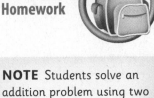

Solving a Problem in Two Ways

NOTE Students solve an addition problem using two different methods.

SMH 20–24

Solve the addition problem below in 2 different ways. Write equations to show each way you solved it. You may also draw number lines to show your solutions.

45 + 78

This is the first way I solved it:

This is the second way I solved it:

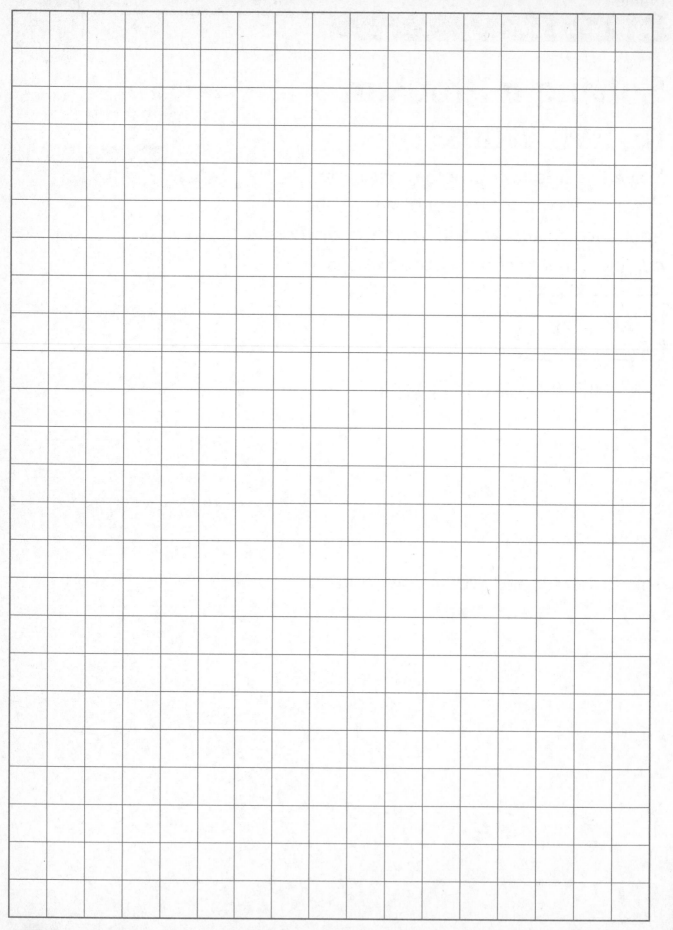

What Did You Learn from Your Survey? (page 1 of 2)

1. What was your survey question?

_____

_____

_____

_____

2. What did you find out about our class?

_____

_____

_____

_____

_____

_____

_____

_____

What Did You Learn from Your Survey? (page 2 of 2)

3. What did you find out about the other class?

_____

_____

_____

_____

_____

_____

_____

4. How are the two classes similar or different?

_____

_____

_____

_____

_____

_____

_____

_____

Jigsaw Puzzles

For each problem, write an equation that represents what the problem is asking. Then solve the problem and show your work.

NOTE Students write equations to match story problems, and then solve the equations.

SMH 20–24, 32–34

1. Denzel is putting together a jigsaw puzzle. The puzzle has 100 pieces. So far, he has put together 53 pieces. How many pieces does Denzel have left to finish the puzzle?

2. a. Kim and Gil are putting together a jigsaw puzzle. The puzzle has 100 pieces. So far, Kim has put together 37 pieces, and Gil has put together 23 pieces. How many pieces have they put together so far?

b. How many pieces do Kim and Gil have left to finish the puzzle?

3. Kelley is also putting together a jigsaw puzzle. The puzzle has 200 pieces. So far, she has put together 121 pieces. How many pieces does Kelley have left to finish the puzzle?

Reach for the Sky! (page 1 of 2)

The students in Mr. Burke's class used centimeters to measure how high they could reach without standing on their tiptoes. Here are their data:

NOTE Students represent and describe a set of data.

SMH 95–96

Keisha	148	Nicholas	150	Gina	156	Kelley	155
Pilar	150	Kelley	153	Kenji	152	Jung	154
Benjamin	155	Jane	152	Oscar	150	Adam	157
Denzel	154	Nancy	156	Inez	154	Keith	153

1. Use the data to make a line plot.

2. The students' reaches ranged

from _____ to _____ centimeters.

Reach for the Sky! (page 2 of 2)

3. Describe 2 things you notice about the data, including where data are spread out or are concentrated, where there are few data, and whether there are outliers.

_____

_____

_____

_____

_____

_____

Ongoing Review

4. What was the typical reach for this class?

A. 3 cm   **B.** 150 cm   **C.** 154 cm   **D.** 157 cm

Measuring

1. Foot Length (in inches)

   a. How long is your foot?

   _____

   b. Is your foot a foot long, or is it shorter or longer than a foot?

   _____

   _____

   _____

2. Pattern Block Distance (in inches or in feet and inches)

   a. How far did you blow the pattern block?

   _____

3. Classroom Length (in feet and inches)

   a. First time: _____

   b. Second time: _____

4. Jump Distance (in feet and inches and in inches)
   How far did you jump?

   a. _____ feet and _____ inches

   b. _____ inches

Foot Findings

Colin measured the length of every teacher's foot to the nearest inch. Here are the data:

NOTE Students analyze data on a line plot.

SMH 97–98

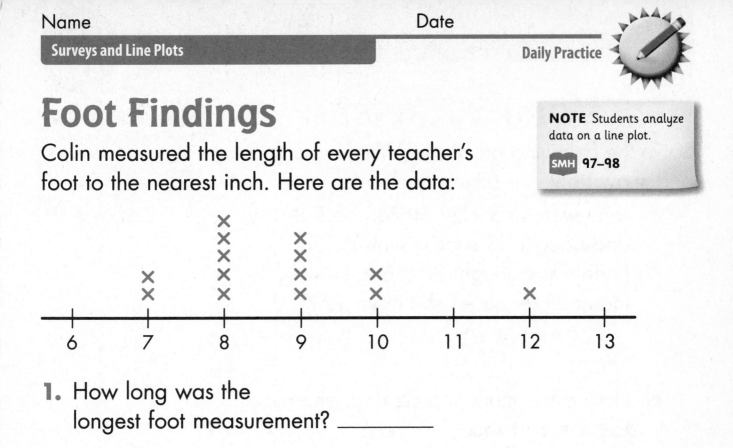

1. How long was the longest foot measurement? _____

2. What was the typical length for all? _____

3. How did you determine the typical length for all feet measured?

4. Describe 2 things you notice about the data, including where data are spread out or concentrated, where there are few data, and what the range is.

How Many Stickers?

Solve the following problems. Write equations and show how you solved each one.

NOTE Students practice solving addition and subtraction problems.

SMH 20–24, 32–35

1. a. Jane went to Sticker Station on Tuesday and bought 43 soccer stickers. On Friday, she bought 28 more. How many stickers does she have now?

b. How many more stickers does she need to have 100 soccer stickers?

2. a. Benjamin has 74 baseball stickers. He went to Sticker Station and bought 46 more baseball stickers. How many baseball stickers does he have now?

b. How many more baseball stickers does he need to buy to have 200 baseball stickers?

Coin Jar

Becky has these coins in her coin jar:

NOTE Students practice solving addition and subtraction problems using coins.

 37–38

1. What is the total amount of money in Becky's coin jar?

2. If Becky spends all of the **dimes,** how much money does she have left?

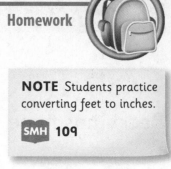

Standing Broad
Jump Distances ✏️WRITING

NOTE Students practice converting feet to inches.

SMH 109

On Field Day, Mr. Keith's Grade 3 group recorded the following distances for the standing broad jump:

Denzel jumped 3 feet.	Adam jumped 33 inches.
Bridget jumped 40 inches.	Elena jumped 2 feet and 1 inch.

1. Who had the longest jump? How do you know?

_____

_____

_____

2. Who had the shortest jump? How do you know?

_____

_____

_____

Feet and Inches (page 1 of 2)

In a Grade 3 class, some students were playing Blowing a Pattern Block. They measured how far each student blew the block.

> Benjamin: 1 ruler and 3 more inches
> Jung: 1 ruler and 6 more inches
> Chris: 2 rulers
> Elena: 1 ruler and $\frac{1}{2}$ a ruler

1. Use rulers to show how far each student blew the pattern block. How far did each block go in inches? How far did each block go in feet and inches?

   How far did the students blow the pattern block?

	Inches	**Feet and Inches**
Benjamin		
Jung		
Chris		
Elena		

Feet and Inches (page 2 of 2)

Later, the same students were jumping with both feet. They measured their jumps by putting rulers end to end.

Here is how long the jumps were:

Benjamin: 4 rulers and 2 more inches
Jung: 3 rulers and 4 more inches
Chris: 5 rulers
Elena: 4 rulers and 11 more inches

2. Use rulers to show how far each student jumped. How far did each student jump in inches? How far did each student jump in feet and inches?

How far did the students jump?

	Inches	**Feet and Inches**
Benjamin		
Jung		
Chris		
Elena		

Mouse Trips (page 1 of 2)

Mike the Mouse comes out of his mouse hole (Start) and takes a walk to find some cheese (End).

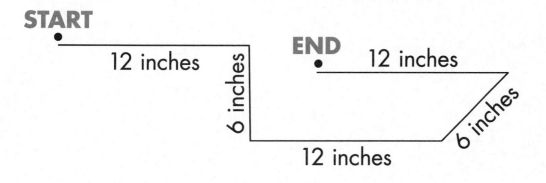

START

12 inches

6 inches

END

12 inches

12 inches

6 inches

1. How far does Mike travel? _____

2. Some other mice traveled to find some cheese. The table shows how far each mouse went. Fill in the rest of the table.

Mouse's Name	Inches	Feet and Inches
Mary	40 in.	
Mo		2 ft 6 in.
Missy	66 in.	
Mario		3 ft 11 in.

Mouse Trips (page 2 of 2)

3. How did you figure out how many feet and inches Mary walked?

4. How did you figure out how many inches Mo walked?

Today's Number

Today's Number is 157.

NOTE Students practice creating equations that equal today's number.

SMH 25, 36

Write 3 equations that equal 157. You must do the following:

- Use both addition and subtraction in each equation.
- Use 2 multiples of 10 in each equation.

Equation 1: _____

Equation 2: _____

Equation 3: _____

Running Broad Jump Distances

On field day, some of Mr. Keith's students wanted to see how far they could jump if they took a running start. They recorded the following distances for the running broad jump:

NOTE On this page, students practice converting feet to inches.

SMH 109

Oscar jumped 56 inches.	Jane jumped 5 feet.
Becky jumped 4 feet and 5 inches.	Gil jumped 51 inches.

1. Who had the longest jump? How do you know?

_____

_____

_____

2. Who had the shortest jump? How do you know?

_____

_____

_____

How Far Can a Grade 3 Student Blow a Pattern Block? ✏️ WRITING

1. On another sheet of paper, make a graph to show the data from your class.

2. Write at least 3 things you notice about the data. (If you have more to say, you can write more ideas on a blank sheet of paper.)

a. _____

_____

_____

b. _____

_____

_____

c. _____

_____

_____

3. If someone asked you, "How far can a Grade 3 student blow a pattern block?" what would you say, according to the data?

_____

_____

_____

Making Graphs

The table below shows the number of books read by students in a third-grade class in one month.

NOTE Students are able to use data to create a line plot and a bar graph.

SMH 95–96

Name	Number of Books Read	Name	Number of Books Read
Ines	8	Chris	7
Philip	9	Gina	9
Jane	18	Adam	8
Oscar	11	Murphy	9
Edwin	7	Kenji	10
Jung	8	Bridget	6
Nancy	9	Zhang	6
Gil	4	Elena	22
Kim	9	Keisha	12

1. On a separate sheet of paper, make a line plot using the data from the table.

2. On another sheet of paper, make a bar graph using the same data.

An Internet Survey

The graph below shows the results of a survey that many people completed over the Internet.

NOTE Students solve real-world problems involving the math content of this unit.

SMH 92

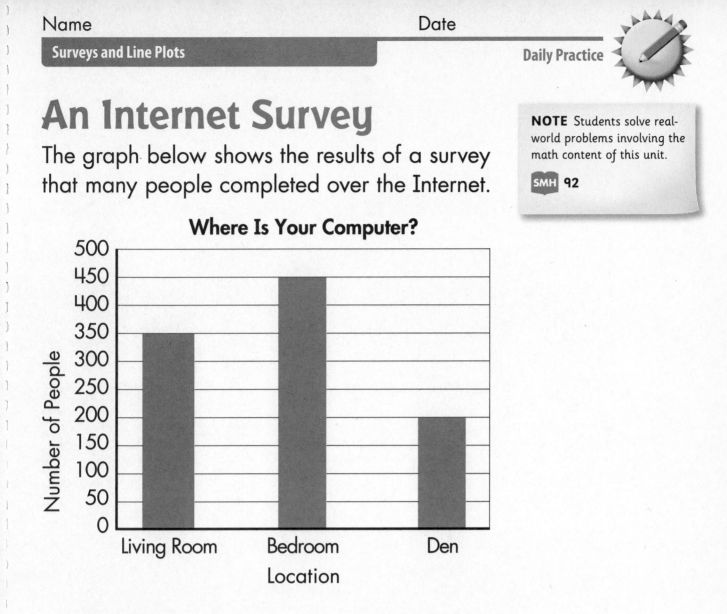

Where Is Your Computer?

1. Write three things you can tell from looking at the graph.

_____

_____

_____

_____

_____

2. Write a question for another Internet survey.

_____

_____

Ikenaga 2 Jos Leys

"A relatively simple formula can generate immensely complex images." – Jos Leys

Investigations

IN NUMBER, DATA, AND SPACE®

Collections and Travel Stories

Investigation 4

Finding Numbers on the 1,000 Chart

1. Look at each set of numbers. Find the spaces on your 1,000 chart where each number should be located. Then, write each number in the correct space.

Set A:	43	143	643	843
Set B:	378	358	328	318
Set C:	775	275	575	975
Set D:	813	833	853	873
Set E:	67	267	467	667
Set F:	227	257	277	297

2. Choose one set of numbers and explain how you found those numbers on your 1,000 chart.

_____

_____

_____

_____

_____

_____

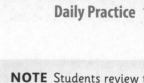

Addition and the 700 Chart

Solve these problems. Fill in the sums on the 700 chart.

NOTE Students review the place value of 3-digit numbers as they add 10s to any number. They also find and write the sums on the 700 chart.

SMH 10, 36

1. 616 + 50 = _____

2. 613 + 60 = _____

3. 688 + 10 = _____

4. 611 + 20 = _____

5. 602 + 40 = _____

6. 664 + 20 = _____

7. 608 + 20 = _____

8. 609 + 50 = _____

9. 600 + 10 = _____

601			604					609	
					616				
	622								630
				635					
641						647			
		653							
							668		
					676				680
	682								
			694			697			700

Ongoing Review

10. The sum of which expression does **not** belong on the 700 chart?

   A. 634 + 70

   B. 601 + 40

   C. 684 + 10

   D. 617 + 80

Collections: Smallest to Largest

1. Make a list of the Collection Card categories.

_____   _____

_____   _____

_____   _____

_____   _____

2. Choose two categories and pull out all of the cards in those categories. You will have 8 cards to put in order. Starting with the smallest number and moving to the largest, write the number of items in each collection in order.

Collection Categories: _____ and _____

Smallest   to   Largest

↙ _____ _____ _____ _____ _____ _____ _____ _____ ↘

3. Find each of these numbers on your 1,000 chart and write in any numbers that are not already there.

Book Fair

Solve the problems. For each story problem, first write an equation that represents what the problem is asking, and then solve the problem.

NOTE Students practice adding and subtracting with 2- and 3-digit numbers.

SMH 20–24, 32–35

1. $\begin{array}{r} 84 \\ + 37 \\ \hline \end{array}$

2. Jane has $3.00 to spend at the book fair. She buys a book that costs $2.25. How much money does she have left?

3. Zhang buys a journal for $1.75 and a book for $1.50. How much does he spend at the book fair?

Ongoing Review

4. Which expression is closest to 100?

    A. 55 + 40   **C.** 21 + 70

    B. 39 + 59   **D.** 30 + 77

Adding and Subtracting 10s

NOTE Students practice adding and subtracting multiples of 10.

SMH 36

Solve each set of problems below.

1. $55 + 20 =$ _____

$55 + 40 =$ _____

$55 + 60 =$ _____

2. $123 - 10 =$ _____

$133 - 10 =$ _____

$143 - 10 =$ _____

3. $167 + 10 =$ _____

$167 + 20 =$ _____

$167 + 30 =$ _____

4. $91 - 20 =$ _____

$91 - 30 =$ _____

$91 - 40 =$ _____

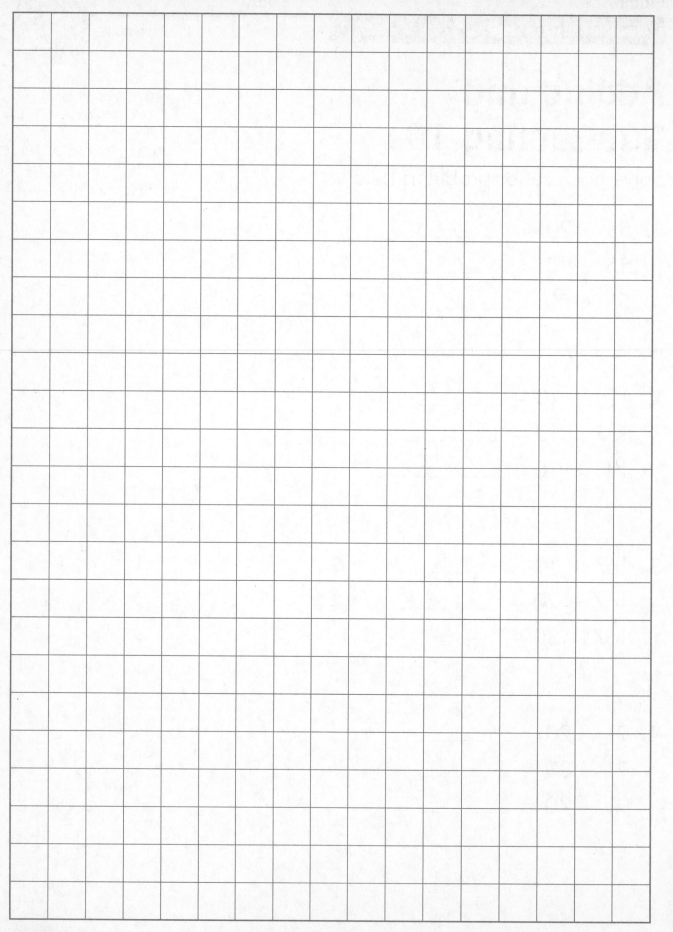

6 Unit 3

Go Collecting Recording Sheet

Collection Quantities	How Many Hundreds?/Score
Example: __138__ + __376__	__5__
1. _____ + _____	_____
2. _____ + _____	_____
3. _____ + _____	_____
4. _____ + _____	_____
5. _____ + _____	_____
6. _____ + _____	_____
7. _____ + _____	_____
8. _____ + _____	_____
9. _____ + _____	_____
10. _____ + _____	_____

Total: _____

Close to 100 Recording Sheet

Game 1   Score

Round 1: _____ _____ + _____ _____ = _____ _____

Round 2: _____ _____ + _____ _____ = _____ _____

Round 3: _____ _____ + _____ _____ = _____ _____

Round 4: _____ _____ + _____ _____ = _____ _____

Round 5: _____ _____ + _____ _____ = _____ _____

TOTAL SCORE _____ _____

Game 2   Score

Round 1: _____ _____ + _____ _____ = _____ _____

Round 2: _____ _____ + _____ _____ = _____ _____

Round 3: _____ _____ + _____ _____ = _____ _____

Round 4: _____ _____ + _____ _____ = _____ _____

Round 5: _____ _____ + _____ _____ = _____ _____

TOTAL SCORE _____ _____

Pairs That Make 100

NOTE Students practice finding combinations of 2-digit numbers that add to 100.

SMH 32, G5

1. Connect the pairs of numbers that make 100.

47	36
31	42
64	69
72	7
12	28
93	53
58	88

2. Complete these equations.

_____ + 45 = 100

32 + _____ = 100

17 + _____ = 100

_____ + 78 = 100

3. Write pairs of numbers that make 100.

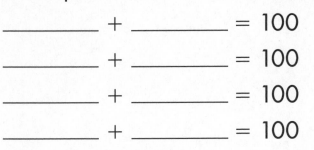

_____ + _____ = 100

_____ + _____ = 100

_____ + _____ = 100

_____ + _____ = 100

Collections and Travel Stories

How Many 10s? Part 1 (page 1 of 2) ✏️WRITING

Solve the problems below. You may use your
1,000 chart to help you.

1. The students in Mr. Jackson's class are collecting
pennies. They decide to display them in stacks
of 10. How many stacks can they make with
345 pennies? How many single pennies will
they have left?

Explain how you figured it out.

2. The students in Ms. Kennedy's class are collecting
stamps from old letters. They are displaying the
stamps in rows of 10. How many rows can they
make with 428 stamps?

Explain how you figured it out.

How Many 10s? Part 1 (page 2 of 2) ✏️WRITING

3. The students in Ms. Vega's class are collecting pull tabs from juice cans. They are hanging them on a bulletin board in bags of 10. On Wednesday, they had 536 pull tabs. How many bags of 10 were on the board? How many single pull tabs were left over?

Explain how you figured it out.

4. On Friday, the students in Ms. Vega's class had 58 bags of pull tabs on their bulletin board and 7 single pull tabs on the counter. How many pull tabs did they have?

Explain how you figured it out.

How Many 100s?
How Many 10s?

> **NOTE** Students find the number of 10s and 100s in 3-digit numbers.

Solve the problems below. You may use your 1,000 chart to help you.

1. Beatriz is reading a book that has 530 pages. If she reads 10 pages a day, how many days will it take her to finish the book?

2. Kenji has 714 postcards to put in an album. Each page of the album holds 10 postcards. How many pages does Kenji need for his postcards?

3. Benjamin and his sister collected 423 seashells. They put 100 seashells in each jar. How many jars did they fill completely? How many seashells were left?

4. Benjamin's parents also collect seashells. They have 6 jars with 100 seashells in each. They have one jar with 57 seashells. How many seashells do they have?

Ongoing Review

5. Which equation is **not** true?

   A. $168 - 40 = 128$ **C.** $168 - 80 = 88$

   B. $168 - 60 = 108$ **D.** $178 - 40 = 128$

How Many 10s? Part 2

NOTE Students find how many groups of 10 are in some 3-digit numbers.

SMH 7–8, 37–38

1. Ms. Ahmed went to Sticker Station and bought strips of 10 stickers to give to her students. She bought 250 stickers. How many strips of 10 did she buy?

2. Gina and her brother are collecting pennies at home. They have 382 pennies so far. If they trade the pennies for dimes, how many dimes will they have? How many pennies will be left over?

3. At the end of week 3, Ms. Santos' class had 629 bottle caps in their class collection. They are displaying the bottle caps in bags of 10. How many bags of 10 do they have? How many bottle caps are left over?

Unit 3

Class Collection Data— Week 1 (page 1 of 3)

For each problem, write an equation, solve the problem, and show your solution.

The students in Mr. Jackson's third-grade class collected pennies for their Class Collection. For week 1, they had a goal of collecting 250 pennies. On Wednesday, they looked at their Class Collection Data. It looked like this:

Monday	66 pennies
Tuesday	60 pennies
Wednesday	57 pennies

1. How many pennies did the class have so far?

_____

2. How many more pennies did they need to reach their goal of 250 pennies? _____

Collections and Travel Stories

Class Collection Data—
Week 1 (page 2 of 3)

On Friday, the students looked at their data again.
It looked like this:

Thursday	53 pennies
Friday	48 pennies

3. How many pennies did the students collect on
Thursday and Friday? _____

4. How many pennies did the students in Mr.
Jackson's class collect altogether in week 1?

Collections and Travel Stories

Class Collection Data—
Week 1 (page 3 of 3)

5. Did they reach their goal of 250 for the week?
If not, how far from the goal were they?

6. On Wednesday of the second week, Mr.
Jackson's students had a total of 387 pennies.
Their goal for the week was 500. How many
more pennies did they need to reach their goal?

How Many 10s? Part 3

Solve the problems below. You may use your 1,000 chart to help you.

1. Mr. Jackson's class now has 623 pennies. They are displaying them in stacks of 10. How many stacks of 10 are there? How many single pennies are left over?

Explain how you figured it out.

2. Ms. Vega's class now has 56 bags of pull tabs hanging on the bulletin board and 4 single pull tabs on the counter. How many pull tabs are in their collection? Remember that there are 10 pull tabs in each bag.

Explain how you figured it out.

3. At the end of week 3, Ms. Kennedy's class had 735 stamps in their collection. How many rows of 10 were in their display?

Explain how you figured it out.

Coupon Cutting

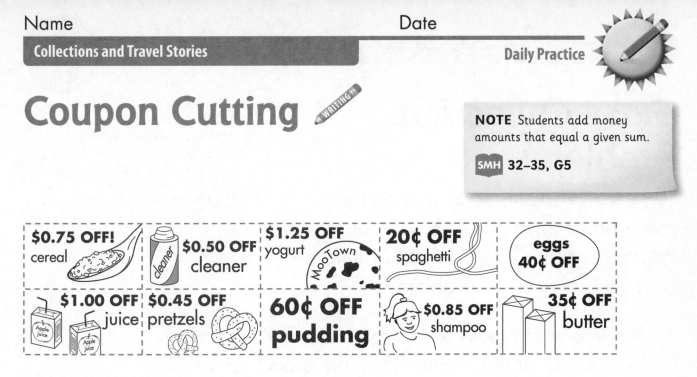

> **NOTE** Students add money amounts that equal a given sum.
>
> **SMH** 32–35, G5

1. Find and list coupons that add up to $3.00.

2. Find and list **three** coupons that add up to $1.50.

3. Will the savings on cereal, yogurt, and eggs be more or less than $2.00? Explain.

Ongoing Review

4. Adam's goal is to collect 500 signatures for a petition. He has collected 382 signatures so far. How many more signatures does he need to reach his goal?

   A. 100   **B.** 118   **C.** 218   **D.** 582

Class Collection Problems

For each problem, write an equation, solve the problem, and show your solution. You may use a number line to help you solve these problems.

NOTE Students practice finding the difference between two 3-digit numbers. Ask your child to explain how he or she solved each problem.

SMH 29–30, 32–35

1. Mr. Vasquez's class wants to collect 700 pennies by the end of the month. They have 535 so far. How many more do they need to collect to reach 700?

2. The students in Ms. Chin's class are collecting ring pulls from juice cans. Their goal for the week is 450. They have 379 so far. How many more do they need to reach their goal?

Today's Number: 59

1. Circle all of the expressions that equal 59.

$60 - 1 + 10 + 20 - 30$	$80 - 11 - 10$
$9 + 20 + 20 + 20$	$4 + 5 + 20 + 30$
$100 - 20 - 20 + 1$	$100 - 50 + 4 + 4 + 1$
$50 + 1 + 2 + 3 + 4$	$8 + 10 + 40 - 1$
$5 + 10 + 15 + 25 + 4$	$19 + 20 + 20$

2. Show four more ways to make 59.

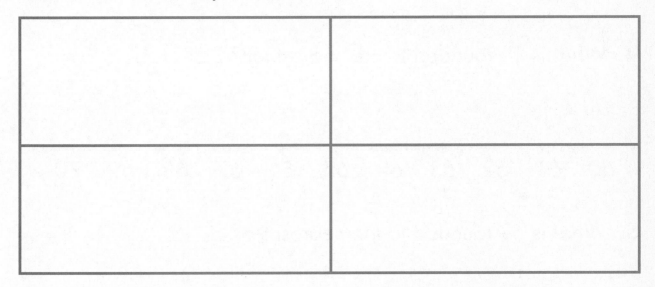

Rounding to Tens

Use the number lines to help you answer the problems.

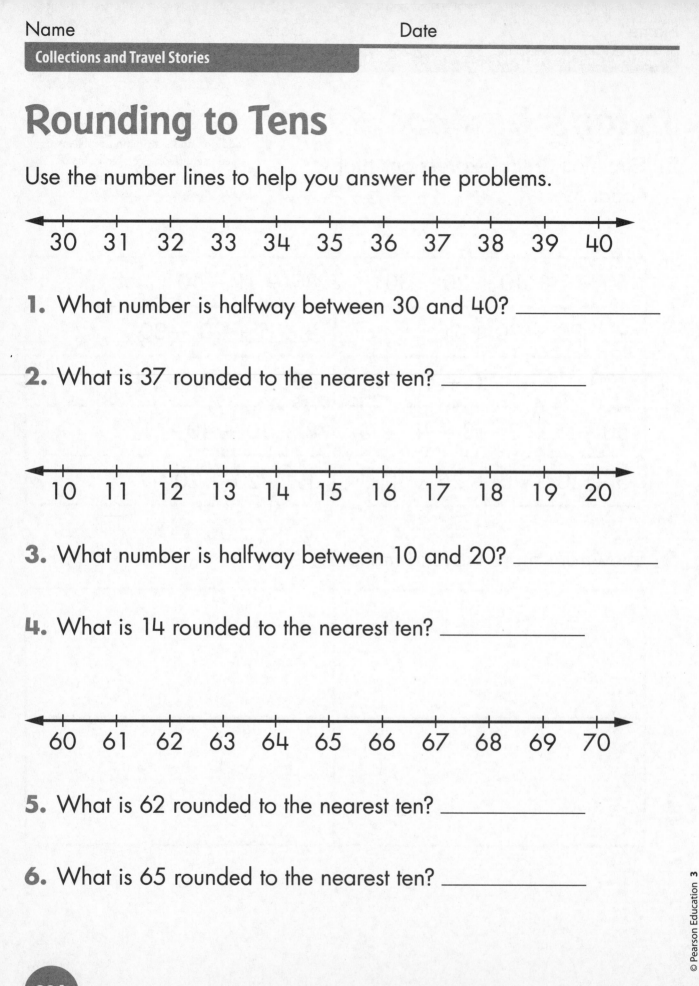

1. What number is halfway between 30 and 40? _____

2. What is 37 rounded to the nearest ten? _____

3. What number is halfway between 10 and 20? _____

4. What is 14 rounded to the nearest ten? _____

5. What is 62 rounded to the nearest ten? _____

6. What is 65 rounded to the nearest ten? _____

Rounding to Hundreds

Use the number lines to help you answer the problems.

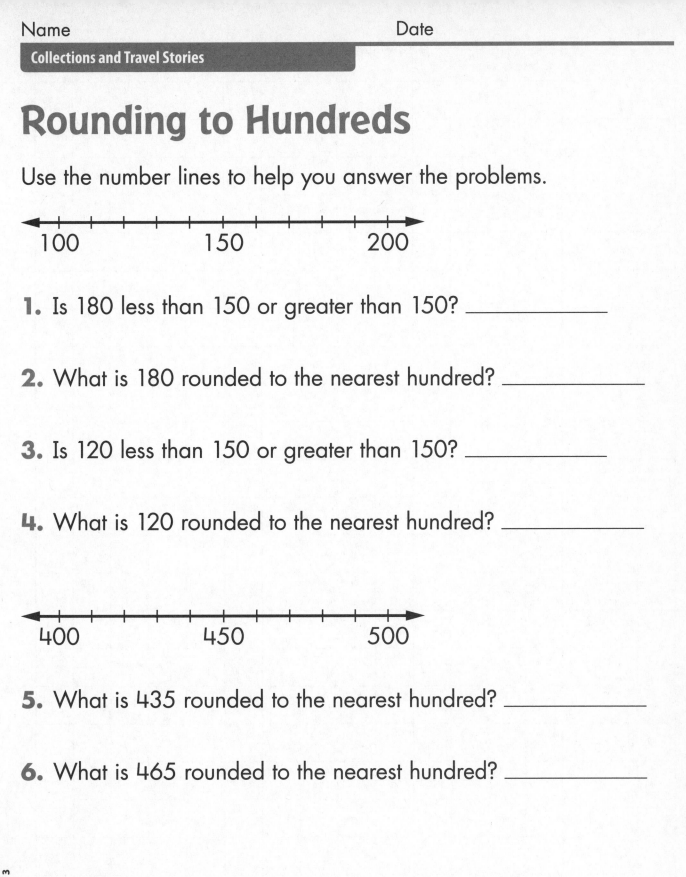

1. Is 180 less than 150 or greater than 150? _____

2. What is 180 rounded to the nearest hundred? _____

3. Is 120 less than 150 or greater than 150? _____

4. What is 120 rounded to the nearest hundred? _____

5. What is 435 rounded to the nearest hundred? _____

6. What is 465 rounded to the nearest hundred? _____

22C

Rounding to Tens and Hundreds

NOTE Students round whole numbers to the nearest ten and hundred.

SMH 6, 10–11

For each problem, write the number in expanded form and then round to the nearest ten and hundred.

1. 138

Expanded form: _____

What is 138 rounded to the nearest ten? _____

What is 138 rounded to the nearest hundred? _____

2. 459

Expanded form: _____

What is 459 rounded to the nearest ten? _____

What is 459 rounded to the nearest hundred? _____

3. 392

Expanded form: _____

What is 392 rounded to the nearest ten? _____

What is 392 rounded to the nearest hundred? _____

4. 750

Expanded form: _____

What is 750 rounded to the nearest ten? _____

What is 750 rounded to the nearest hundred? _____

Collecting Stickers and Pennies (page 1 of 2)

For each problem, write an equation, solve the problem, and show your solution.

Remember that stickers come in sheets of 100, strips of 10, and as single stickers.

1. Oscar collects animal stickers. He has 135 stickers in his collection. With his birthday money, he buys 1 sheet, 1 strip, and 2 single stickers to add to his collection. How many animal stickers does Oscar have now?

2. Gina collects dog stickers. In her sticker book, she has 2 full pages of 100 stickers and 1 page with 7 single stickers. For her birthday, her friends give her 4 strips and 8 single dog stickers. How many dog stickers does Gina have now?

3. Jung collects sports stickers. In her sticker box, she has 258 soccer stickers. She also has 127 tennis stickers. How many soccer and tennis stickers does Jung have in all?

Collecting Stickers and Pennies (page 2 of 2)

For each problem, write an equation, solve the problem, and show your solution.

Remember to write your answers as dollars and cents.

4. Last month, Lucas collected 97 pennies. This month, he collected 143 pennies. How much money does Lucas have now?

5. Kim had $2.64 in her penny collection. Her aunt gave her 108 more pennies. How much money does Kim have now?

6. Cristobal had 352 pennies in his collection. His younger brother had 49¢ in his penny collection. How much money did they have in all?

94 Stickers

Solve the problems below and show your work. Write an equation for each combination of strips and singles. The first equation is started for you.

NOTE Students practice making the number 94 with different combinations of 10s and 1s.

SMH 7–8, 9

1. Arthur bought 94 stickers at Sticker Station. He bought 9 strips of 10 and some singles. How many singles did he buy?

$$90 + \underline{\hspace{3cm}} = 94$$

2. Keith bought 94 stickers as well. He bought 8 strips of 10 and some singles. How many singles did he buy?

3. David also bought 94 stickers. He bought 2 strips of 10 and many singles. How many singles did he buy?

4. Deondra bought 94 stickers, too. She bought some strips of 10 and 34 singles. How many strips of 10 did she buy?

Combining Collections (page 1 of 3)

1. If these two Negro Leagues memorabilia collections were put together, how many items would there be in all? First, make an estimate. Then, write an equation, solve the problem, and show your solution below.

SPORTS C	**SPORTS** D
Negro Leagues Memorabilia Collection	**Negro Leagues Memorabilia Collection**
Location: Plainville, Michigan	**Location:** Birdsong, Alabama
Owner: John and Mildred Hayes	**Owner:** Birdsong Sports Museum
Number: 84 items	**Number: 137** items
Details: In the first decades of the 1900s, when baseball was a segregated sport, many African American players broke world records and made a name for themselves in the Negro Leagues.	**Details:** Here is a collection of posters, photographs, uniforms, and artifacts connected with some of the greatest ballplayers in history.

Estimate: _____

Equation: _____

How did you solve the problem?

Combining Collections (page 2 of 3)

2. If these two dragonfly collections were put together, how many dragonflies would there be in all? First, make an estimate. Then, write an equation, solve the problem, and show your solution below.

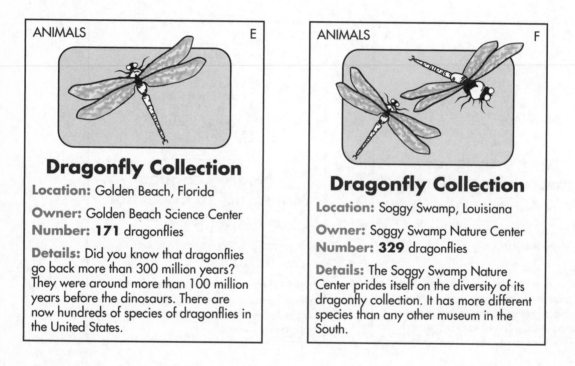

Estimate: _____

Equation: _____

How did you solve the problem?

Combining Collections (page 3 of 3)

3. If these two teddy bear collections were put together, how many teddy bears would there be in all? First, make an estimate. Then write an equation, solve the problem, and show your solution below.

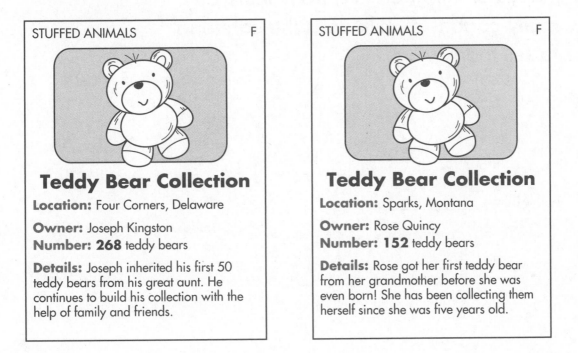

STUFFED ANIMALS F	STUFFED ANIMALS F
Teddy Bear Collection	**Teddy Bear Collection**
Location: Four Corners, Delaware	**Location:** Sparks, Montana
Owner: Joseph Kingston	**Owner:** Rose Quincy
Number: 268 teddy bears	**Number: 152** teddy bears
Details: Joseph inherited his first 50 teddy bears from his great aunt. He continues to build his collection with the help of family and friends.	**Details:** Rose got her first teddy bear from her grandmother before she was even born! She has been collecting them herself since she was five years old.

Estimate: _____

Equation: _____

How did you solve the problem?

Addition Problems

Solve each problem and show your solution. Write an equation to go with the story problem.

NOTE Students solve addition problems with 2- and 3-digit numbers.

SMH 20–24

1. The cafeteria received 285 cartons of milk today. 134 cartons of milk were left from yesterday. How many cartons of milk does the cafeteria have to sell today?

2. $391 + 88 =$ _____

3. $\begin{array}{r} 126 \\ + 275 \\ \hline \end{array}$

Ongoing Review

4. Which expression does **not** equal 100?

   A. $65 + 35$ **C.** $13 + 87$

   B. $48 + 52$ **D.** $29 + 81$

Combining Stamp Collections

NOTE Students practice solving addition problems with 3-digit numbers.

SMH 20–24

Write an equation, solve the problem, and show your solution.

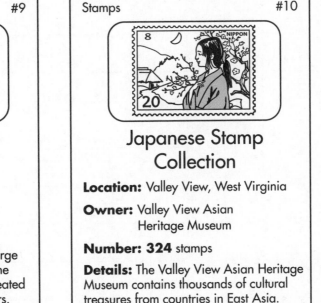

Stamps   #9

Canadian Stamp Collection

Location: Greenville, Connecticut

Owner: Greenville City Museum

Number: 145 stamps

Details: Greenville is home to a large community of French Canadians. The Canadian Stamp Collection was created from the donations of local collectors.

Stamps   #10

Japanese Stamp Collection

Location: Valley View, West Virginia

Owner: Valley View Asian Heritage Museum

Number: 324 stamps

Details: The Valley View Asian Heritage Museum contains thousands of cultural treasures from countries in East Asia.

The Greenville City Museum is loaning its stamp collection to the Valley View Asian Heritage Museum for a special showing. When the two collections are combined, how many stamps will there be in all?

Capture on the 300 Chart Recording Sheet

Record as an equation your starting number, the cards you use, and your ending number for each move.

Example: $116 + 50 + 10 - 3 = 173$
1.
2.
3.
4.
5.
6.
7.
8.
9.
10.
11.
12.

How Many More?

Solve the problems below. Show your solutions on the number lines.

NOTE Students find the missing number to make an addition equation correct.

SMH 32, 37–38

1. $136 +$ _____ $= 255$

2. $86 +$ _____ $= 279$

3. $334 +$ _____ $= 500$

4. $215 +$ _____ $= 401$

Ongoing Review

5. Which group of coins makes $1.85?

A. 6 quarters, 1 dime

C. 7 quarters, 1 nickel, 1 dime

B. 7 quarters, 5 nickels, 15 pennies

D. 3 dimes, 5 pennies, 6 quarters

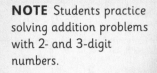

Solving Addition Problems

Solve each problem and show your solution.
For Problem 3, write an equation to go with
the story problem.

NOTE Students practice
solving addition problems
with 2- and 3-digit
numbers.

SMH 20–24

1. 215 + 78 = _____

2. 157 + 121 = _____

3. The students in Ms. Suarez's class had 320 bottle
caps in their collection at the end of last week.
This week, the students collected 64 more bottle
caps. How many bottle caps do they have now?

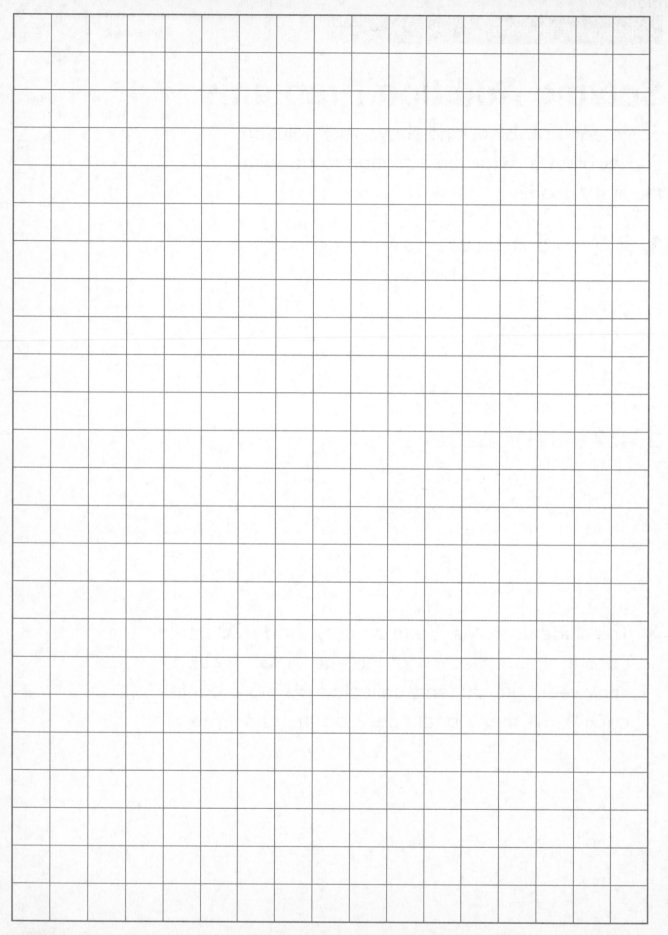

Collections Story Problems

For each problem, write an equation, solve the problem, and show your solution.

1. The students in Ms. Greene's third grade class are collecting pennies. At the end of week 1, they had 126 pennies. In week 2, they collected 176 pennies. How many pennies did they have in all at the end of week 2? How much money is that?

2. The students in Mr. River's third grade class are collecting bottle caps. At the end of week 1, they had 247 bottle caps. In week 2, they collected 184 bottle caps. How many bottle caps did they have in all at the end of week 2?

3. Jane and Ines both have stamp collections. Jane has 135 stamps in her collection, and Ines has 229 stamps in her collection. They brought their collections to school to show their class. How many stamps did the two girls have in all?

4. In Ms. Silvie's third grade class, many of the students collect stickers. The boys in the class have 158 stickers and the girls in the class have 302 stickers. How many stickers do Ms. Silvie's third graders have in all?

Fisherman's Log

Fishermen log how many fish they catch each day. Use this fisherman's log to solve the problems below. Write an equation and show your solution for each problem.

NOTE Students practice solving addition problems with 3-digit numbers.

SMH 20–24, 32–35

Day	Monday	Tuesday	Wednesday	Thursday
Count	276	230	239	257

1. How many fish did the fisherman catch on Monday and Tuesday?

2. How many fish did the fisherman catch on Wednesday and Thursday?

3. The fisherman's weekly goal is to catch 1,000 fish. Did he meet his goal? How far over or under is he from his goal?

Ongoing Review

4. $36 +$ _____ $= 100$

A. 55 **B.** 64 **C.** 74 **D.** 76

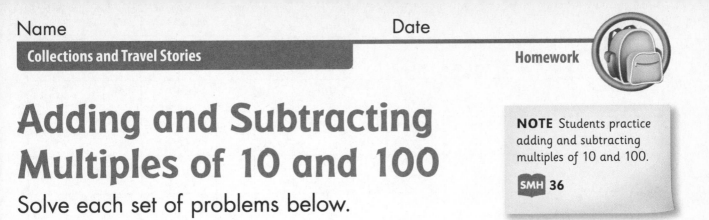

Adding and Subtracting Multiples of 10 and 100

Solve each set of problems below.

NOTE Students practice adding and subtracting multiples of 10 and 100.

SMH 36

1. 125 + 100 = _____

125 + 200 = _____

125 + 300 = _____

2. 346 − 100 = _____

346 − 200 = _____

346 − 300 = _____

3. 207 + 40 = _____

207 + 60 = _____

207 + 80 = _____

4. 172 − 50 = _____

172 − 70 = _____

172 − 90 = _____

38 Unit 3

Addition Starter Problems (page 1 of 3)

In each set of problems below, solve all three Starter Problems. Then solve the final problem, and show your solution. If you used a Starter Problem to help you solve the final problem, tell which one.

1. $100 + 100 =$ _____

$146 + 100 =$ _____

$140 + 120 =$ _____

$146 + 124 =$ _____

2. $200 + 100 =$ _____

$263 + 7 =$ _____

$260 + 140 =$ _____

$263 + 139 =$ _____

Addition Starter Problems (page 2 of 3)

In each set of problems below, solve all three Starter
Problems. Then solve the final problem, and show
your solution. If you used a Starter Problem to help
you solve the final problem, tell which one.

3. $100 + 300 =$ _____

$316 + 100 =$ _____

$130 + 310 =$ _____

$137 + 316 =$ _____

4. $100 + 200 =$ _____

$154 + 200 =$ _____

$54 + 46 =$ _____

$154 + 248 =$ _____

Addition Starter Problems (page 3 of 3)

In each set of problems below, solve all three Starter Problems. Then solve the final problem, and show your solution. If you used a Starter Problem to help you solve the final problem, tell which one.

5. 200 + 100 = _____

271 + 100 = _____

271 + 200 = _____

271 + 199 = _____

6. 200 + 300 = _____

220 + 350 = _____

225 + 350 = _____

225 + 357 = _____

More Starter Problems

In each set of problems below, solve all three Starter Problems. Then solve the final problem, and show your solution. If you used a Starter Problem to help you solve the final problem, tell which one.

NOTE Students solve Starter Problems and then use one of the Starter Problems to solve the final problem.

SMH 20–24

1. $200 + 300 =$ _____

   $317 + 300 =$ _____

   $17 + 58 \ \ =$ _____

   $217 + 358 =$ _____

2. $100 + 298 =$ _____

   $119 + 300 =$ _____

   $100 + 200 =$ _____

   $119 + 298 =$ _____

Ongoing Review

3. Which equation is **not** true?

   A. $35 + 43 = 80$ **C.** $63 + 17 = 80$

   B. $25 + 55 = 80$ **D.** $45 + 35 = 80$

Combining Collections: How Many Altogether?

Choose three of the matches you made when you played *Collections Match*. Make addition problems about combining the two collections in each match, and solve each problem. Show your solutions.

1. Category of Collections: _____

Addition Problem: _____ + _____ = _____

2. Category of Collections: _____

Addition Problem: _____ + _____ = _____

3. Category of Collections: _____

Addition Problem: _____ + _____ = _____

How Many More?

Solve the problems below. Show your solutions on the number lines.

NOTE Students practice finding combinations of numbers that add to a given total.

SMH 32

1. $34 +$ _____ $= 100$

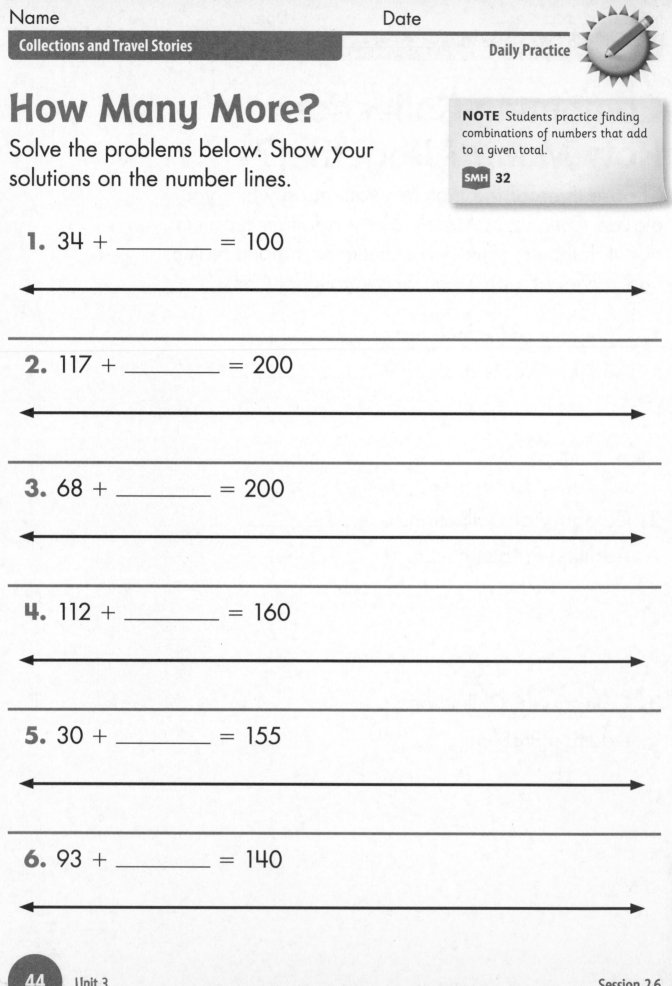

2. $117 +$ _____ $= 200$

3. $68 +$ _____ $= 200$

4. $112 +$ _____ $= 160$

5. $30 +$ _____ $= 155$

6. $93 +$ _____ $= 140$

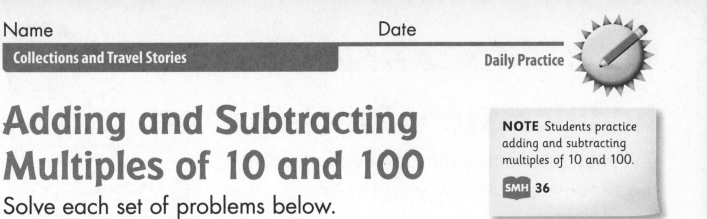

NOTE Students practice adding and subtracting multiples of 10 and 100.

SMH 36

Adding and Subtracting Multiples of 10 and 100

Solve each set of problems below.

1. 381 − 50 = _____

381 − 70 = _____

381 − 90 = _____

2. 239 + 100 = _____

239 + 200 = _____

239 + 400 = _____

3. 157 + 40 = _____

157 + 60 = _____

157 + 80 = _____

4. 862 − 50 = _____

862 − 150 = _____

862 − 200 = _____

Ongoing Review

5. 135 + _____ = 300

A. 65   **B.** 165   **C.** 175   **D.** 235

Addition Story Problems

For each problem, write an equation, solve the problem, and show your solution.

NOTE Students practice solving addition story problems with 2- and 3-digit numbers.

SMH 12, 20–24

1. The South City Soccer League has 133 players on all of the teams. The Rivertown Soccer League has 148 players. When all of the players in both leagues get together for a tournament, how many players will there be?

2. The South City Soccer League bought 140 small T-shirts and 85 large T-shirts to give to the players, the parents, and the coaches. How many T-shirts did the league buy?

3. To pay for new equipment, the Rivertown Soccer League raised $161 from a bake sale and $244 from a car wash. How much money did the league raise in total?

Addition and the 200 Chart

Solve these problems. Fill in the totals on the 200 chart.

> **NOTE** Students review the place value of 3-digit numbers as they add 10s to any number. Students fill in the missing numbers on the 200 chart.
>
> **SMH** 10, 36

1. 114 + 60 = _____

2. 127 + 30 = _____

3. 134 + 10 = _____

4. 139 + 40 = _____

5. 101 + 40 = _____

6. 166 + 20 = _____

7. 108 + 20 = _____

8. 123 + 70 = _____

9. 150 + 40 = _____

10. 142 + 20 = _____

11. 115 + 50 = _____

12. 111 + 70 = _____

101		103			106				
								119	
121									130
		133							
	142			145					
	152							159	
			164				168		
171						177			180
			184					189	
191						197			200

Practicing With Subtraction Cards

Choose 6 Subtraction Card problems from your "working on" pile, and write these on the blank cards below. Practice these at home with a friend or family member.

NOTE Students practice subtraction facts, which are related to the addition combinations up to 10 + 10. Ask your child to explain how the addition clues help him or her solve these subtraction problems.

SMH 31

____ – ____ = ____

____ – ____ = ____

Addition Clue: _____

____ – ____ = ____

____ – ____ = ____

Addition Clue: _____

____ – ____ = ____

____ – ____ = ____

Addition Clue: _____

____ – ____ = ____

____ – ____ = ____

Addition Clue: _____

____ – ____ = ____

____ – ____ = ____

Addition Clue: _____

____ – ____ = ____

____ – ____ = ____

Addition Clue: _____

Distance Riddles (page 1 of 2)

Solve the riddles below. Put the two numbers you find on the number line. Then find the difference between each pair of numbers. Write the addition and subtraction equations that show the distance between the numbers.

1. The distance between 100 and me is 28.
What numbers can I be?

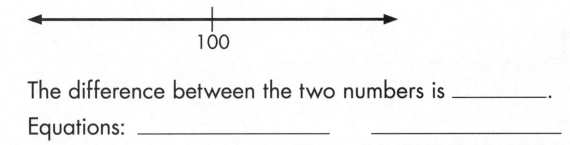

100

The difference between the two numbers is _____.

Equations: _____   _____

2. The distance between 100 and me is 44.
What numbers can I be?

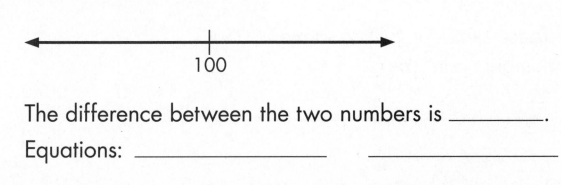

100

The difference between the two numbers is _____.

Equations: _____   _____

Distance Riddles (page 2 of 2)

3. The distance between 100 and me is 57.
What numbers can I be?

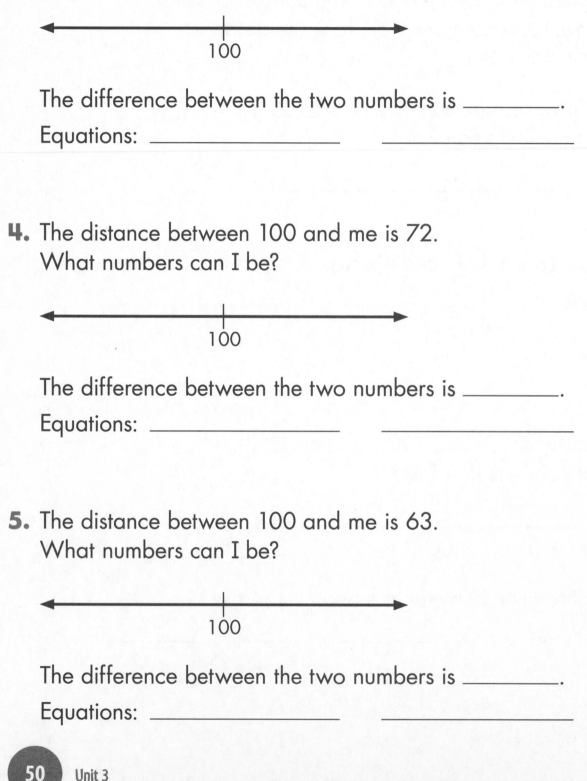

100

The difference between the two numbers is _____.

Equations: _____   _____

4. The distance between 100 and me is 72.
What numbers can I be?

100

The difference between the two numbers is _____.

Equations: _____   _____

5. The distance between 100 and me is 63.
What numbers can I be?

100

The difference between the two numbers is _____.

Equations: _____   _____

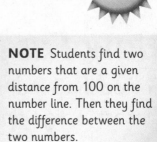
More Distance Riddles

Solve the riddles below. Write the two numbers you find on the number line. Then find the difference between each pair of numbers. Write the addition and subtraction equations that show the distance between the numbers.

> **NOTE** Students find two numbers that are a given distance from 100 on the number line. Then they find the difference between the two numbers.
>
> **SMH** 20–24, 32–35

1. The distance between 100 and me is 31. What numbers can I be?

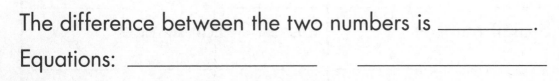

100

The difference between the two numbers is _____.

Equations: _____   _____

2. The distance between 100 and me is 86. What numbers can I be?

100

The difference between the two numbers is _____.

Equations: _____   _____

Ongoing Review

3. There were 100 paper clips in a box. Gina used 29 clips for a project. How many were left?

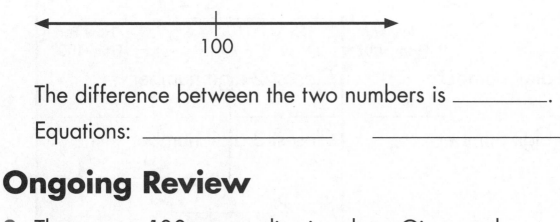

A. 81   **B.** 70   **C.** 71   **D.** 129

How Far From 100? Recording Sheet

For each round, write your cards and find the closest 2-digit and 3-digit numbers you can make. Figure out how far each number is from 100.

Remember to keep a ⌐ 1 ¬ to use for each round.

Round 1 Cards	**Round 2 Cards**
___ ___ ___ ___ ___ **How Far From 100?**	___ ___ ___ ___ ___ **How Far From 100?**
Closest 2-digit number	Closest 2-digit number
___ ___ _____	___ ___ _____
Closest 3-digit number	Closest 3-digit number
___ ___ ___ _____	___ ___ ___ _____
Score: _____	Score: _____
Round 3 Cards	**Round 4 Cards**
___ ___ ___ ___ ___ **How Far From 100?**	___ ___ ___ ___ ___ **How Far From 100?**
Closest 2-digit number	Closest 2-digit number
___ ___ _____	___ ___ _____
Closest 3-digit number	Closest 3-digit number
___ ___ ___ _____	___ ___ ___ _____
Score: _____	Score: _____

Total Score: _____

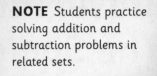

Related Problem Sets

Solve each set of related problems. Think about how to use one problem to solve the next one.

NOTE Students practice solving addition and subtraction problems in related sets.

SMH 20–24, 32, 36

1. 128 − 10 = _____

128 − 20 = _____

128 − 30 = _____

128 − 40 = _____

2. 50 + 47 = _____

60 + 47 = _____

70 + 47 = _____

80 + 47 = _____

3. 90 + _____ = 93

80 + _____ = 93

60 + _____ = 93

30 + _____ = 93

4. 85 + 5 = _____

85 + 15 = _____

85 + 25 = _____

85 + 35 = _____

Travel Problems:
The Santos Family Vacation

Answer the questions below and show your solutions. Write equations for each problem.

1. <u>Keisha's Question</u>

When the Santos family stopped at the diner, they had traveled 36 miles from their home. At the gas station, the trip meter read 79 miles. How far did they travel from the diner to the gas station?

2. <u>Edwin's Question</u>

The Santos family had driven 79 miles when they stopped at the gas station. How much farther will they have to drive to reach 100 miles?

3. <u>Question for the Class</u>

When the Santos family stopped at the gas station, the trip meter read 79 miles. When they arrived at their grandparents' house, it read 128 miles. How far did they travel from the gas station to their grandparents' house?

© Pearson Education 3

What's the Number?

NOTE Students review place value of 3-digit numbers.

SMH 9, 32–35, 36

1. What number is 60 more than 823?

_____

2. What number is 60 less than 345? _____

3. What number is 140 more than 361? _____

4. What number is 270 less than 631? _____

5. What number has 7 hundreds, 9 tens, and 7 ones? _____

6. What number has 42 tens and 16 ones?

_____

7. What number has 2 hundreds and 5 ones?

_____

8. What number has 3 hundreds and 18 tens?

_____

Ongoing Review

9. Which number has 91 tens and 12 ones?

A. 910 **C.** 921

B. 912 **D.** 922

Problems About *Capture* on the 300 Chart ✏️

NOTE Students solve problems related to a game in which they move on a 300 chart by adding 10s and 1s.

SMH G4

Jane and Edwin are playing *Capture on the 300 Chart.* Answer the following questions about their game. You may use a 300 chart to help you.

1. Jane's game piece was on 139. She used these cards to capture a marker:

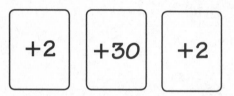

What number did she land on?

Explain how you figured it out.

2. Edwin's game piece was on 216. He used these cards to capture a marker:

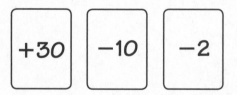

What number did he land on?

Explain how you figured it out.

More Distance Riddles

1. I am 20 less than 100. What number am I? _____

I am 52 more than 100. What number am I? _____

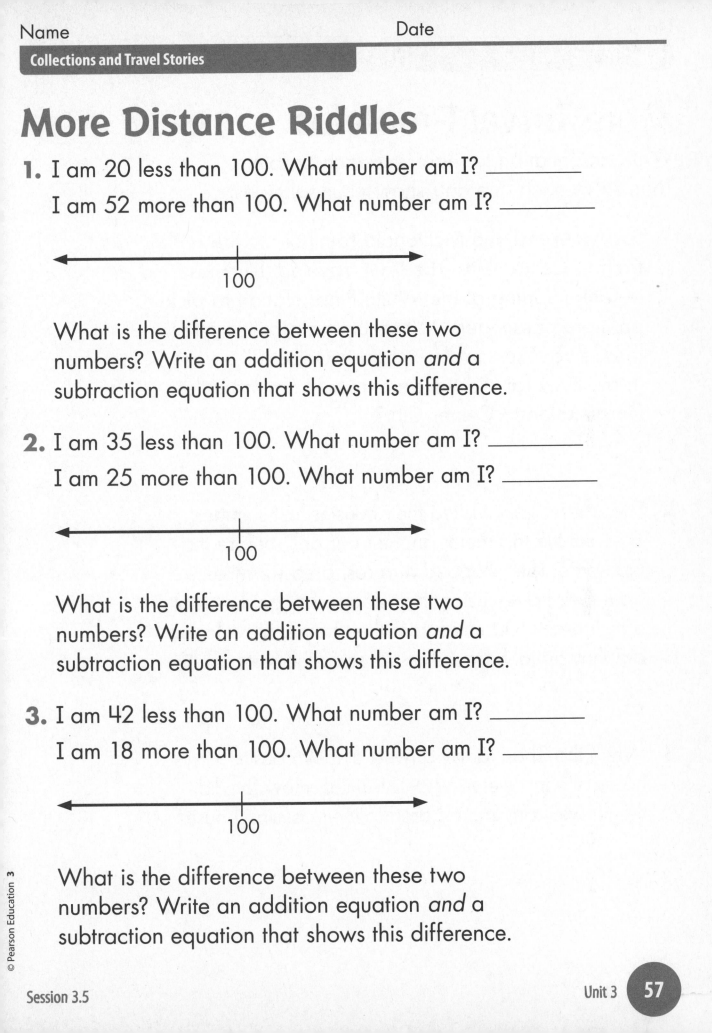

What is the difference between these two numbers? Write an addition equation *and* a subtraction equation that shows this difference.

2. I am 35 less than 100. What number am I? _____

I am 25 more than 100. What number am I? _____

What is the difference between these two numbers? Write an addition equation *and* a subtraction equation that shows this difference.

3. I am 42 less than 100. What number am I? _____

I am 18 more than 100. What number am I? _____

What is the difference between these two numbers? Write an addition equation *and* a subtraction equation that shows this difference.

More Travel Problems

Write an equation to represent each problem.
Then solve each one and show your solutions.

1. Last weekend, the McDonald family took the train to Center City. The train traveled 16 miles before stopping at the White Pines station to pick up more passengers. When the train pulled into the Center City station, it had traveled 93 miles in all. How far did the train travel from the White Pines station to Center City?

2. The Chan family visited their cousins last summer. They set the trip meter on their car at 0 before they left home. They stopped at a rest area 42 miles from their home. Later, they stopped to get lunch at a restaurant 100 miles from their home. How far did they travel from the rest area to the restaurant?

3. When the Chan family arrived at their cousins' house, the trip meter read 138 miles. How far did they travel from the rest area to their cousins' house?

Biking Trip

Write an equation, solve each problem, and show your solution for each problem.

NOTE Students solve distance problems to practice subtraction.

SMH 26–28, 32–35

1. Philip and Keith are on a 3-day biking trip. Their final destination is 138 miles away. On the first day, they rode 51 miles. How much farther do they have to bike?

2. On the second day, they biked through some steep hills and rode only 37 miles. How far have they biked so far?

3. How much farther do they have to bike to reach their destination?

Ongoing Review

4. $69 + $ _____ $= 143$

   A. 64   **C.** 84

   B. 74   **D.** 86

Addition Practice

For each problem, write an equation, solve the problem, and show your solution.

NOTE Students practice solving story problems involving the addition of 3-digit numbers. Ask your child to explain how he or she solved each problem.

SMH 12, 20–24

1. Last summer, the Smith family traveled to their cousins' house. The trip took two days. They drove 246 miles on the first day of their trip and 318 miles on the second day. How far did they travel in all?

2. The West Side Toy Museum has 372 toy cars in its collection. Mr. Jones is donating his collection of 153 toy cars to the museum. How many cars will the West Side Toy Museum have then?

3. The students in a third-grade class at Beech Street School collected 298 pennies the first week of their class collection. They collected 282 pennies the second week. How many pennies in total did the students collect in the first two weeks of their class collection?

Sticker Station

For each problem, write an equation that represents what the problem is asking. Then solve the problem and show your work.

NOTE Students practice adding and subtracting 2-digit numbers.

SMH 12, 20–24, 26–28, 32–35

1. Gina went to Sticker Station and bought 64 lion stickers and 30 boat stickers. How many stickers did she buy?

2. Gina went back the next day and bought 33 more stickers. How many does she have now?

3. David had 86 stickers. He gave 41 stickers to his best friend, Nancy. How many stickers does David have now?

4. Philip had 79 stickers. He went to Sticker Station and bought 15 more stickers. How many stickers does Philip have now?

More Trips Home

Solve the problems below. Be sure to show how you got your answer. Write equations that show what you did.

1. Last summer, the Soeng family visited an amusement park 136 miles from their home. On the way back home, they stopped to see their aunt. She lives 72 miles from their home. How far is it from the amusement park to their aunt's home?

2. During spring vacation, the Davis family drove 152 miles to visit the science museum in their state capital. On the way home, they stopped at the Dinosaur Tracks State Park. The park is 43 miles from their home. How far was the drive from the science museum to the State Park?

3. Last weekend, the Smith family drove 179 miles to Ocean Beach State Park. On the way home, they stopped for dinner at the Green Mountain Family Restaurant. The restaurant is 65 miles from their home. How far was the drive from Ocean Beach State Park to the restaurant?

Marbles

For each problem, write an equation that represents what the problem is asking. Then solve the problem and show your work.

NOTE Students practice adding and subtracting 2-digit numbers.

SMH 12, 20–24, 26–28, 32–35

1. Richard has 53 green marbles and 28 orange marbles. How many marbles does he have altogether?

2. Christopher had 68 marbles. His uncle gave him 20 marbles and his cousin gave him 30 marbles. How many marbles does Christopher have now?

3. Kim had 89 marbles. She gave 42 marbles to her sister. How many marbles does Kim have now?

Comparing Lengths and Heights (page 1 of 2)

For each problem, write an equation, solve the problem, and show your solution. You may use cubes, number lines, or drawings if it will help you explain your thinking.

1. Ms. Martinez is 67 inches tall. Philip is 52 inches tall. How much taller is Ms. Martinez than Philip?

2. A basketball player is 82 inches tall. How much taller is the basketball player than Ms. Martinez?

3. How much would Philip have to grow to be as tall as the basketball player?

© Pearson Education 3

Comparing Lengths and Heights (page 2 of 2)

The Nature Center has a collection of snakes. The table at the right shows some of the snakes and their lengths. Use the information in the table to answer the questions. Remember to write an equation and show your solution.

Kind of Snake	Length in Inches
Timber rattlesnake	56 inches
Ring-necked snake	15 inches
Rainbow snake	53 inches
Boa constrictor	84 inches
Garter snake	18 inches
Black Rat snake	92 inches

4. How much longer is the timber rattlesnake than the garter snake?

_____

5. Which snake in the collection is the longest?

_____

Which snake in the collection is the shortest? _____

How much would the shortest snake have to grow to be as long as the longest snake? _____

6. Make up your own snake problem. Then solve it.

How much longer is the _____

snake than the _____ snake? _____

Adding Up Coins

1. What is the value of these coins?
Show how you figured it out.

> **NOTE** Students practice adding money amounts and using different combinations of coins to equal the same amount.
>
> **SMH** 37–38

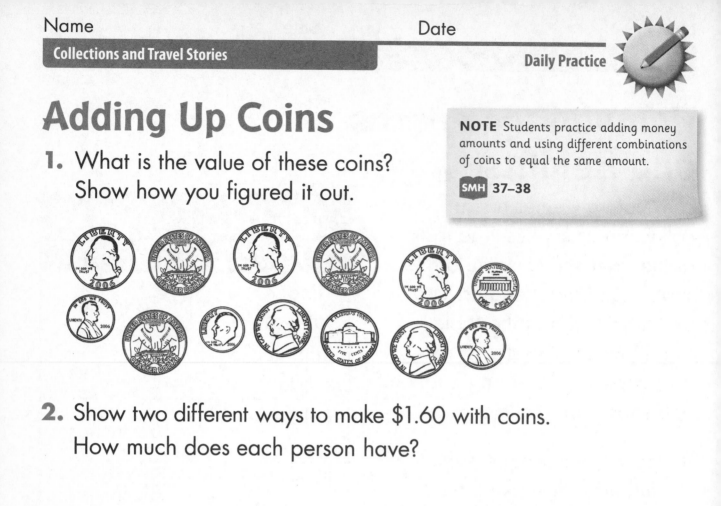

2. Show two different ways to make $1.60 with coins.
How much does each person have?

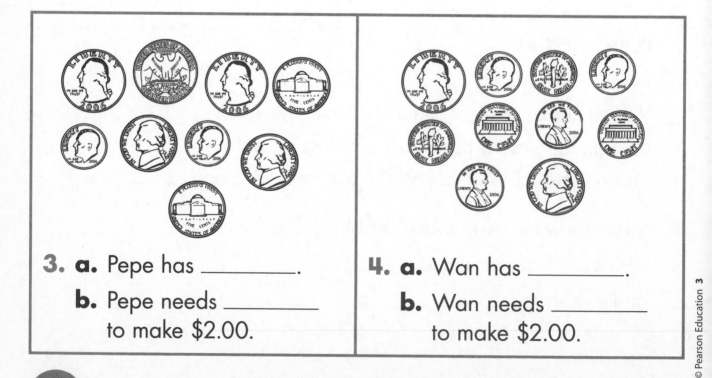

3. a. Pepe has _____.

   b. Pepe needs _____
       to make $2.00.

4. a. Wan has _____.

   b. Wan needs _____
       to make $2.00.

Comparing Collections: How Many More?

For each problem, write an equation, solve the problem, and show your solution.

1. Denzel and Jung each collect marbles. Denzel has 104 marbles, and Jung has 65 marbles. How many more marbles does Denzel have than Jung?

2. Keith has 92 stickers in his sticker book. Nancy has 58 stickers in her book. How many more stickers does Keith have than Nancy?

3. Ms. Santos' class collected 86 bottle caps in the first two days of their Class Collection. Mr. Singh's class collected 123 bottle caps. How many more bottle caps did Mr. Singh's class collect than Ms. Santos' class?

4. The Ocean Park Aquarium has 95 tropical fish and 67 jellyfish in their collection. How many more tropical fish than jellyfish does the Aquarium have?

Oldest Animals

The animals in the table lived a record number of years.

NOTE Students solve comparison problems to practice subtraction.

SMH 26–28, 32–35

1. How many more years did the oldest monkey live than the oldest parrot?

Animal	Record Ages
Parrot	35 years
Monkey	53 years
Alligator	66 years
Eel	88 years

2. How many more years would the oldest alligator have to have lived to live as long as the oldest eel?

3. A young alligator is 9 years old. How many more years will it need to live to tie the record for the oldest alligator?

4. Explain the strategy you used to find the answer in Problem 3.

Ongoing Review

5. How much longer did the oldest eel live than the oldest parrot?

A. 35 years   **C.** 53 years

B. 50 years   **D.** 55 years

All About the Number

Answer the following questions about the number 432. You may use your 1,000 chart to help you.

NOTE Students use a 1,000 chart to answer questions about a given 3-digit number.

SMH 9, 10–11, 36

1. Is 432 closer to 400 or 500?

_____

How do you know?

2. Choose a landmark number that is close to 432. _____

3. Is 432 more or less than that landmark number?

_____

4. How many 100s are in 432? _____

5. How many 10s are in 432? _____

6. What number is 30 more than 432? _____

7. What number is 20 less than 432? _____

Unit 3

Related Problems (page 1 of 2)

Solve the problems. Think about how solving the first one in each set might help you solve the others. Show your solutions. Write equations for the story problems.

Set 1. Kelley had 88 pennies in her piggy bank. She spent 50¢ on a get-well card for her grandmother. How much money does Kelley have left?

Nicholas' mom gave him the loose change from her purse, which came to 88¢. He spent 40¢ on a sticker for his collection. How much money does Nicholas have left?

Set 2. $95 - 30 =$ _____ $95 - 20 =$ _____ $95 - 15 =$ _____	**Set 3.** $\begin{array}{r} 100 \\ -\ 70 \\ \hline \end{array}$ $\begin{array}{r} 105 \\ -\ 70 \\ \hline \end{array}$ $\begin{array}{r} 115 \\ -\ 70 \\ \hline \end{array}$
Set 4. $160 - 20 =$ _____ $160 - 25 =$ _____ $160 - 27 =$ _____	**Set 5.** $\begin{array}{r} 135 \\ -\ 30 \\ \hline \end{array}$ $\begin{array}{r} 135 \\ -\ 40 \\ \hline \end{array}$ $\begin{array}{r} 135 \\ -\ 38 \\ \hline \end{array}$

Related Problems (page 2 of 2) ✎ WRITING

Solve the problems. Think about how solving the first one in each set might help you solve the others. Show your solutions. Write equations for the story problems.

Set 6. Bridget has 100 stickers. Gil has 67 stickers. How many more stickers does Gil need to have the same number as Bridget?

On Monday, Mr. Li's students brought in 112 pennies for their Class Collection. Ms. Trenton's students brought in 67 pennies on the same day. How many more pennies did the students in Mr. Li's class bring to school than the students in Ms. Trenton's class?

| **Set 7.** $100 - 50 = $ _____ $120 - 50 = $ _____ $120 - 54 = $ _____ | **Set 8.** $\begin{array}{r} 200 \\ -150 \end{array}$ $\begin{array}{r} 210 \\ -150 \end{array}$ $\begin{array}{r} 210 \\ -145 \end{array}$ |
| **Set 9.** $230 - 100 = $ _____ $230 - 90 = $ _____ $230 - 95 = $ _____ | **Set 10.** $\begin{array}{r} 300 \\ -25 \end{array}$ $\begin{array}{r} 301 \\ -25 \end{array}$ $\begin{array}{r} 301 \\ -26 \end{array}$ |

Choose one set of problems on either page 71 or page 72. On a separate sheet of paper, explain how you used each problem in the set to help you solve the next problem.

How Much Longer?
How Much Taller?

For each problem, write an equation, solve the problem, and show your solution.

1. The Burmese python at the Riverview Zoo is 132 inches long. The boa constrictor is 87 inches long. How much longer is the Burmese python than the boa constrictor?

2. Keisha is 54 inches tall. Her younger sister Mimi is 37 inches tall. How much would Mimi need to grow to be as tall as Keisha is now?

3. Anna and Gil are growing sunflowers in their gardens. Anna's sunflower is 116 inches tall. Gil's sunflower is 49 inches tall. How much taller is Anna's sunflower than Gil's sunflower?

Picking Apples

Solve each problem. Show your work and write an equation.

NOTE Students practice adding and subtracting 2-digit numbers.

SMH 20–24, 32–35

1. While she was at the farm, Amy picked 62 apples in the morning and 54 apples in the afternoon. How many apples did Amy pick in all?

2. Adam picked 73 apples in the morning and 47 apples in the afternoon. How many apples did Adam pick in all?

3. Lana picked 86 apples at the farm. When she got home, she and her mother used 24 apples to make apple pies. How many apples were left?

How Many Are Left? (page 1 of 2)

For each problem, write an equation, solve the problem, and show your solution.

Remember that there are 100 stickers on a sheet and 10 stickers on a strip.

1. Kathryn had 5 sheets of baseball stickers. She gave 40 stickers to her friend for a birthday present. How many stickers did Kathryn have left?

2. Edwin had 3 sheets of insect stickers. He gave 12 dragonfly stickers to the science teacher. How many stickers did Edwin have left?

3. Gil had 2 sheets and 5 strips of famous people stickers. He sold 65 of them at a yard sale. How many stickers did Gil have left?

4. Kelley had 4 sheets of cat stickers. Her dog chewed up 2 sheets, plus 47 more from another sheet. How many stickers did Kelley have left?

How Many Are Left? (page 2 of 2)

For each problem, write an equation, solve the problem, and show your solution.

5. The Greenville City Museum had 145 stamps in its Canadian stamp collection. The museum sold 60 of them to another collector. How many are left?

6. Ms. Heston had 253 puzzles in her collection. She sold 130 of them to the children's museum. How many are left?

7. The Flagtown Aquarium had 282 tropical fish in its collection. Last winter 106 got sick and died. How many are left?

8. Mr. Aboud had 222 basketball trading cards in his collection. He gave 182 of them to his niece and nephew. How many are left?

Parking Garage

The parking attendant keeps a log of the number of cars parked in the garage each day. The table shows the count for last week.

Use the information about the parking garage. For Problems 2 and 3, write an equation, solve the problem, and show your solution.

NOTE Students order and subtract with 3-digit numbers.

SMH 10–11, 32–35

Day	Number of Cars
Sunday	178
Monday	224
Tuesday	230
Wednesday	237
Thursday	215
Friday	261
Saturday	268

1. Write the number of cars in order, from the least to the greatest, on the number line below.

⟵――――――――――――――――――――――⟶

2. How many more cars were parked on Saturday than on Sunday? _____

3. The maximum capacity of the garage is 305 cars. How many more cars could have been parked on Monday? _____

Ongoing Review

4. Which number has 26 10s?

A. 26   **B.** 126   **C.** 226   **D.** 260

How Far From 100?
Story Problems

Solve the problems below. Be sure to show how you got your answers. Write equations that show what you did.

> **NOTE** Students find 2-and 3-digit numbers that are close to 100.
>
> **SMH** G15

1. Oscar and Becky are playing *How Far From 100?* In Round 1, Becky is dealt the following cards:

Becky says that 126 is the closest three-digit number to 100 that she can make. Is there a *2-digit number* she can make that will get her closer to 100?

2. While playing *How Far From 100?*, Mia makes a number that is 31 away from 100. What could her number be? Gil makes a different number that is 31 away from 100. What could his number be?

3. Elena makes a number that is 19 away from 100. What two numbers could she have made? Explain how you know.

© Pearson Education 3

Solving Subtraction Problems

Solve the following problems and show your
solutions. Write an equation for the story problem.

1. $242 - 160 =$ _____

2. Ms. Santos' class has collected 208 cans for the
third grade's recycling project. Mr. Rivers' class
has collected 88 cans. How many more cans has

Ms. Santos' class collected? _____

3.
$$
\begin{array}{r}
168 \\
-\ 73 \\
\hline
\end{array}
$$

4. Write a story for this problem, and then solve
the problem.

$194 - 112 =$ _____

Subtraction Problems

Solve each problem and show
your solution.

> **NOTE** Students solve subtraction problems.
>
> **SMH** 32–35

1. $184 - 65 = $ _____

2. $\begin{array}{r} 105 \\ -\ 32 \\ \hline \end{array}$

3. $274 - 159 = $ _____

Ongoing Review

4. Which expression does **not** equal 100?

    A. $135 - 40 + 5$

    B. $68 + 50 - 20 + 2$

    C. $75 + 40 - 25$

    D. $66 + 50 - 10 - 10 + 4$

Addition and Subtraction Practice

Solve the following problems and show your solutions.

NOTE Students practice solving addition and subtraction problems with 2- and 3-digit numbers.

SMH 20–24, 32–35

1. 145 + 68 = _____

2. 227 + 114 = _____

3. 171 − 83 = _____

4. 250 − 166 = _____

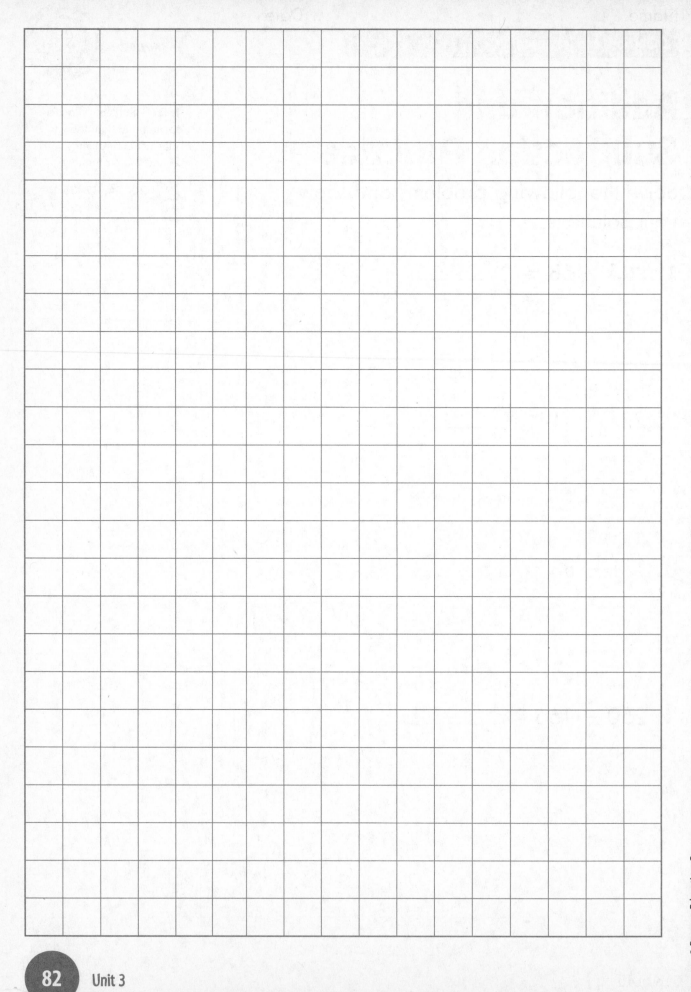

Adding and Subtracting in Our Solar System

NOTE Students solve real-world problems involving the math content in this unit.

SMH 26–28, 29–30, 32–35

Earth	Mars	Mercury	Venus
365 days to revolve around the Sun	687 days to revolve around the Sun	88 days to revolve around the Sun	225 days to revolve around the Sun
Average temperature: 59°F	Average temperature: −81°F	Average temperature: 333°F	Average temperature: 867°F

Use the data in the pictures to help you solve the problems.

1. How much hotter is it on Venus than on Mercury?

2. Which planet takes 450 days to revolve around the Sun two times?

3. One planet takes 462 more days to revolve around the Sun than another planet. Which planets are they? Explain how you found your answer.

Ikenaga 2 Jos Leys

"A relatively simple formula can generate immensely complex images." – **Jos Leys**

Investigations
IN NUMBER, DATA, AND SPACE®

Perimeter, Angles, and Area

Perimeter, Angles, and Area

Finding Lengths

Use a ruler, yardstick, and meterstick to find objects that are about the same length as these measurement units. Record the objects that you find for each unit.

Centimeter	Inch
Example: The tip of my pencil	

Foot	Yard/Meter

What's the Number?

Answer the following questions.

NOTE Students work on place value in 3-digit numbers.

SMH 7–8, 9, 36

1. What number is 50 more than 824? _____

2. What number is 40 less than 567? _____

3. What number is 80 more than 365? _____

4. What number is 30 less than 215? _____

5. What number is 200 more than 439? _____

6. What number has 5 hundreds, 3 tens, and 2 ones? _____

7. What number has 31 tens and no ones? _____

8. What number has 6 hundreds and 8 ones? _____

9. What number has 4 hundreds and 13 tens? _____

10. What number has 16 tens and 15 ones? _____

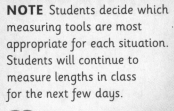

Choosing Measurement Tools and Units (page 1 of 2)

NOTE Students decide which measuring tools are most appropriate for each situation. Students will continue to measure lengths in class for the next few days.

SMH 105, 106, 107

What measurement tool (ruler, yardstick, or meterstick) would you use for each situation? What unit of measure (centimeter, inch, foot, yard, or meter) would you use?

Explain why you chose that tool and that unit of measure.

1. I need to know the length of a fence that will go around the basketball court.

Tool: _____   Unit of Measure: _____

I chose these because . . .

2. I need to know how long the strap is on my book bag.

Tool: _____   Unit of Measure: _____

I chose these because . . .

Choosing Measurement Tools and Units (page 2 of 2) ✏️WRITING

3. I need to know the width of my foot at its widest point.

Tool: _____ Unit of Measure: _____

I chose these because . . .

4. I want to buy material for a bedspread. I need to know how long and how wide my bed is.

Tool: _____ Unit of Measure: _____

I chose these because . . .

Finding and Measuring Perimeters (page 1 of 2)

Choose 5 objects in the classroom that have perimeters you can measure, such as a bulletin board, the top of a table, or the side of the teacher's desk. Measure their perimeters and record your work below.

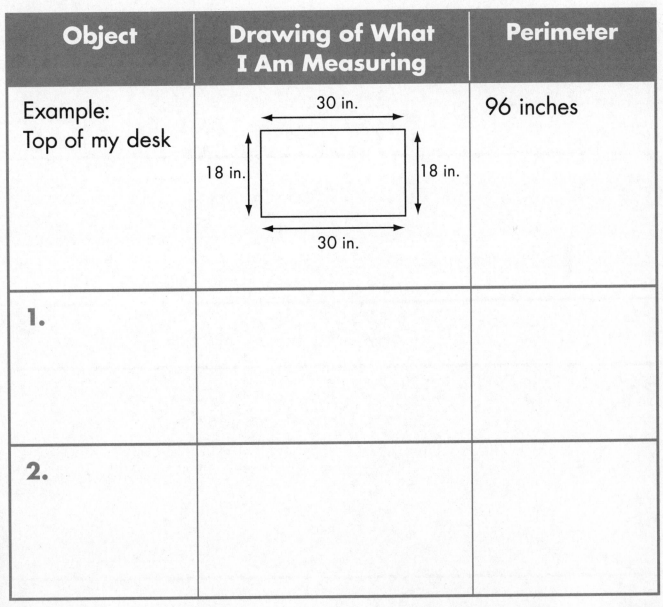

Object	Drawing of What I Am Measuring	Perimeter
Example: Top of my desk	30 in. / 18 in. / 18 in. / 30 in.	96 inches
1.		
2.		

Finding and Measuring Perimeters (page 2 of 2)

Object	Drawing of What I Am Measuring	Perimeter
3.		
4.		
5.		

Adding 10s and 100s

Solve the following sets of related problems.
How would you use one problem to solve
the next one?

NOTE Students practice solving addition problems in related sets.

SMH 20–24, 36

1. $168 + 30 =$ _____

$168 + 40 =$ _____

$168 + 50 =$ _____

2. $249 + 100 =$ _____

$249 + 200 =$ _____

$249 + 300 =$ _____

3. $67 + 40 =$ _____

$67 + 140 =$ _____

$67 + 240 =$ _____

4. $282 + 10 =$ _____

$282 + 20 =$ _____

$282 + 30 =$ _____

5. $206 + 30 =$ _____

$236 + 30 =$ _____

$266 + 30 =$ _____

6. $234 + 150 =$ _____

$234 + 160 =$ _____

$234 + 170 =$ _____

Perimeters at Home

Measure the perimeters of at least two objects at home. Record your work below.

NOTE Students practice measuring the perimeter of objects, such as the top edge of the kitchen table or the front of the refrigerator door.

SMH 110–111, 112–113

Object	Drawing of What I Am Measuring	Perimeter

© Pearson Education 3

Perimeter Problems (page 1 of 2) ✏️ *WRITING*

1. Your teacher wants to put a tape around the edge of the largest table in the classroom. How much tape will she need? Explain how you got the answer.

2. The perimeter of Pilar's yard is 100 feet. Draw a picture of what her yard might look like, and label each side.

Perimeter, Angles, and Area

Perimeter Problems (page 2 of 2)

3. Draw three different rectangles below that each have a perimeter of 20 centimeters.

Making Shapes

Draw a sketch of each given shape.
Label the length of each side.

NOTE Students draw and label shapes with given perimeters.

SMH 112

1. Square with a perimeter of 80 units

2. Rectangle with a perimeter of 120 units

3. Square with a perimeter of 160 units

4. Rectangle with a perimeter of 180 units

Ongoing Review

5. What is the perimeter of a square with 6-inch sides?

A. 12 **B.** 18 **C.** 24 **D.** 36

Perimeter, Angles, and Area

Ordering Shapes
by Perimeter (page 1 of 2)

1. Look at the shapes below. Put them in order
   from the shortest to the longest perimeter
   without measuring.

_____   _____   _____   _____

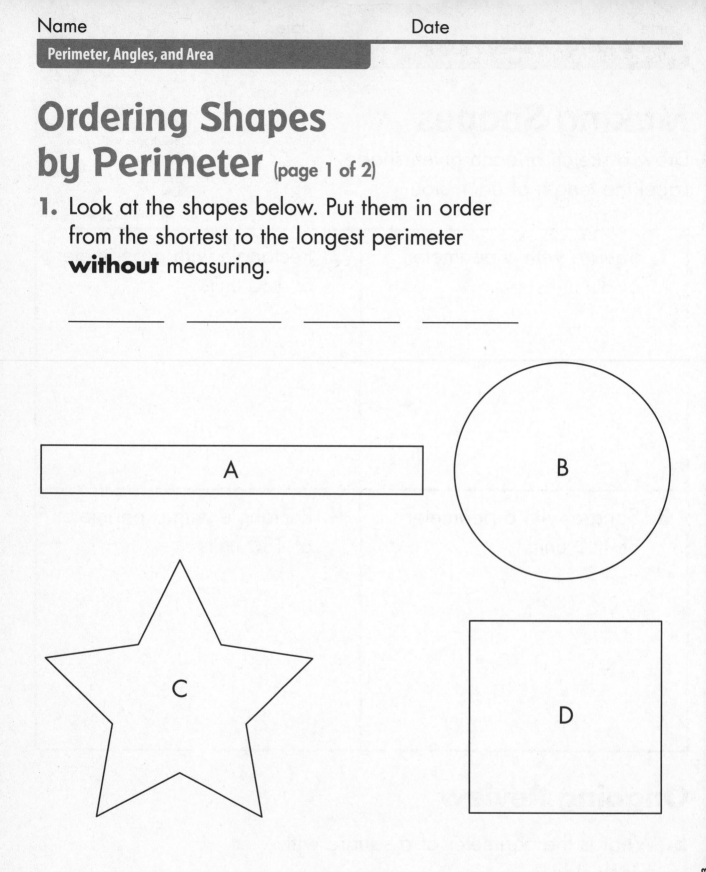

Ordering Shapes
by Perimeter (page 2 of 2)

2. Now choose a measurement tool and measure
the perimeter of each shape. Put them in order
from shortest to longest. Write the perimeter of
each shape.

Measurement tool you chose: _____

_____   _____   _____   _____

3. Compare the lists you made before and after
you measured. Did anything surprise you about
the perimeters of these shapes? Explain what you
found out.

Crossing Over 100

Solve the following sets of related problems. How would you use one problem to solve the next one?

> **NOTE** Students practice solving subtraction problems in related sets.
>
> **SMH** 32–35

1. 100 – 54 = _____

110 – 54 = _____

120 – 54 = _____

2. 100 – 86 = _____

112 – 86 = _____

132 – 86 = _____

3. 100 – 92 = _____

121 – 92 = _____

141 – 92 = _____

4. 100 – 37 = _____

110 – 37 = _____

120 – 37 = _____

5. 100 – 49 = _____

120 – 49 = _____

124 – 49 = _____

6. 100 – 83 = _____

130 – 83 = _____

138 – 83 = _____

Frog Jumps (page 1 of 2)

NOTE Students practice adding and subtracting centimeters.

SMH 25, 106

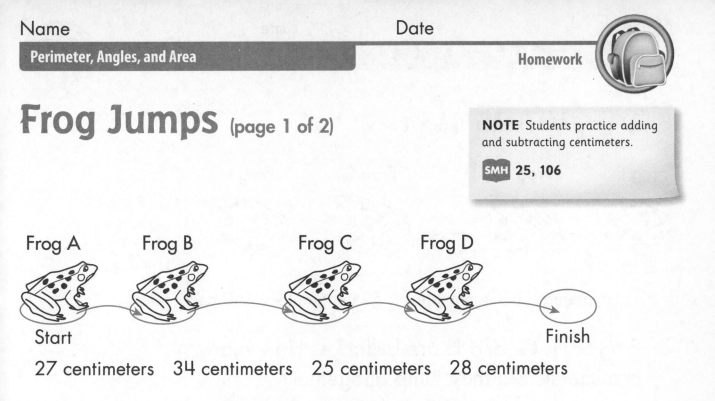

Frog A   Frog B   Frog C   Frog D

Start   Finish

27 centimeters   34 centimeters   25 centimeters   28 centimeters

1. Frogs A, B, C, and D had a jumping relay race. How many centimeters did they jump altogether?

2. Did they jump more or less than one meter? Explain how you know.

Frog Jumps (page 2 of 2)

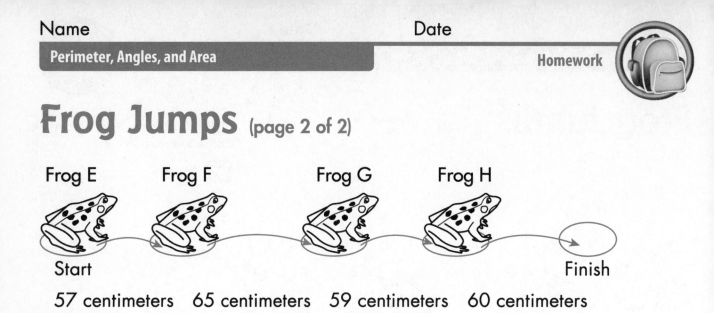

Frog E   Frog F   Frog G   Frog H

Start   Finish

57 centimeters   65 centimeters   59 centimeters   60 centimeters

3. Frogs E, F, G, and H are bullfrogs. How many
centimeters did they jump altogether?

4. How much farther did they jump than Frogs A,
B, C, and D?

Building Shapes

Aaron combined two of these shapes
to make a new shape.

NOTE Students combine shapes and
find the perimeter of the new shape.

SMH 110–111

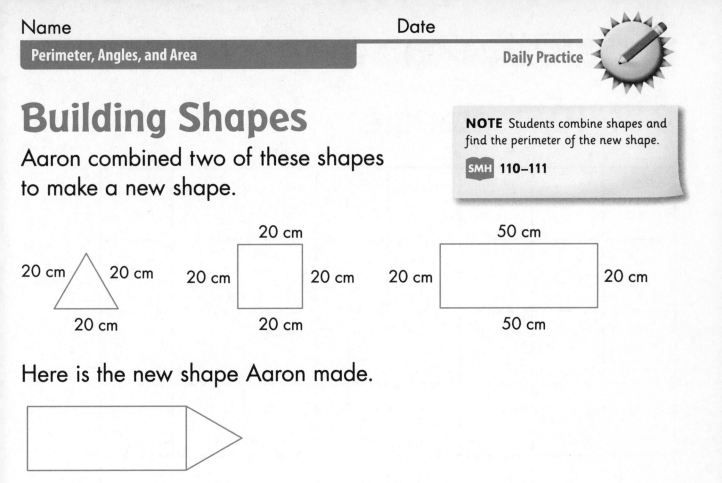

Here is the new shape Aaron made.

1. What is the perimeter of Aaron's new shape? _____

2. Combine the rectangle and the square.
Draw the new shape. Find the perimeter. _____

3. Combine the square and the triangle.
Draw the new shape. Find the perimeter. _____

8 × 10 Rectangle

Perimeter, Angles, and Area

The Perfect Cover-Up (page 1 of 2)

1. Choose one of the tetromino shapes. Draw the shape in the first column of the chart on the next page. Use 10–15 of that shape to cover as many squares as you can on the 8 × 10 rectangle on page 18.

2. Do you think this shape will completely cover the whole rectangle? How do you know? Answer this question in the second column of the chart.

3. If you are not sure whether it will cover the entire rectangle, you can do one of the following:

a. Build more of the same tetromino shape and continue to cover the rectangle.

b. On the rectangle, color the tetromino shapes you have already covered. Color all 4 squares in one tetromino shape the same color, but make each tetromino a different color. Then, try to cover the rest of the rectangle by moving the tetromino shapes or by coloring where additional tetrominoes will fit.

4. Answer the questions in the other columns of the chart.

5. Repeat these steps with the other tetromino shapes.

Perimeter, Angles, and Area

The Perfect Cover-Up (page 2 of 2)

Tetromino Shape	Will it be a "perfect cover-up"? Yes or No	Why or why not?	How many cover the rectangle?

6. Which tetromino shapes were not a "perfect cover-up"? Explain why you think each one did not cover the 8 by 10 rectangle.

How Many More?

Solve the following problems and show
your solutions on the number lines provided.

NOTE Students find the
missing number to make an
addition equation correct.

SMH 27

1. 116 + _____ = 250

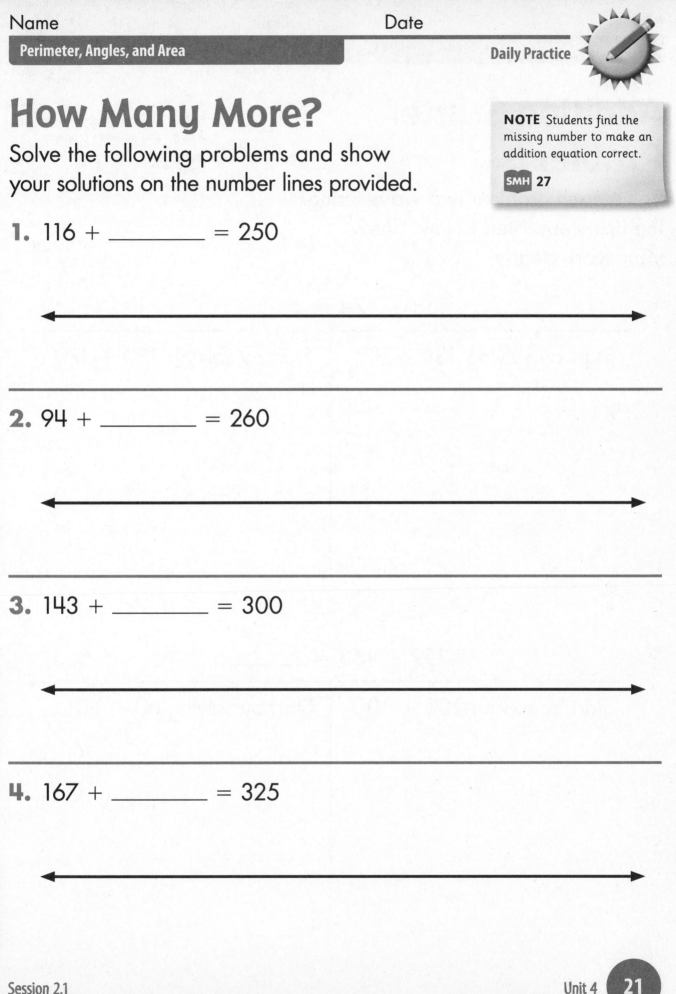

2. 94 + _____ = 260

3. 143 + _____ = 300

4. 167 + _____ = 325

Addition Starter Problems

NOTE Students practice flexibility
with solving addition problems.

SMH 20–24

Solve each problem two ways, using
the first steps listed below. Show
your work clearly.

1. $138 + 174 =$ _____

Start by solving $138 + 4$.	Start by solving $130 + 170$.

2. $259 + 163 =$ _____

Start by solving $200 + 100$.	Start by solving $60 + 60$.

Puzzle Pieces

Which pieces fit in the holes? Draw a line
from each hole in the puzzle to the piece
that will fit exactly. The pieces are painted
on one side only. You can turn pieces, but
do not flip them! Carefully cut out the pieces.
Glue in place the ones that fit.

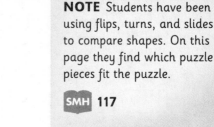

NOTE Students have been
using flips, turns, and slides
to compare shapes. On this
page they find which puzzle
pieces fit the puzzle.

SMH 117

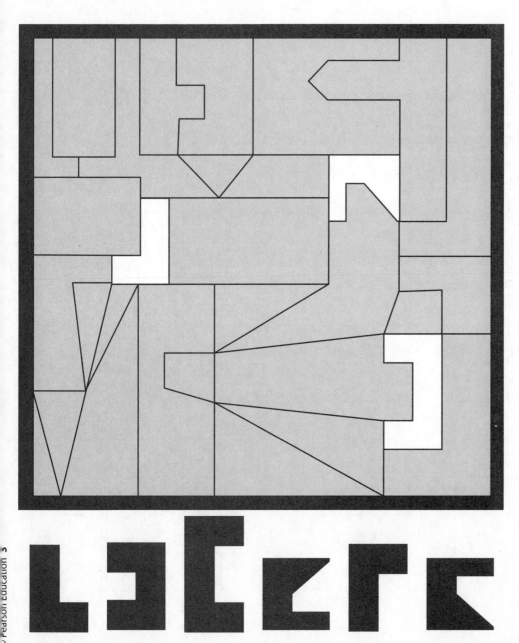

© Pearson Education 3

24 Unit 4

Perimeter, Angles, and Area

Tetromino Puzzle (page 1 of 2)

Perimeter, Angles, and Area

Tetromino Puzzle (page 2 of 2)

The Perfect Fit

NOTE Students use puzzle pieces to practice geometry and spatial relationships.

SMH 117

1. Draw a line from each hole in the puzzle to the piece that will fit there exactly. You can turn pieces, but do **not** flip them!

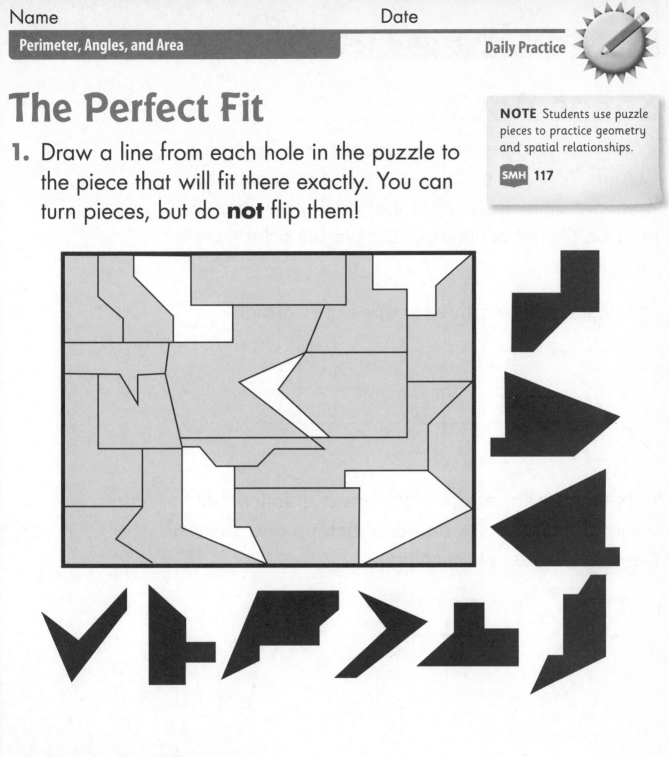

Ongoing Review

2. How was this tetromino moved?

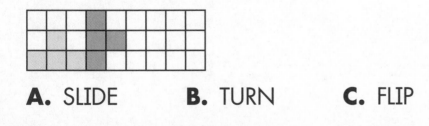

A. SLIDE   **B.** TURN   **C.** FLIP

Shape Poster

With your partner, use the Square and Triangle Cutouts (M17) to make new shapes with exactly 4 square units. Remember that each new shape must be like tetrominoes and have full sides touching.

For example, these three shapes are correct.

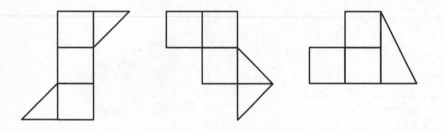

These three shapes are **not** correct. (Notice that some of the full sides do not match up and some of the corners are not touching.)

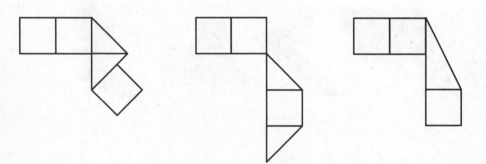

Tape or glue any new shapes you make onto a large sheet of construction paper.

Perimeter, Angles, and Area

What's the Area? (page 1 of 2) ✏️

The drawings below show different sections of
Mr. Tyler's room. Part of the tiled floor has been
covered with a rug. Determine how many tiles are
in the entire rectangle and explain how you found
your answer.

1.

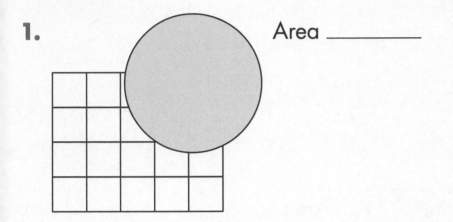

Area _____

2.

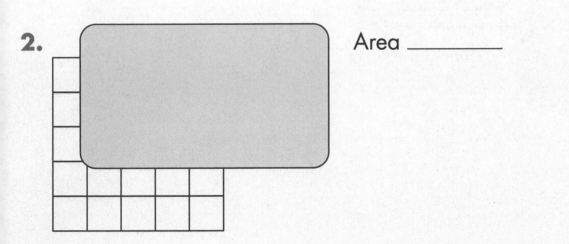

Area _____

What's the Area? (page 2 of 2)

3.

Area _____

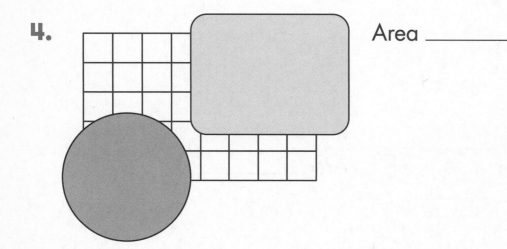

4.

Area _____

Class Collections

For each problem, write an equation, solve the problem, and show your solution. You may use a number line or your 1,000 chart to help you solve these problems.

NOTE Students find the difference between 3-digit numbers. Ask your child to explain how he or she solves each problem.

SMH 29–30, 32–35, 106

1. The students in Ms. Ahmed's class are collecting bottle caps. Their goal is to collect 500. They have 317 so far. How many more do they need to reach their goal?

2. The students in Ms. Kennedy's class are collecting pennies. Their goal is to collect $7.00. So far they have 426 pennies. How many more do they need to reach their goal?

Ongoing Review

3. The perimeter of a rectangle is 39 centimeters. The perimeter of a circle is 39 inches. Which statement about the two shapes is correct?

   A. The rectangle has a larger perimeter.

   B. The circle has a larger perimeter.

   C. The rectangle and the circle have the same perimeter.

Make Some Frog Jumps

Answer the questions below, and
explain how you solved the problem.

NOTE Students practice
solving addition problems
by finding 3 or 4 addends
that equal the given sum.

SMH 25

1. Three frogs jumped a total of 115 centimeters.
How far could each frog have jumped?

Frog 1_____   Frog 2_____   Frog 3_____

How did you solve it?

2. Four frogs jumped a total of 185 centimeters.
How far could each frog have jumped?

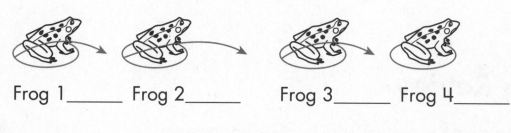

Frog 1_____   Frog 2_____   Frog 3_____   Frog 4_____

How did you solve it?

© Pearson Education 3

What's the Area? (page 1 of 2)

Use color tiles to find the area of the rectangles.

1. Area: _____ square inches

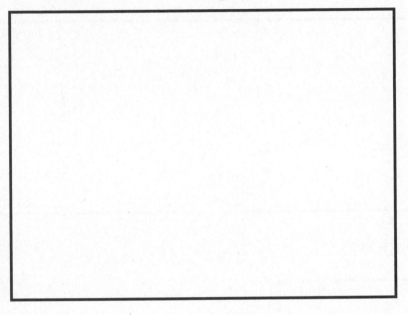

2. Area: _____ square inches

3. Area: _____ square inches

What's the Area? (page 2 of 2)

Use color tiles to find the area of the rectangles.

4. Area: _____ square inches

5. Area: _____ square inches

Find the Area

Each rectangle has a perimeter of 12 inches. Find the area.

1. Area: _____ square inches

2. Area: _____ square inches

3. Area: _____ square inches

Area and Perimeter (page 1 of 2)

NOTE Students find the area and perimeter of rectangles.

SMH 110–111, 114–115

1. Each rectangle has an area of 20 square units. Find the perimeter of each rectangle.

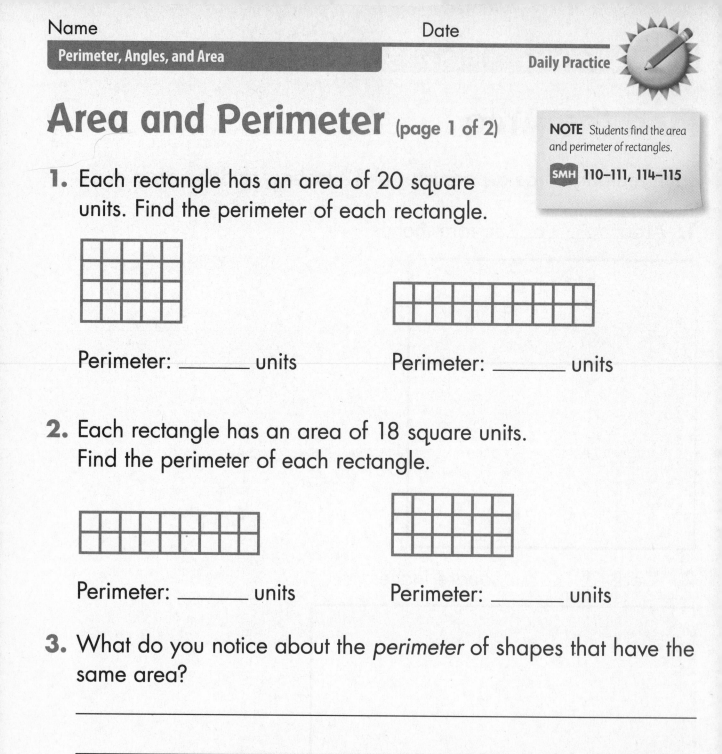

Perimeter: _____ units

Perimeter: _____ units

2. Each rectangle has an area of 18 square units. Find the perimeter of each rectangle.

Perimeter: _____ units

Perimeter: _____ units

3. What do you notice about the *perimeter* of shapes that have the same area?

_____

_____

_____

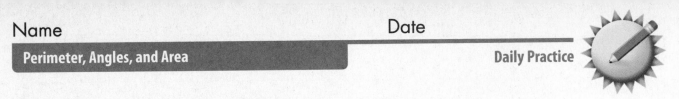

Area and Perimeter (page 2 of 2)

4. Each rectangle has a perimeter of 16 units.
Find the area of each rectangle.

Area: _____ square units   Area: _____ square units

5. Each rectangle has a perimeter of 14 units.
Find the area of each rectangle.

Area: _____ square units   Area: _____ square units

6. What do you notice about the *area* of shapes that have the same perimeter?

_____

_____

_____

How Big Is Your Foot? ✏️WRITING✎

Find the perimeter and area of your foot.
Then answer the following questions.

1. What is the perimeter of your foot?

Describe how you measured the perimeter.

2. What is the area of your foot?

Explain how you found your answer.

Seven-Unit Shapes

NOTE Students build shapes with an area of 7 square units.

SMH 115

Use the Square and Triangle Cutouts (M17) to make three new shapes with an area of seven square units. Remember that each new shape must, like tetrominoes, have full sides touching.

Tape or glue the new shapes you make on a large piece of paper. You may also draw the new shapes.

1. Use only squares in your first shape.

2. Use only triangles in your second shape.

3. Use both squares and triangles in your third shape.

Ongoing Review

4. What is the area of the following shape?

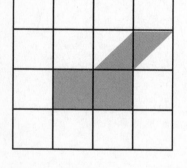

A. 2 square units

B. 3 square units

C. $3\frac{1}{2}$ square units

D. 4 square units

Session 2.5

How Many 10s?

Solve each problem below. You may use your 1,000 chart to help you. Explain how you figured out each problem.

NOTE Students find groups of 10s in 3-digit numbers.

SMH 9

1. Mr. Jackson went to Sticker Station and bought strips of 10 stickers to give to his students. He bought 270 stickers. How many strips of 10 did he buy?

2. Ms. Donaldson's class has collected 375 stamps from old letters. They are displaying the stamps in rows of 10. How many rows can they make? How many stamps will be left over?

3. Ms. Vega's class is collecting bottle caps. They are displaying them in stacks of 10. So far they have 41 stacks of bottle caps and 3 single bottle caps. How many bottle caps do they have?

4. Philip and his sister are collecting pennies at home. They have 256 pennies so far. If they trade the pennies for dimes, how many dimes will they have? How many pennies will be left over?

More Perimeter Problems

NOTE Students practice making rectangles and squares that have given perimeters.

SMH 112–113

1. Draw at least two different rectangles, each with a perimeter of 160 units. Label the length of each side.

2. My perimeter is 200. The length of one of my sides is 75. Draw the rest of my sides to make me a whole rectangle. Label the length of each side.

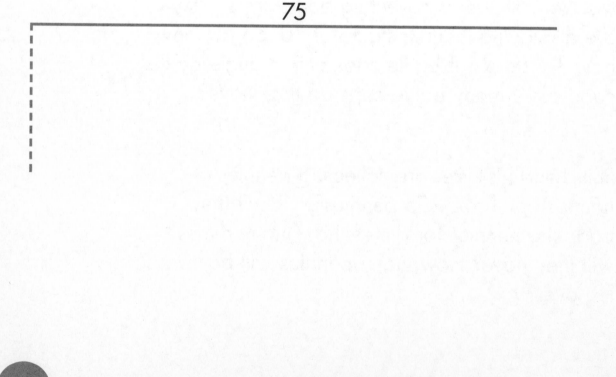

75

Building Triangles (page 1 of 2)

Follow the directions below to make triangles with your straw building kit. Draw a picture of each triangle you make, and label the lengths of the straws you used for each side.

1. Make a triangle with all sides the same length.

2. Make a triangle from a 3-inch, a 4-inch, and a 5-inch straw.

Building Triangles (page 2 of 2)

3. Make a triangle with two sides the same length and one side a different length.

4. Can you find three straws that will not make a triangle? Draw them and label their lengths. Why do you think they will not make a triangle?

Collecting Stickers and Pennies

NOTE Students practice solving addition problems that involve 2- and 3-digit numbers. Ask your child to explain how he or she solves each problem.

SMH 20–24

For each problem, write an equation, solve the problem, and show your solution.

1. Jung collects animal stickers. She has 158 stickers in her collection. On her birthday, her mother gave her 64 more stickers to add to her collection. How many animal stickers does Jung have now?

2. Oscar collects sports stickers. In his sticker box, he has 213 baseball stickers and 189 tennis stickers. How many of these sports stickers does Oscar have altogether?

3. Last month Kim collected 130 pennies. This month she collected 82 pennies. How much money does Kim have now?

4. Gil had 298 pennies in his collection. His younger sister had 112 pennies in her collection. They combined their collections to buy a present for their parents. How much money did they have altogether?

Perimeter, Angles, and Area

Tricky Triangles

Which Are Triangles? (page 1 of 2) ✏️WRITING

1. Which of the Tricky Triangles on page 40 are actually triangles? Without showing your partner, list the letter of each shape in the box below where you think it belongs.

These shapes are triangles:	These shapes are **not** triangles:

2. Now compare your list with your partner's. Discuss any shapes on which you disagree.

3. After you have discussed the Tricky Triangles with your partner, write why you think certain shapes are triangles and others are not triangles.

Which Are Triangles? (page 2 of 2)

4. Draw some shapes that are triangles and some that are **not** triangles. Then trade this sheet with your partner. Put the letter *T* in each shape your partner drew that is a triangle, and put the letters *NT* in each shape your partner drew that is **not** a triangle.

Make It a Triangle

Look at each shape below. Explain why these shapes are **not** triangles.

NOTE Students use their knowledge of properties of a triangle to explain why a shape is not a triangle.

SMH 118, 120

Shape	This shape is not a triangle because . . .
Example:	the sides are not closed.
1.	
2.	
3.	
4.	

Ongoing Review

5. Circle the correct statement about triangles.

    A. Triangles have 4 sides.

    B. Triangles must have a 90-degree angle.

    C. Triangles have 3 vertices.

    D. Triangles must have 3 equal sides.

Perimeter, Angles, and Area   Homework

Related Problems

Solve the following sets of related problems. How would you use one problem to solve the next one?

NOTE Students practice solving addition and subtraction problems in related sets.

1. 250 − 100 = _____

   250 − 90 = _____

   250 − 95 = _____

   250 − 105 = _____

2. 280 + _____ = 283

   270 + _____ = 283

   250 + _____ = 283

   220 + _____ = 283

3. 53 + 47 = _____

   153 + 147 = _____

   253 + 147 = _____

   253 + 247 = _____

4.   400   401   401
        − 25   − 25   − 26

Building Quadrilaterals (page 1 of 2)

Follow the directions below to make quadrilaterals with your straw building kit.

1. Make a square and a rectangle. Draw them here and label which is the square and which is the rectangle.

How are they the same?

How are they different?

2. Make two different rectangles. Draw them here and label the length of each of the sides.

How are they the same?

How are they different?

Building Quadrilaterals (page 2 of 2)

Follow the directions below to make quadrilaterals
with your straw building kit.

3. Make two different squares. Draw them here,
   and label the length of each of the sides.

   How are they the same?

   How are they different?

4. Make two different quadrilaterals that are not
   squares or rectangles. Draw them here, and
   label the length of each of the sides.

   How are they the same?

   How are they different?

How Many Are Left?

For each problem, write an equation, solve the problem, and show your solution.

NOTE Students practice solving 2- and 3-digit subtraction problems. Ask your child to explain how he or she solves each problem.

SMH 32–35

1. Keith had 300 animal stickers. He gave 28 tiger stickers to the science teacher. How many stickers did Keith have left?

2. Jane had 250 mouse stickers. Her cat scratched up 62 stickers. How many stickers did Jane have left?

3. Ms. Donaldson had 280 teddy bears in her collection. She sold 146 of them to the Children's Museum. How many are left?

4. Ms. Patel had 134 mystery books in her collection. She sold 65 of them to another collector. How many are left?

Finding Triangles and Quadrilaterals at Home

NOTE Students have been using materials to build shapes that have three and four sides and identifying the characteristics of triangles and quadrilaterals. In this homework, they find these shapes in real-life objects.

SMH 120–121

Find examples of these shapes at home. List or draw them below.

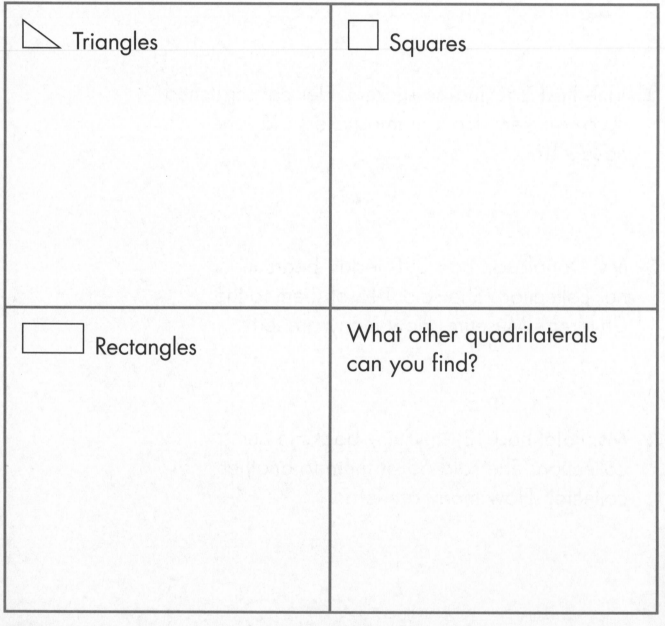

△ Triangles

□ Squares

□ Rectangles

What other quadrilaterals can you find?

Perimeter, Angles, and Area

Finding Angles (page 1 of 2)

Use your straws to make angles of different sizes.
Draw a picture of each angle you make. Then find 2
or 3 objects in the room that have angles that match
these sizes, and record the name of each object.

1. Make a right angle (90 degrees).

Draw your angle.   Objects with this angle:

2. Make an angle that is smaller than a right angle.

Draw your angle.   Objects with this angle:

3. Make an angle that is larger than a right angle.

Draw your angle.   Objects with this angle:

Finding Angles (page 2 of 2)

Use your straws to make angles of different sizes.
Draw a picture of each angle you make. Then find
2 or 3 objects in the room that have angles that match
these sizes, and record the name of each object.

4. Make an angle that is much smaller than a right angle.

Draw your angle.   Objects with this angle:

5. Make an angle that is much larger than a right angle.

Draw your angle.   Objects with this angle:

6. List at least three things you know about angles.
You may draw pictures if that will help you explain.

Is It a Quadrilateral?

Look at each shape below. For each shape that is **not** a quadrilateral, explain why it is not one.

> **NOTE** Students use their knowledge of properties of a quadrilateral to determine whether a shape is a quadrilateral and to explain why a shape is not a quadrilateral.
>
> **SMH** 118, 121

Shape	This shape is not a quadrilateral because . . .
Example:	it has five sides.
1.	
2.	
3.	
4.	

Ongoing Review

5. Circle the statement that is **not** true.

   A. A right angle has 90 degrees.

   B. All quadrilaterals have 4 right angles.

   C. A triangle can have a right angle.

   D. All squares have right angles.

Building More Triangles and Quadrilaterals (page 1 of 2)

Follow the directions below to make triangles and quadrilaterals with your straw building kit. Draw a picture of each shape you make, and label the lengths of the straws you used for each side.

1. Make two different triangles that have all sides the same length.

2. Make a triangle that has a right angle.

3. Make a triangle that has three different side lengths.

Building More Triangles and Quadrilaterals (page 2 of 2)

4. Make a quadrilateral that has at least one right angle.

5. Make a quadrilateral that has at least one angle that is smaller than a right angle.

6. Make a quadrilateral that has at least one angle that is larger than a right angle.

Perimeter, Angles, and Area   **Daily Practice**

Make $1.00, Make $2.00

NOTE Students practice finding combinations of amounts that add to a given total.

1. Fill in the blanks to make combinations of four amounts that add up to $1.00.

Example:

___$0.25___ + ___0.25___ + ___0.40___ + ___0.10___ = $1.00

_____ + ___0.15___ + _____ + _____ = $1.00

_____ + _____ + ___0.10___ + _____ = $1.00

_____ + ___0.30___ + _____ + _____ = $1.00

2. Now fill in the blanks to make combinations of four amounts that add up to $2.00.

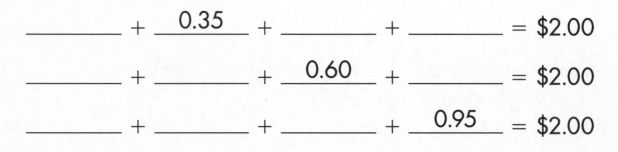

_____ + ___0.35___ + _____ + _____ = $2.00

_____ + _____ + ___0.60___ + _____ = $2.00

_____ + _____ + _____ + ___0.95___ = $2.00

How Much Taller?
How Much Longer?

NOTE Students compare heights and lengths in centimeters.

SMH 28, 32–35

For each problem, write an equation, solve the problem, and show your solution. You may use number lines or drawings to help you explain your thinking.

1. Mr. Vega is 185 centimeters tall. Oscar is 129 centimeters tall. How much taller is Mr. Vega than Oscar?

2. An NBA basketball player is 216 centimeters tall. How much taller is the basketball player than Mr. Vega?

3. The Burmese python at the Midtown Zoo is 330 centimeters long. The boa constrictor is 217 centimeters long. How much longer is the Burmese python?

How Big Is Our Classroom?

> **NOTE** Students identify and accurately measure the perimeter of a shape using U.S. Standard and metric units.
>
> **SMH** 110–111, 112

1. Estimate how many yardstick lengths it will take to measure the perimeter of your classroom.

2. Multiply the number of yardsticks by 3 to get an accurate estimate of the perimeter in feet.

3. Measure the perimeter of the room as best you can. You may want to have one person measure with the yardstick and the other person keep a tally of how many yardstick lengths you use.

4. After you have measured the actual perimeter of your classroom, skip count or multiply by 3 to get the measurement in feet (instead of yards).

Answer the following questions:

1. How many yardstick lengths do you think it will take to find the perimeter of your classroom? _____

2. What do you estimate the perimeter of your classroom to be in feet? _____

3. How many yardstick lengths did it actually take to measure the perimeter of your classroom? _____

4. What is the perimeter of your classroom in feet? _____

5. Do you think you made an accurate estimate of the classroom's perimeter? Explain why or why not.

_____

_____

Ikenaga 2 Jos Leys

"A relatively simple formula can generate immensely complex images." – Jos Leys

Investigations
IN NUMBER, DATA, AND SPACE®

Equal Groups

Investigation 3

Investigation 4

Wheels, Apples, and Days

Solve the problems and show your solutions.

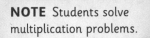
NOTE Students solve multiplication problems.

SMH 40–41

1. There are 5 cars parked in the driveway. How many wheels are there altogether?

2. I have 3 bags of apples. Each bag has 6 apples. How many apples do I have?

3. My birthday is 3 weeks away. Each week has 7 days. How many days away is my birthday?

Ongoing Review

4. 8 + 8 + 8 = _____

A. 16   **B.** 23   **C.** 24   **D.** 25

Things That Come in Groups

Talk with family members—or look around your home or in a store—to find things that come in groups of 2 to 12. Write the name of each item and the quantity the item comes in. See whether you can find things that come in groups of 7 or 11!

NOTE Students have been solving multiplication problems about things that come in groups of a certain amount. For example, there are 4 wheels on a car, juice boxes are packaged in groups of 3, and so on. Help your child find things at home, outside, or in a store that come in equal groups.

SMH 39

Item	Comes in Groups of This Many

Fingers and Eyes ✎ WRITING

NOTE Students write and solve multiplication problems.

📖 SMH 39, 40–41

Solve the problems and show your solutions.

1. There are 4 people sitting at my table.
   Each person has 5 fingers on each hand.
   How many fingers are there altogether?

2. There are 12 people in my group. Each
   person has 2 eyes. How many eyes are
   there altogether?

3. Write a story problem that represents 4×3.

Ongoing Review

4. $5 \times 3 =$ _____

   A. 9   **B.** 12   **C.** 15   **D.** 25

Equal Groups

Picture Problems (page 1 of 3)

For each problem, write a multiplication equation, solve the problem, and show your solution.

1. There are 10 apples in a basket.
Each apple has 4 worms.
How many worms do the apples have in all?

2. There are 4 sports bags.
Each bag has 9 balls inside.
How many balls are there in all?

Picture Problems (page 2 of 3)

For each problem, write a multiplication equation,
solve the problem, and show your solution.

3. Alan sees 6 cars.
Each car has 4 wheels.
How many wheels does Alan see?

4. Mia has 5 packs of juice boxes.
There are 30 juice boxes in all.
The same number of juice boxes is in each pack.
How many juice boxes are in each pack?

Equal Groups

Picture Problems (page 3 of 3)

For each problem, write a multiplication equation, solve the problem, and show your solution.

5. Rosi has 3 bags of marbles.
There are 12 marbles in each bag.
How many marbles does Rosi have?

6. Jack drew some hexagons.
Each hexagon has 6 sides.
There are 30 sides in all.
How many hexagons did Jack draw?

Equal Groups

What's the Number?

Answer the following questions.

NOTE Students practice place-value concepts with 3-digit numbers.

SMH 9, 10–11, 36

1. What number is 40 more than 717? _____

2. What number is 60 less than 485? _____

3. What number is 90 more than 236? _____

4. What number is 20 less than 119? _____

5. What number is 300 more than 331? _____

6. What number has 4 hundreds, 2 tens, and 8 ones? _____

7. What number has 23 tens and no ones? _____

8. What number has 7 hundreds and 2 ones? _____

9. What number has 5 hundreds and 12 tens? _____

Chapters, Slices, and Miles

Write multiplication equations, solve the problems, and show your solutions.

NOTE Students solve multiplication problems.

SMH 40–41

1. There are 3 books in a series. Each book has 11 chapters. If I read all of the books, how many chapters will I read altogether?

2. I have 4 pizzas. Each pizza has 8 slices. How many slices are there altogether?

3. George ran for 6 days. He ran 5 miles each day. How many miles did he run altogether?

Ongoing Review

4. Circle the equation that goes with the story below.
   Orange juice comes in packs of 4 cans. I have 5 packs of orange juice. How many cans of orange juice do I have?

   A. $20 \times 4 = ?$ **C.** $9 \times 6 = ?$

   B. $5 \times 4 = ?$ **D.** $5 \times 20 = ?$

More Picture Problems

For each problem, write a multiplication equation, solve the problem, and show your solution.

NOTE Students practice solving multiplication problems.

SMH 39, 40–41

1. In Kelley's picture there are 6 shirts. Each shirt has 6 buttons. How many buttons are there altogether?

2. Pilar brought 5 packs of crayons. There are 8 crayons in each pack. How many crayons are there altogether?

3. Benjamin drew a picture of some dogs. Each dog has 4 legs. There are 28 legs in the picture. How many dogs did he draw?

Rounding to Tens and Hundreds

NOTE Students round whole numbers to the nearest ten and hundred.

SMH 6, 10–11

For each problem, write the number in expanded form and then round to the nearest ten and hundred.

1. 267

Expanded form: _____

What is 267 rounded to the nearest ten? _____

What is 267 rounded to the nearest hundred? _____

2. 124

Expanded form: _____

What is 124 rounded to the nearest ten? _____

What is 124 rounded to the nearest hundred? _____

3. 848

Expanded form: _____

What is 848 rounded to the nearest ten? _____

What is 848 rounded to the nearest hundred? _____

4. 581

Expanded form: _____

What is 581 rounded to the nearest ten? _____

What is 581 rounded to the nearest hundred? _____

Groups, Groups, Everywhere!

NOTE Students solve multiplication problems.

SMH 40–41

1. There are 4 wheels on a car.
   How many wheels are on 5 cars? _____

2. There are 2 wings on a bird.
   How many wings are on 6 birds? _____

3. There are 10 dimes in a dollar.
   How many dimes are in 4 dollars? _____

4. There are 7 days in a week.
   How many days are in 2 weeks? _____

5. There are 6 muffins in a box.
   How many muffins are in 5 boxes? _____

6. There are 8 legs on a spider.
   How many legs are on 3 spiders? _____

7. There are 12 months in a year.
   How many months are in 2 years? _____

Ongoing Review

8. Which multiplication expression equals 30?

   A. 4×5 **B.** 5×6 **C.** 10×2 **D.** 7×4

Equal Groups   Homework

Saving Nickels

Solve these problems and show
your solutions.

NOTE Students practice multiplying by 5s. All four problems are related to one another, and students may use the answer to one problem to help them find the answer to another.

SMH 40–41, 43

1. Adam decided to save a nickel
every day. How much money did
Adam have after 2 days?

2. How much money did Adam have after 5 days?

3. How much money did he have after 10 days?

4. How much money did he have after 20 days?

Animal Groups

Write the multiplication sentence that goes with the picture.

NOTE Students solve multiplication problems.

SMH **39, 40–41**

1. 4 nests with 3 birds each

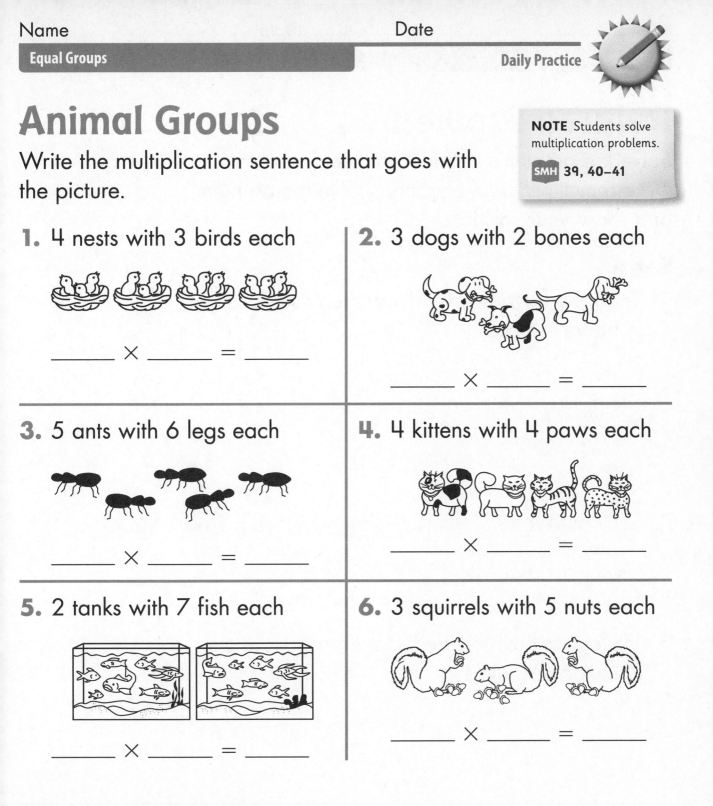

_____ × _____ = _____

2. 3 dogs with 2 bones each

_____ × _____ = _____

3. 5 ants with 6 legs each

_____ × _____ = _____

4. 4 kittens with 4 paws each

_____ × _____ = _____

5. 2 tanks with 7 fish each

_____ × _____ = _____

6. 3 squirrels with 5 nuts each

_____ × _____ = _____

Ongoing Review

7. Each cube tower has 10 cubes. How many cubes are in 5 towers?

A. 55   **B.** 50   **C.** 30   **D.** 25

Equal Groups

Related Problems (page 1 of 3)

Solve the problems in Set A. For each problem,
write a multiplication equation, solve the problem,
and show your solution.

Set A

1. Triangles have 3 sides. How many sides do
7 triangles have?

2. Hexagons have 6 sides. How many sides do
7 hexagons have?

Related Problems (page 2 of 3)

Solve the problems in Set B. For each problem, complete the multiplication equation, solve the problem, and show your solution.

Set B

1. Nancy and Philip were finding multiples on their skip counting charts. They circled 42 on the 6s chart. How many jumps of 6 did they take to get to 42?

_____ × 6 = 42

2. Deondra and Kenji circled 42 on the 3s chart. How many jumps of 3 did they take to get to 42? Show how you got your answer.

_____ × 3 = 42

Related Problems (page 3 of 3)

Solve the problems in Set C and Set D. For each problem, write a multiplication equation, solve the problem, and show your solution.

Set C

1. Oscar bought juice boxes that come in packages of 6. He bought 5 packs. How many juice boxes did he buy?

2. Pilar bought 8 packs of juice boxes. How many juice boxes did she buy?

Set D

1. Deondra noticed 7 children outside her house, each riding a tricycle. How many wheels were there altogether?

2. Two more children rode up on tricycles. How many wheels were there then?

Choose one set (A, B, C, or D) and explain how the first problem could help you solve the second problem. Write your answer on another sheet of paper.

Multiplication Match

NOTE Students solve multiplication problems.

SMH 40–41

1. Match the problem to the solution.

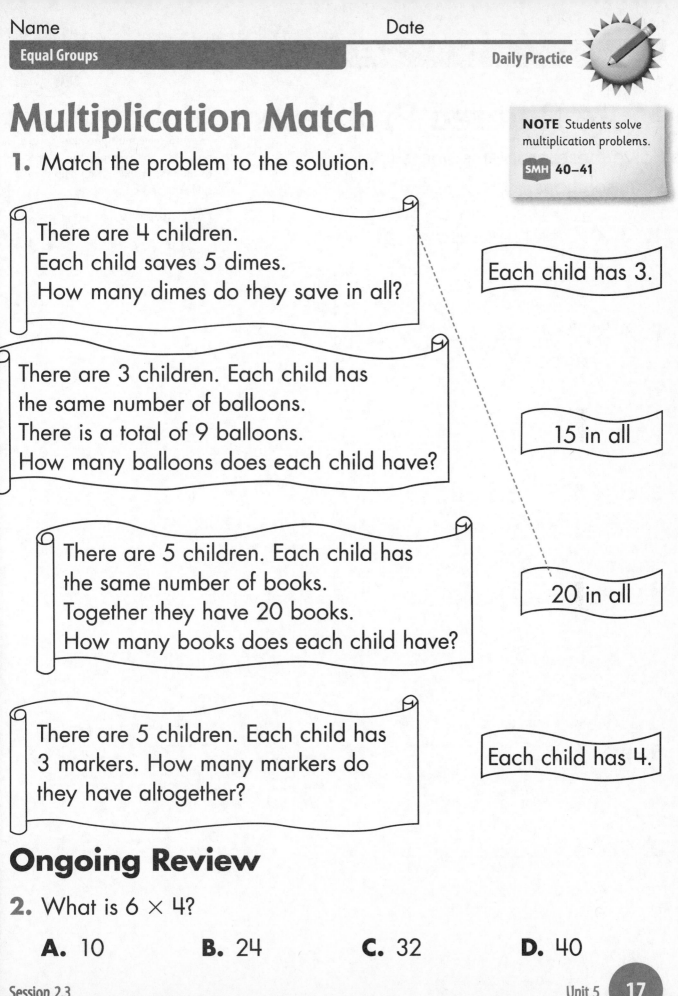

There are 4 children.
Each child saves 5 dimes.
How many dimes do they save in all?

Each child has 3.

There are 3 children. Each child has
the same number of balloons.
There is a total of 9 balloons.
How many balloons does each child have?

15 in all

There are 5 children. Each child has
the same number of books.
Together they have 20 books.
How many books does each child have?

20 in all

There are 5 children. Each child has
3 markers. How many markers do
they have altogether?

Each child has 4.

Ongoing Review

2. What is 6 × 4?

A. 10   **B.** 24   **C.** 32   **D.** 40

More Related Problems

Solve these problems and show your solutions.

NOTE Students use what they know to solve multiplication problems. For example, the answer to the first problem may help them solve the second problem.

SMH 40–41, 44

1. $3 \times 7 =$ _____

2. $6 \times 7 =$ _____

3. $3 \times 5 =$ _____

4. $6 \times 5 =$ _____

5. $4 \times 6 =$ _____

6. $9 \times 6 =$ _____

© Pearson Education 3

Counting Around by 3s and 6s

One day Ms. Johnson's class counted around the room by 6s. The 30th person said 180.

The next day they counted around by 3s. Some students in the class said they knew that this time the 30th person would say 90.

Use a number line, a 100 chart, or a picture to show if that is true.

Bags of Apples

Ms. Ross owns an apple orchard. She was making bags that each held 6 apples. In order to fill up 30 bags, she used 180 apples.

The next day she was filling bags that held 3 apples. She knew that this time she would need only 90 apples to fill up 30 bags.

Use a number line, 100 chart, or picture to show whether that is true.

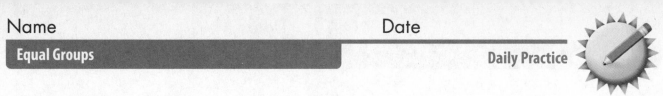

Daily Practice

Adding 10s and 100s

Solve the following sets of related problems.
Think about how to use one problem to solve
the next one.

> **NOTE** Students practice
> solving addition problems
> in related sets.
>
> SMH **20–24, 36**

---

1. $175 + 20 =$ _____

$175 + 30 =$ _____

$175 + 40 =$ _____

2. $235 + 100 =$ _____

$235 + 200 =$ _____

$235 + 300 =$ _____

---

3. $72 + 30 =$ _____

$72 + 130 =$ _____

$72 + 230 =$ _____

4. $264 + 30 =$ _____

$264 + 40 =$ _____

$264 + 50 =$ _____

---

5. $308 + 40 =$ _____

$328 + 40 =$ _____

$348 + 40 =$ _____

6. $144 + 130 =$ _____

$144 + 140 =$ _____

$144 + 150 =$ _____

How Many Legs?

Solve the problems and show your solutions.

1. Cats have 4 legs.

How many legs are on 3 cats?

How many legs are on 7 cats?

How many legs are on 26 cats?

2. Insects have 6 legs.

How many legs are on 3 insects?

How many legs are on 7 insects?

How many legs are on 15 insects?

Equal Groups

How Much Taller?

For each problem, write an equation, solve the problem, and show your solution.

> **NOTE** Students use addition and/or subtraction to compare two different heights.
>
> **SMH** 28, 32–35

Average Giraffe Heights

Female Adult: 168 inches   Baby: 72 inches   Male Adult: 216 inches

1. How much taller is a female giraffe than a baby giraffe?

2. How much taller is a male giraffe than a female giraffe?

3. How much taller is a male giraffe than a baby giraffe?

Spiders, Cats, and People ✎

NOTE Students practice multiplying by 2s, 4s, and 8s.

SMH **40–41, 49–51**

Solve the problems and show your solutions.

In an old house, there live some spiders, cats, and people.

| Cats have 4 legs.   Spiders have 8 legs.   People have 2 legs. |

1. In one room, there are 4 cats and 3 spiders. How many legs are there altogether?

2. In another room, there are 3 people and 5 cats. How many legs are there altogether?

3. In another room, there are 16 legs. What could be in that room? Can you find more than one possibility? Explain your thinking.

Equal Groups

How Many Towers?

Color the towers to help you solve the problem.

NOTE Students solve multiplication problems.

SMH 42–43

1. How many 3s are there in 36?

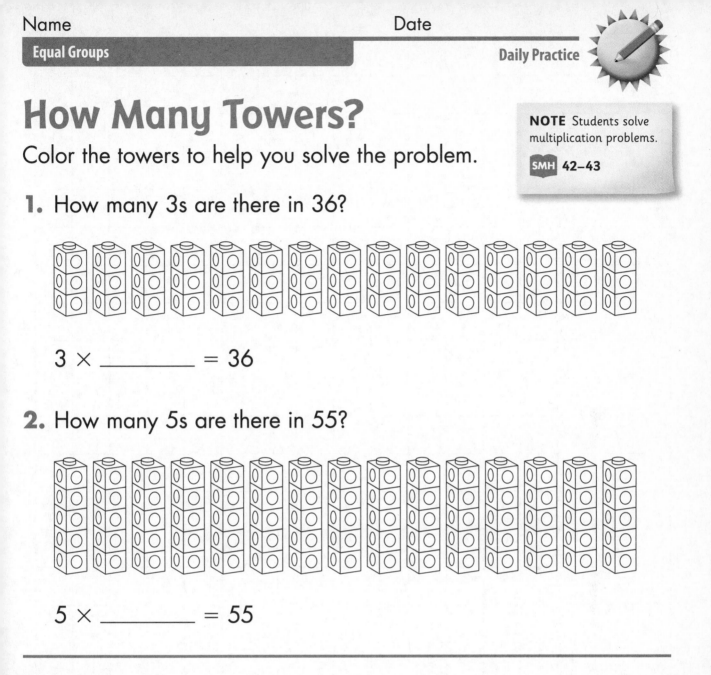

$$3 \times \underline{\hspace{2cm}} = 36$$

2. How many 5s are there in 55?

$$5 \times \underline{\hspace{2cm}} = 55$$

Ongoing Review

3. If I start at 0 and count by 6s, which number will I **not** land on?

A. 6   **B.** 24   **C.** 30   **D.** 32

Finding the Area (page 1 of 4)

Use color tiles to completely fill each rectangle. Label each rectangle with the dimensions. Then find the area of the rectangle.

1.

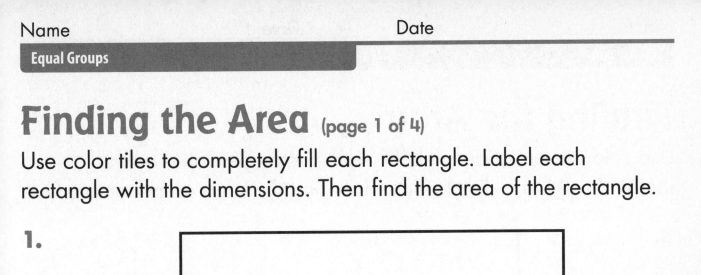

_____ inches

_____ inches

A

What is the area of the rectangle? _____ square inches

2.

_____ inches

B

_____ inches

What is the area of the rectangle? _____ square inches

Equal Groups

Finding the Area (page 2 of 4)

Use color tiles to completely fill each rectangle. Label each rectangle with the dimensions. Then find the area of the rectangle.

3.

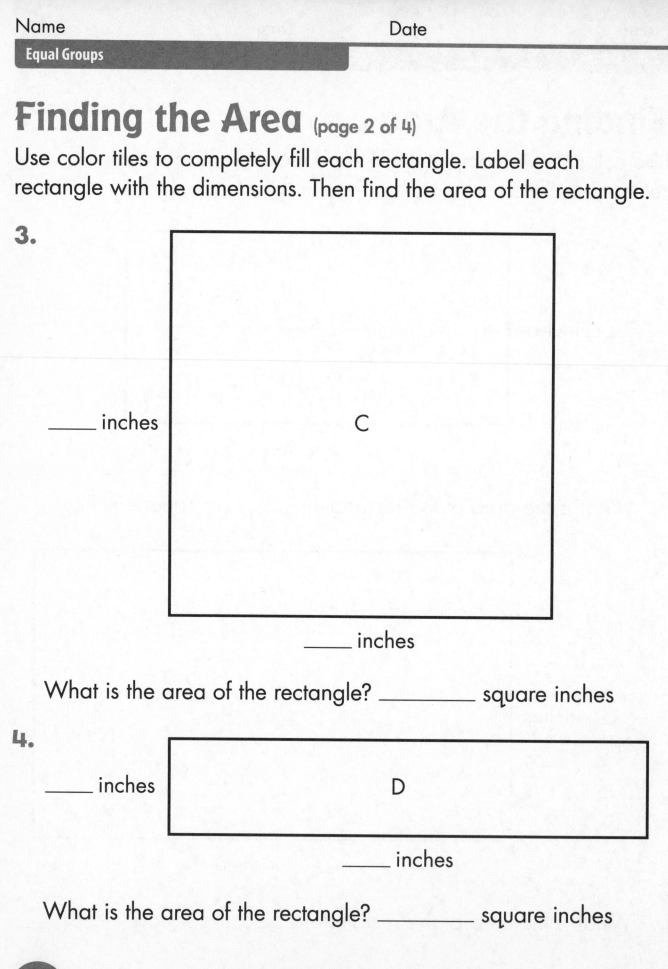

_____ inches

C

_____ inches

What is the area of the rectangle? _____ square inches

4.

_____ inches

D

_____ inches

What is the area of the rectangle? _____ square inches

Finding the Area (page 3 of 4)

5. Use tiles to build a rectangle that has one side that is
8 tiles long and another side that is 3 tiles long. Think
of this as Rectangle E. Record the dimensions and area
of the rectangle below.

Dimensions: _____ by _____   Area: _____ square inches

6. Use tiles to build a rectangle that is 7 tiles by 4 tiles.
Think of this as Rectangle F. Record the dimensions
and area of the rectangle below.

Dimensions: _____ by _____   Area: _____ square inches

7. Use tiles to build a rectangle that is 5 tiles by 5 tiles.
Think of this as Rectangle G. Record the dimensions
and area of the rectangle below.

Dimensions: _____ by _____   Area: _____ square inches

8. Use tiles to build a rectangle with the dimensions
6 tiles by 5 tiles. Think of this as Rectangle H. Record
the dimensions and area of the rectangle below.

Dimensions: _____ by _____   Area: _____ square inches

Finding the Area (page 4 of 4)

Complete the table by recording the dimensions
and the area of each rectangle.

	Dimensions (in inches)	**Area (in square inches)**
Example:	5 by 7	35
Rectangle A		
Rectangle B		
Rectangle C		
Rectangle D		
Rectangle E		
Rectangle F		
Rectangle G		
Rectangle H		

What's the Area?

Record the dimensions and the area of each rectangle.

NOTE Students find the dimensions and the area of rectangles.

SMH 114

1.

Dimensions: _____ by _____

Area: _____ square units

2.

Dimensions: _____ by _____

Area: _____ square units

Comic Book Collections

NOTE Students order, add, and subtract 3-digit numbers.

SMH 10–11

Collector	Number of Comic Books
Adam	175
Bridget	207
Casawn	250
Denzel	152
Elena	215

1. Write the number of comic books in each collection in order on the number line below.

For each problem, write an equation, solve the problem, and show your solution.

2. How many more comic books are in the largest collection than the smallest collection?

3. If Adam and Denzel put their collections together, how many comic books would they have?

Crossing Over 100

Solve the following sets of related problems. Think about how to use one problem to solve the next one.

NOTE Students practice solving subtraction problems in related sets.

SMH 32–35

1. 100 − 68 = _____

     110 − 68 = _____

     120 − 68 = _____

2. 100 − 74 = _____

     112 − 74 = _____

     132 − 74 = _____

3. 100 − 94 = _____

     113 − 94 = _____

     123 − 94 = _____

4. 100 − 43 = _____

     110 − 43 = _____

     120 − 43 = _____

5. 100 − 37 = _____

     120 − 37 = _____

     124 − 37 = _____

6. 100 − 81 = _____

     130 − 81 = _____

     136 − 81 = _____

Equal Groups

How Many More?

Solve the problems. Show your solutions
on the number lines.

NOTE Students find the missing
number to make an addition
equation correct.

SMH **32**

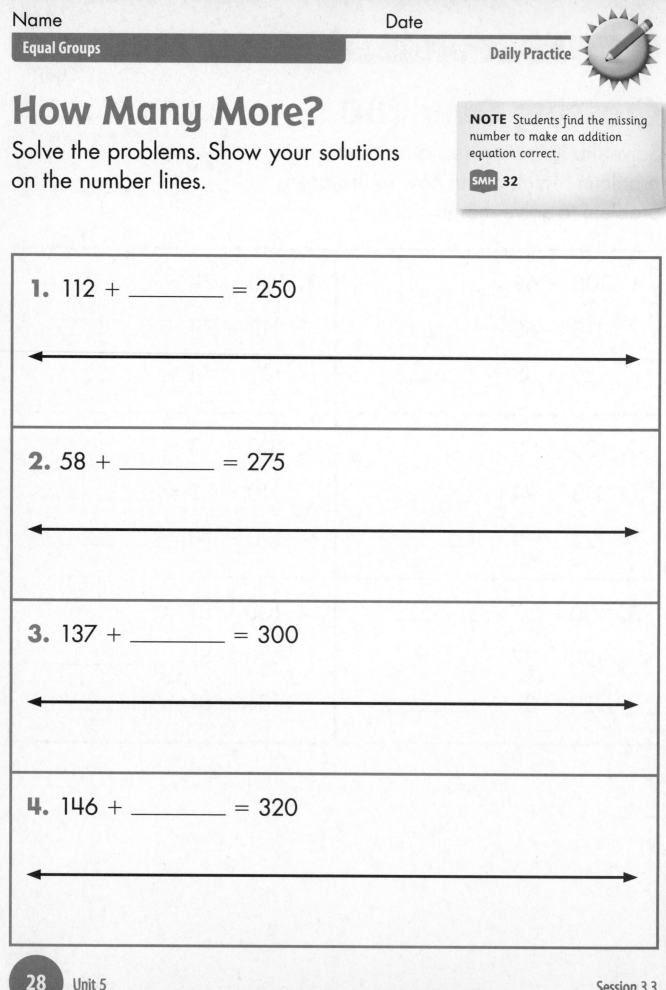

1. $112 +$ _____ $= 250$

2. $58 +$ _____ $= 275$

3. $137 +$ _____ $= 300$

4. $146 +$ _____ $= 320$

Making Array Cards

I started to make my own set of Array Cards in class. Now I will finish making my set for homework.

I have the following items:
- The Array Cards I have made so far
- The sheets I need to cut to make the rest of the cards
- The directions on how to make the cards
- A plastic bag to store the cards in

I need the following items:
- Scissors
- Pencil, marker, or crayon

Here are two different ways to figure out the number of squares in a 4 × 6 array.

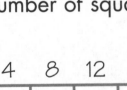

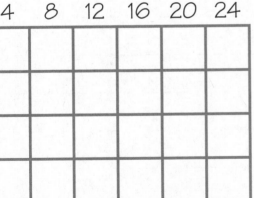

NOTE Students make Array Cards to learn about multiplication and multiplication combinations. Ask your child to explain how he or she is figuring out the total number of squares in each array.

SMH 45, 46

Count by 4s

Count by 6s

30 Unit 5

"Combinations I Know" and "Combinations I'm Working On"

As you play *Factor Pairs*, make a list of the multiplication combinations you know and the ones that you are still working on. This list will change as you learn more of the combinations.

Combinations I Know	Combinations I'm Working On

How Many Are Left?

For each problem, write an equation, solve the problem, and show your solution.

NOTE Students practice solving subtraction problems that involve 2- and 3-digit numbers. Ask your child to explain how he or she solved each problem.

SMH 26–28, 32–35

1. Gina had 300 basketball stickers. She gave 55 of them to her friend for a birthday present. How many stickers did Gina have left?

2. Cristobal had 250 boat stickers. He sold 85 of them at a yard sale. How many stickers did Cristobal have left?

3. The Valley View Asian Heritage Museum had 294 stamps in their Japanese stamp collection. They sold 120 of them to another collector. How many are left?

4. Mr. Jackson had 268 baseball trading cards in his collection. He gave 92 of them to his niece. How many are left?

Playing *Factor Pairs*

Let's play *Factor Pairs* together.

NOTE The game "Factor Pairs" is designed to help your child learn multiplication combinations, sometimes called multiplication "facts." As you play with your child, ask questions about how he or she is figuring out the number of squares on each Array Card.

SMH 45, 46, G10

I have the following items:
- A copy of the game rules
- A list of "Combinations I Know" and a list of "Combinations I'm Working On"
- My Array Cards

Here is one of the Array Cards I will be using in the game.

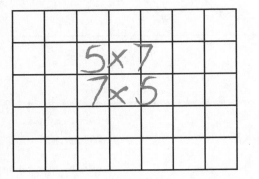

This is how I plan to keep practicing the ones I do **not** know.

_____

_____

_____

_____

How Many Books?

Use the pictograph to answer
the problems.

NOTE Students interpret a pictograph.

Number of Books Read	
Kelley	📖 📖 📖 📖
Murphy	📖 📖 📖 📖 📖 📖
Chiang	📖 📖 📖 📖 📖
Adam	📖 📖 📖

Each 📖 = 5 books

1. Who read the least number of books?

_____

2. How many books did Chiang read?

_____

3. What was the greatest number of books read by one person?

_____

4. How many more books did Murphy read than Adam?

_____

What's the Area?

NOTE Students find the area of rectangles.

SMH 114

Find the area of each rectangle.

1.

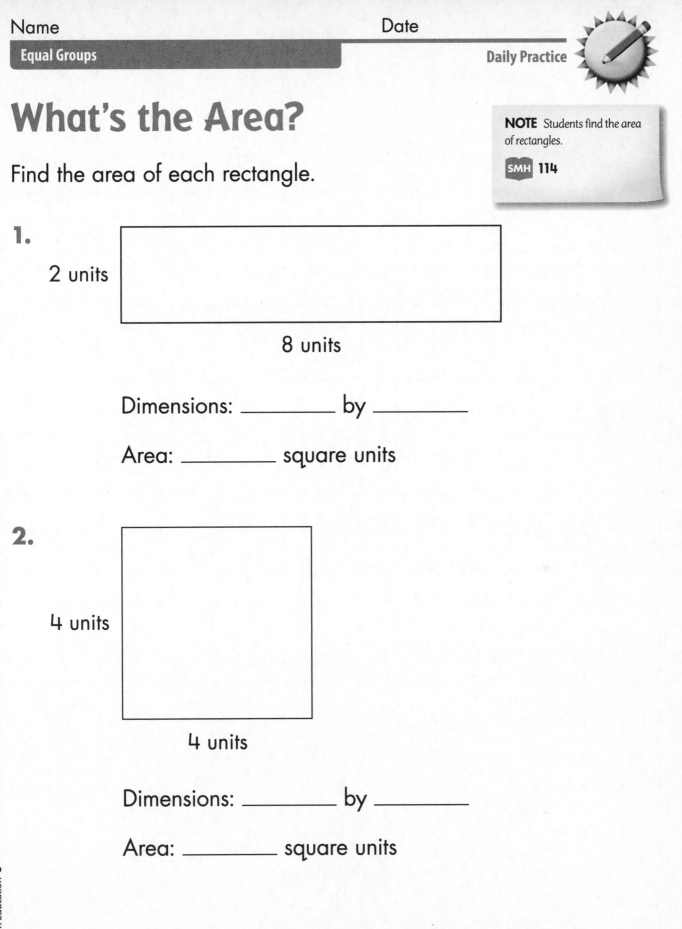

2 units

8 units

Dimensions: _____ by _____

Area: _____ square units

2.

4 units

4 units

Dimensions: _____ by _____

Area: _____ square units

Equal Groups

Spots and Stripes

Solve each problem.

NOTE Students solve multiplication problems.

SMH 39, 40–41

1. This butterfly has 6 spots on each wing.
How many spots are on
5 butterflies like this one? _____

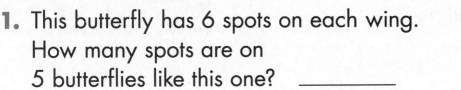

2. This fish has 5 black stripes.
How many stripes are on
8 fish like this one? _____

3. This frog has 7 spots.
How many spots are on
10 frogs like this one? _____

4. This zebra has 9 black stripes.
How many stripes are on
3 zebras like this one? _____

5. This ladybug has 4 spots.
How many spots are on
7 ladybugs like this one? _____

Ongoing Review

6. One spider has 8 legs. How many legs do
5 spiders have?

A. 20 **B.** 40 **C.** 60 **D.** 80

Practicing with Multiplication Cards

Help me practice with my Multiplication Cards.

NOTE Students practice learning multiplication combinations with products up to 50.

SMH 49–51

I have the following items:
- A copy of the directions
- My Multiplication Cards from school or 6 sheets to make new ones

Here are the front and back of one Multiplication Card.

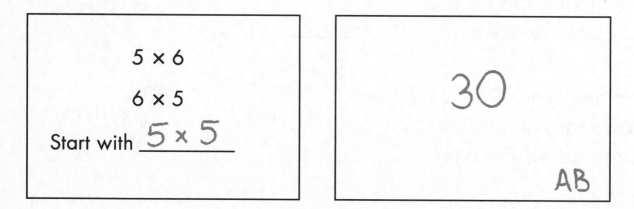

5 × 6

6 × 5

Start with ___5 × 5___

30

AB

Make $1.00, Make $2.00

> **NOTE** Students practice finding combinations of numbers that add up to a given total.

1. Fill in the blanks to make combinations of four amounts that add up to $1.00.

Example:

$0.25 + $0.25 + $0.40 + $0.10 = $1.00

_____ + $0.12 + _____ + _____ = $1.00

_____ + _____ + $0.13 + _____ = $1.00

_____ + $0.33 + _____ + _____ = $1.00

2. Fill in the blanks to make combinations of four amounts that add up to $2.00.

_____ + $0.35 + _____ + _____ = $2.00

_____ + _____ + $0.36 + _____ = $2.00

_____ + _____ + _____ + $0.41 = $2.00

Playing Array Games

Let's play *Count and Compare* together.

I have the following items:
- A copy of the game rules
- A list of "Combinations I Know" and a list of "Combinations I'm Working On"
- My Array Cards

> **NOTE** The new game "Count and Compare" is designed to help your child learn multiplication combinations, sometimes called multiplication facts. As you play with your child, ask questions about how he or she is figuring out the number of squares on each Array Card. Also revisit the array game "Factor Pairs," which you and your child have already played together.
>
> **SMH** 49–51, G9, G10

Let's play *Factor Pairs* together.

I have the following items:
- A copy of the game rules
- My Array Cards

Here are some of my Array Cards that we will be playing with.

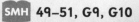

3 × 4
4 × 3

2 × 6
6 × 2

1 × 12   12 × 1

© Pearson Education 3

Problems About Counting Around the Class (page 1 of 2)

Write an equation to represent each problem.
Then solve the problem and show your work.

1. Denzel's class was counting around the class by 10s.
What number did the 6th person say?

Equation: _____

2. Gina's class was counting around the class by 20s.
What number did the 4th person say?

Equation: _____

3. Kenji's class was counting around the class by 30s.
What number did the 5th person say?

Equation: _____

Equal Groups

Problems About Counting Around the Class (page 2 of 2)

Write an equation to represent each problem.
Then solve the problem and show your work.

4. Nancy's class was counting around the class by 60s.
What number did the 3rd person say?

Equation: _____

5. Adam's class was counting around the class by 90s.
What number did the 5th person say?

Equation: _____

6. Keisha's class was counting around the class by 20s.
What number did the 9th person say?

Equation: _____

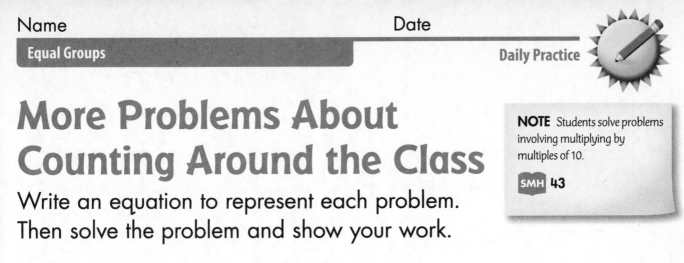

More Problems About Counting Around the Class

NOTE Students solve problems involving multiplying by multiples of 10.

SMH 43

Write an equation to represent each problem.
Then solve the problem and show your work.

1. Edwin's class was counting around the class by 50s.
   What number did the 8th person say?

   Equation: _____

2. Pilar's class was counting around the class by 40s.
   What number did the 7th person say?

   Equation: _____

3. Zhang's class was counting around the class by 70s.
   What number did the 3rd person say?

   Equation: _____

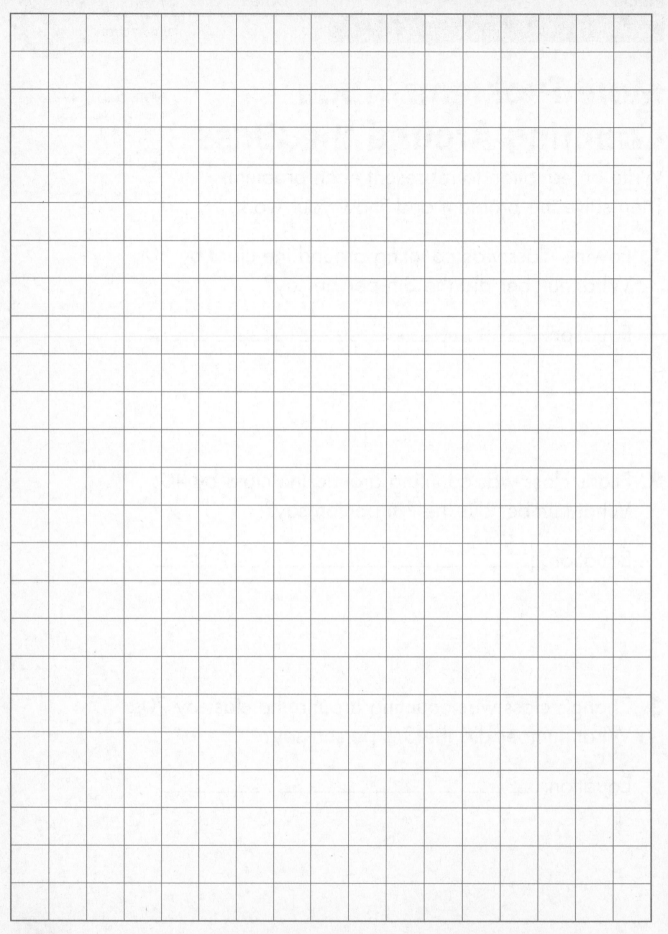

Division Stories (page 1 of 2)

Solve each of the problems below and show your solution clearly.

1. There are 28 desks in the classroom. The teacher puts them in groups of 4. How many groups of desks are in the classroom?

2. Three friends are given a pack of trading cards to share equally. The pack contains 18 cards. How many cards should each person get?

Division Stories (page 2 of 2)

3. Becky has 30 flowers. She wants to put them in bouquets of 5 flowers each. How many bouquets will Becky be able to make?

4. Seven children are building toy cars. They have 28 toy wheels to share equally. How many toy wheels will each child get?

© Pearson Education 3

Addition Starter Problems

Solve each problem two ways, using the first
steps listed below. Show your work clearly.

NOTE Students practice
flexibility with solving
addition problems.

SMH **20–24**

1. $143 + 168 =$ _____

Start by solving $143 + 8$.	Start by solving $140 + 160$.

2. $253 + 149 =$ _____

Start by solving $200 + 100$.	Start by solving $53 + 49$.

Equal Groups

Story Problems (page 1 of 2)

Solve each problem and show how you solved it.

1. A robot has 4 hands. Each hand has 6 fingers. How many fingers does the robot have altogether?

2. We made 20 muffins for the bake sale. We put the muffins in bags to sell. We put 4 muffins in each bag. How many bags of muffins did we have to sell?

3. We bought 5 packs of yogurt cups. Each pack had 4 yogurt cups. How many yogurt cups did we buy?

Story Problems (page 2 of 2)

4. Five children have one book of 35 movie tickets to share equally. Each movie costs one ticket. How many movies can each child see?

5. Before school my mother gave me a pack of 24 new pencils. When I get to school, I want to share them equally among my three friends and me. How many pencils will each of us get?

6. Benjamin drew a picture of 7 pentagons. Each pentagon has 5 sides. How many sides are there in all?

Packs, Students, Sides, and Frogs

NOTE Students solve division problems.

SMH 47, 48

Solve each problem and show your solution.

1. I bought 28 cups of yogurt. Each pack of yogurt has 4 cups. How many packs did I buy?

2. A teacher wants to put 25 students in 5 equal groups. How many students will be in each group?

3. I counted 24 sides on all of the triangles I drew. Each triangle has 3 sides. How many triangles did I draw?

4. There is a group of frogs in a pond. Each frog has 4 legs. I counted 24 legs. How many frogs are in the pond?

Ongoing Review

5. How many days are there in 6 weeks?

A. 42   **B.** 40   **C.** 36   **D.** 24

Addition Story Problems

For each problem, write an equation, solve the problem, and show your solution.

NOTE Students practice solving 2- and 3-digit addition problems. Ask your child to explain how he or she solved each problem.

SMH 20–24

1. The Parktown Soccer League has 144 players. The Riverside Soccer League has 165 players. When the two leagues get together for a tournament, how many soccer players are there altogether if everyone comes?

2. The Parktown Soccer League bought T-shirts for the players, parents, and coaches. They bought 150 large T-shirts and 95 extra-large T-shirts. How many T-shirts did they buy in all?

3. To pay for new equipment, the Riverview Soccer League raised $215 from a bake sale and $287 from a car wash. How much money did they raise altogether?

Missing Factors Recording Sheet

Follow the rules for playing *Missing Factors*. For each array that you keep, write an equation that uses either multiplication or division. Circle the missing factor in each equation.

Example: $2 \times \boxed{8} = 16$ or $16 \div 2 = \boxed{8}$

1.	2.
3.	4.
5.	6.
7.	8.
9.	10.
11.	12.
13.	14.
15.	16.
17.	18.
19.	20.
21.	22.
23.	24.

Multiply or Divide?

Solve each problem and show your solution.

NOTE Students solve multiplication and division problems.

SMH 40–41, 48

1. Zoe and Yuki have a bag of 30 pretzels.
   They want to share them evenly.
   How many pretzels should each student get?

   Did you multiply or divide?

2. Webster has 5 boxes of granola bars for
   his class. Each box has 6 granola bars.
   How many granola bars are there altogether?

   Did you multiply or divide?

3. Latisha picks 24 flowers from her garden.
   She wants to put the same number of
   flowers in each of 3 vases. How many
   flowers should she put in each vase?

   Did you multiply or divide?

Ongoing Review

4. If each letter is worth 5¢, how much money is
   the name **Maurice** worth?

   A. 30¢   **B.** 35¢   **C.** 40¢   **D.** 45¢

Two-Part Problems

Solve these two-part problems and show
your solutions.

NOTE Students solve
multiplication and division
problems.

SMH 40–41, 48

1. Matthew has 30 boxes of raisins. There are
10 raisins in each box. He shares them equally
with the children at his lunch table. There are
6 children altogether. How many raisins does
each child get?

_____ boxes per child

_____ raisins per child

2. Jamal has 2 cats. Each cat has 4 kittens.
Each kitten has 3 toys. How many toys do
the kittens have altogether?

_____ kittens

_____ toys

Ongoing Review

3. There are 46 legs in Room 222, including the
teacher's legs.

How many students are in the class?

A. 20   **B.** 22   **C.** 23   **D.** 25

Match Me Up!

1. Match the picture to the problems. Then solve all of the problems.

NOTE Students solve multiplication and division problems and match each problem with a representation.

SMH 40–41, 47, 48

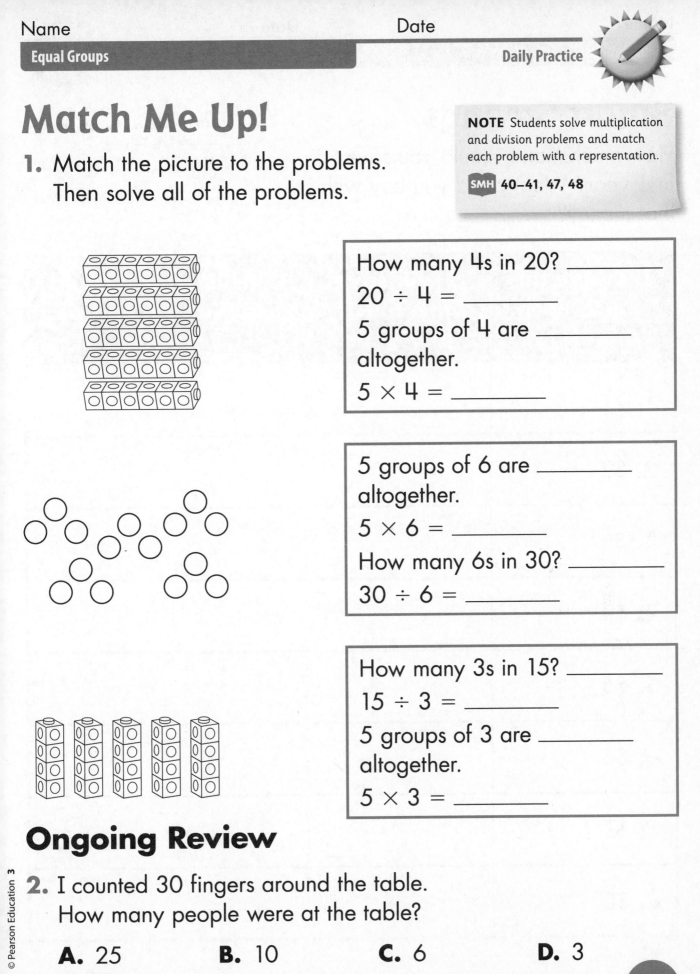

How many 4s in 20? _____

$20 \div 4 =$ _____

5 groups of 4 are _____ altogether.

$5 \times 4 =$ _____

5 groups of 6 are _____ altogether.

$5 \times 6 =$ _____

How many 6s in 30? _____

$30 \div 6 =$ _____

How many 3s in 15? _____

$15 \div 3 =$ _____

5 groups of 3 are _____ altogether.

$5 \times 3 =$ _____

Ongoing Review

2. I counted 30 fingers around the table. How many people were at the table?

A. 25   **B.** 10   **C.** 6   **D.** 3

Smart Savings

How much money could you save in 1 year? What could you buy with that money?

NOTE Students multiply several numbers by 12.

SMH 40–41

If I save this much each month . . .	I will save this much in a year!	This is what I could buy at the end of 1 year.
1. $1		
2. $2		
3. $3		
4. $4		
5. $5		
6. $6		
7. $7		
8. $8		

Ikenaga 2 Jos Leys

"A relatively simple formula can generate immensely complex images." – **Jos Leys**

Investigations
IN NUMBER, DATA, AND SPACE®

Stories, Tables, and Graphs

Temperatures from September to December (page 1 of 3)

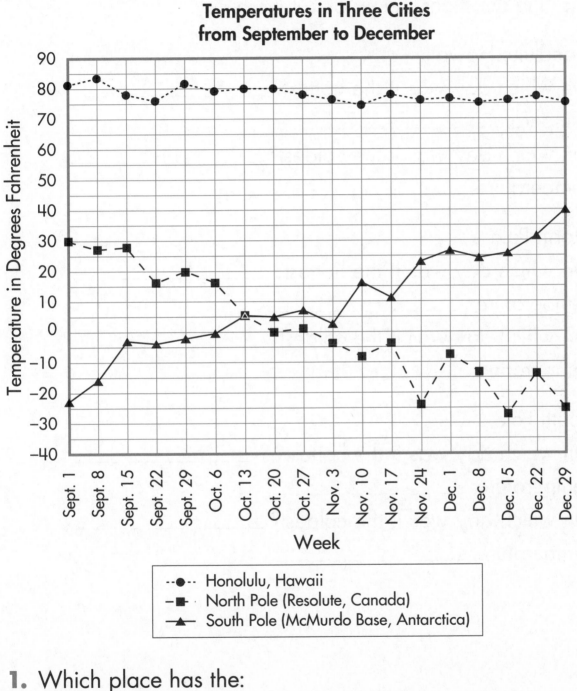

**Temperatures in Three Cities
from September to December**

1. Which place has the:

   Hottest temperature? _____

   Coldest temperature? _____

Temperatures from September to December (page 2 of 3)

2. Answer the questions below about each city.

a. Honolulu, Hawaii

On which day was it the hottest? _____

Temperature: _____

On which day was it the coldest? _____

Temperature: _____

b. North Pole

On which day was it the hottest? _____

Temperature: _____

On which day was it the coldest? _____

Temperature: _____

c. South Pole

On which day was it the hottest? _____

Temperature: _____

On which day was it the coldest? _____

Temperature: _____

Temperatures from September to December (page 3 of 3)

3. a. Choose one of the three
locations. Write it here: _____

b. What is an outdoor activity you would
do there?

c. During which months could you do your
outdoor activity?

d. Could you do your outdoor activity in one of
the other locations? Explain.

4. a. Choose another of these locations. _____

b. How are the temperatures from September to
December different from or similar to the
temperatures where you live?

Practicing with Multiplication Cards

NOTE Students practice multiplication combinations with products to 50. These steps will help students practice.

SMH 49–51

1. Ask someone to help you practice multiplication combinations by showing you the front of each Multiplication Card.

2. Say the answer to the problem as quickly as you can. If you get the correct answer right away, put the card in a pile of facts that you "just know." If you have to stop and figure it out, put it in a pile of facts that you are "working on."

3. Paper clip your "just know" cards together and put them back in your resealable bag.

4. Practice each of the cards in your "working on" pile at least 3 times.

5. Put all your cards back together (including the ones you "just know") and go through them again. Keep practicing over the next few weeks until you have no more cards in your "working on" pile.

Changing Temperatures in a Day

NOTE Students learn to read temperature values on graphs and on a thermometer. Students record temperatures during different times of the day.

 SMH 66–69

Think about the following times of day:

- when you leave for school in the morning
- when you get home from school in the afternoon
- when you go to bed at night

1. Which time of day is usually the warmest?

2. Which time of day is usually the coolest?

3. If you have an outdoor thermometer at home, check the temperature at the three times listed above and write them below.

Temperature when I leave for school: _____

Temperature when I get home from school: _____

Temperature when I go to bed: _____

Stories, Tables, and Graphs

Temperatures over a Year (page 1 of 4)

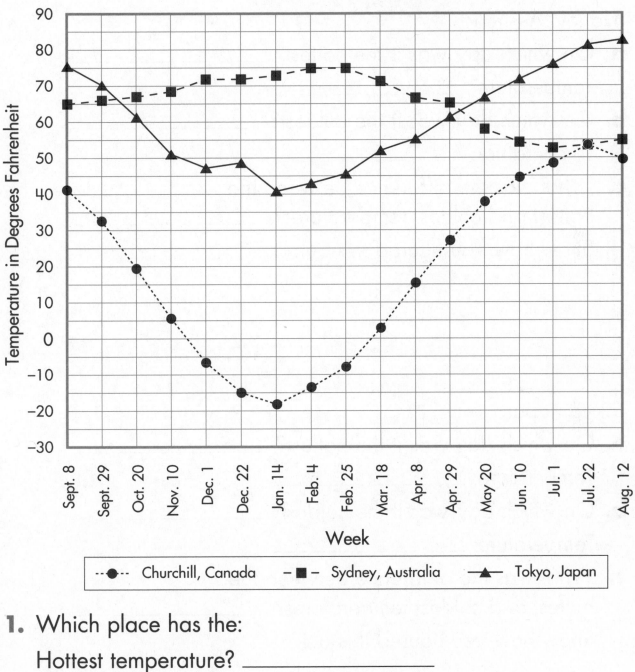

Temperatures in Three Cities

Temperature in Degrees Fahrenheit

Week

--●-- Churchill, Canada   -■- Sydney, Australia   -▲- Tokyo, Japan

1. Which place has the:

Hottest temperature? _____

Coldest temperature? _____

Temperatures over a Year (page 2 of 4)

Answer the questions below about each city.

2. Sydney, Australia

a. On which day was it the hottest? _____

Temperature: _____

b. On which day was it the coldest? _____

Temperature: _____

c. What was the difference between the hottest and coldest temperatures? _____

Show how you figured this out:

3. Tokyo, Japan

a. On which day was it the hottest? _____

Temperature: _____

b. On which day was it the coldest? _____

Temperature: _____

c. What was the difference between the hottest and coldest temperatures? _____

Show how you figured this out:

Temperatures over a Year (page 3 of 4)

4. Churchill, Canada

   a. On which day was it the hottest? _____

      Temperature: _____

   b. On which day was it the coldest? _____

      Temperature: _____

   c. What was the difference between the
      hottest and coldest temperatures? _____
      Show how you figured this out:

Temperatures over a Year (page 4 of 4)

5. Pick one of these three places and imagine that you are going to live there for one year.

a. Place: _____

b. What are three articles of clothing you would want to wear outside?

_____ _____ _____

c. Is that different from what you need at home? Explain.

6. Pick another of these three places and imagine that you are going to live there for one year.

a. Place: _____

b. What are three articles of clothing you would want to wear outside?

_____ _____ _____

c. Is that different from what you need at home? Explain.

Multiplication Combinations of 3s, 6s, and 12s

NOTE Students practice multiplication combinations ("facts"). They look for patterns in the 3s, 6s, and 12s combinations.

SMH 49–51

1. Solve these problems.

$1 \times 3 =$

$2 \times 3 =$ $1 \times 6 =$

$3 \times 3 =$

$4 \times 3 =$ $2 \times 6 =$ $1 \times 12 =$

$5 \times 3 =$

$6 \times 3 =$ $3 \times 6 =$

$7 \times 3 =$

$8 \times 3 =$ $4 \times 6 =$ $2 \times 12 =$

$9 \times 3 =$

$10 \times 3 =$ $5 \times 6 =$

$11 \times 3 =$

$12 \times 3 =$ $6 \times 6 =$ $3 \times 12 =$

2. What patterns do you notice?

Ask someone at home to help you practice the multiplication combinations that you are working on.

High and Low Temperatures

NOTE Students record high and low temperatures of the day.

SMH 66–69

Check the newspaper, radio, television, or Internet for the high and low temperatures of the day.

1. High temperature: _____

2. Low temperature: _____

3. At what time of day do you think the high temperature happened? _____

4. At what time of day do you think the low temperature happened? _____

5. What is the difference between the low and high temperatures? _____

Temperatures over a Day

Use your Temperatures over a Day graph to answer the following questions.

1. On your graph, write what is happening to the temperature above each part of the line that shows the temperature change. You can use these phrases:

   Getting warmer   Getting cooler   Staying the same

2. Describe the shape of the line graph. What does it tell you about this day?

3. How much did the temperature change from 9:00 A.M. to 12:00 NOON?

4. How much did the temperature change from 12:00 NOON to 3:00 P.M.?

5. What is the difference between the highest and lowest temperatures of the day?

   Show how you found the difference.

Preparing for a Party

Solve each problem. Show your work.

NOTE Students solve division problems in a story context.

SMH 47, 48

1. Edwin, Kelley, Keisha, and Dwayne have to blow up 36 balloons for the party. If they each blow up the same number of balloons, how many balloons will each person blow?

2. Kenji has 27 pencils for the gift bags. He will put the same number of pencils in each of the 9 gift bags. How many pencils will he put in each bag?

3. Kim will send out 16 invitations. Invitations are sold in packages of 4. How many packages of invitations does Kim need to buy?

Ongoing Review

4. Which number is **not** a factor of 24?

A. 2 **B.** 3 **C.** 4 **D.** 14

Summer Days

Read each story below, and then match it
with its graph on pages 16–18.

Story 1: Thursday

On Thursday, I woke up and it was hot. During the
day it got even hotter! It was much too hot to go out
to play. At night, the temperature went down, but it
was still too hot.

Story 2: Friday

On Friday, when I woke up, it was still hot outside
and started to get hotter. But when I was eating
lunch, a big storm came and after the rain stopped,
it was much cooler. In the afternoon, I went for a
bike ride, and in the evening, I had to put on
a sweatshirt.

Story 3: Saturday

On Saturday, when I woke up, it was chilly outside.
By noon, it was warm enough that I didn't need my
sweater and my family went out for a picnic. In the
evening, it got cool again, but not as cool as it was
in the morning.

Summer Days Graphs (page 1 of 3)

Summer Days: Graph 1

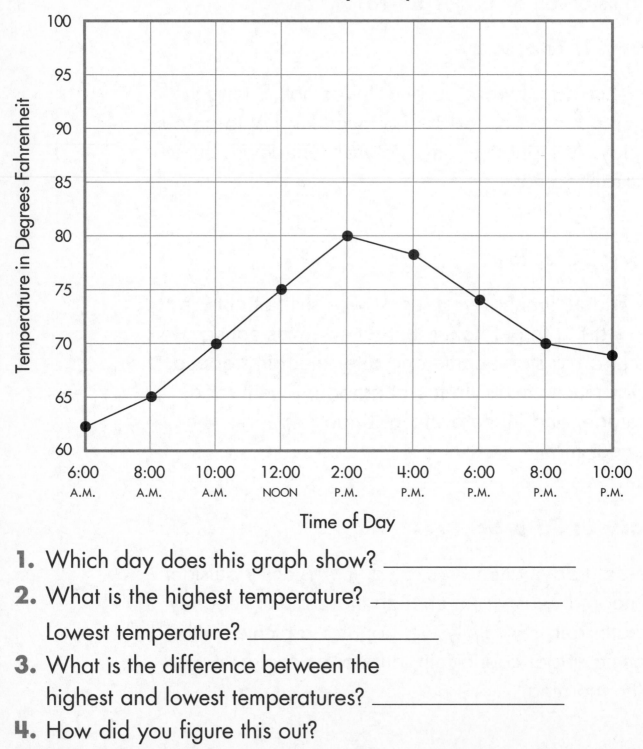

1. Which day does this graph show? _____

2. What is the highest temperature? _____

   Lowest temperature? _____

3. What is the difference between the highest and lowest temperatures? _____

4. How did you figure this out?

Stories, Tables, and Graphs

Summer Days Graphs (page 2 of 3)

Summer Days: Graph 2

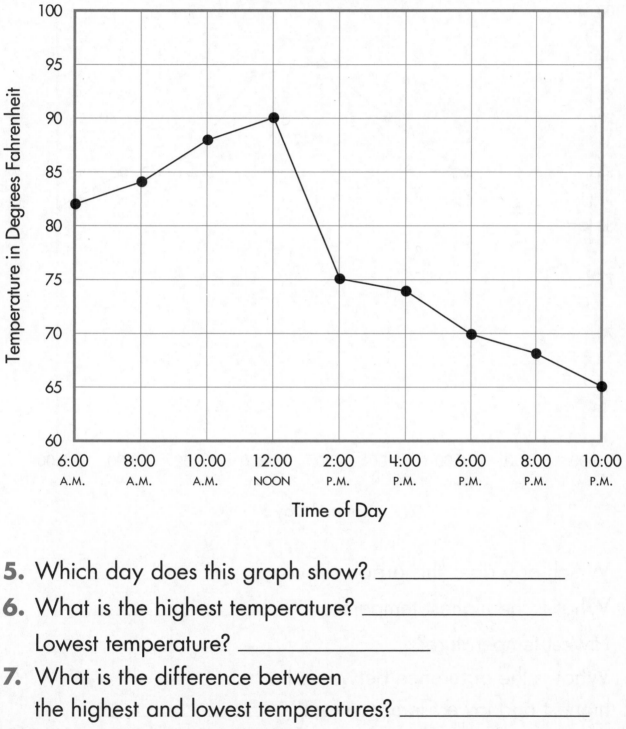

5. Which day does this graph show? _____

6. What is the highest temperature? _____

Lowest temperature? _____

7. What is the difference between
the highest and lowest temperatures? _____

8. How did you figure this out?

Summer Days Graphs (page 3 of 3)

Summer Days: Graph 3

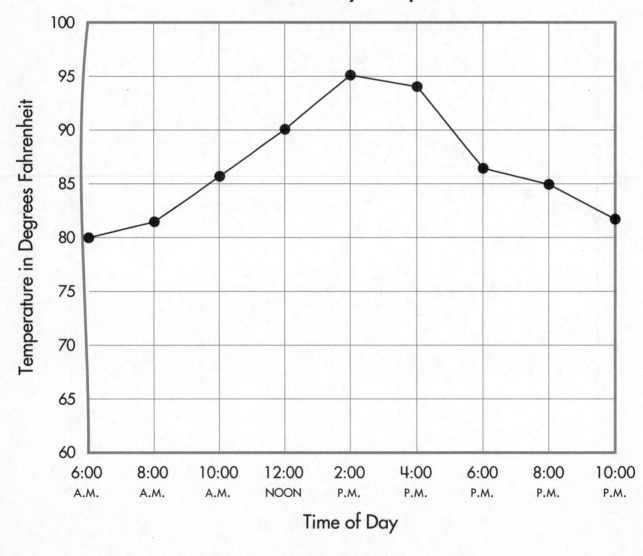

9. Which day does this graph show? _____

10. What is the highest temperature? _____
    Lowest temperature? _____

11. What is the difference between the highest and lowest temperatures? _____

12. How did you figure this out?

Winter Days (page 1 of 2) ✏ WRITING

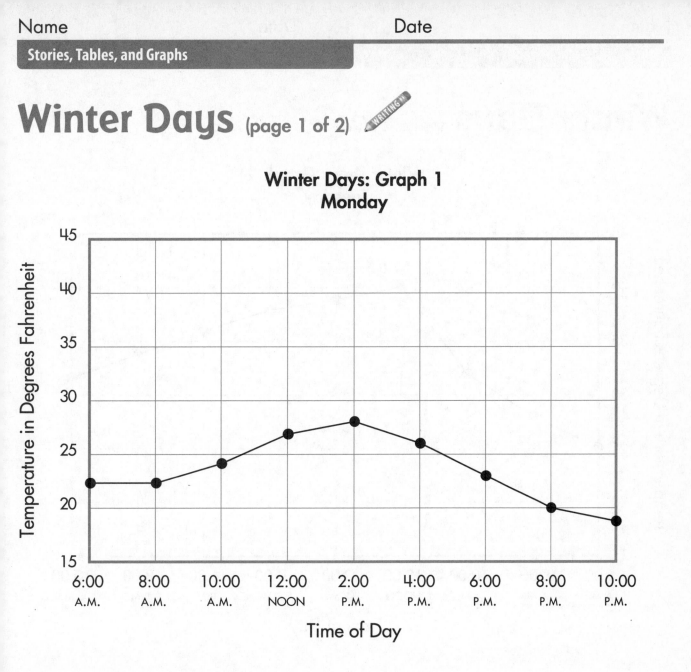

Winter Days: Graph 1
Monday

Write your story below.

Winter Days (page 2 of 2) ✎WRITING

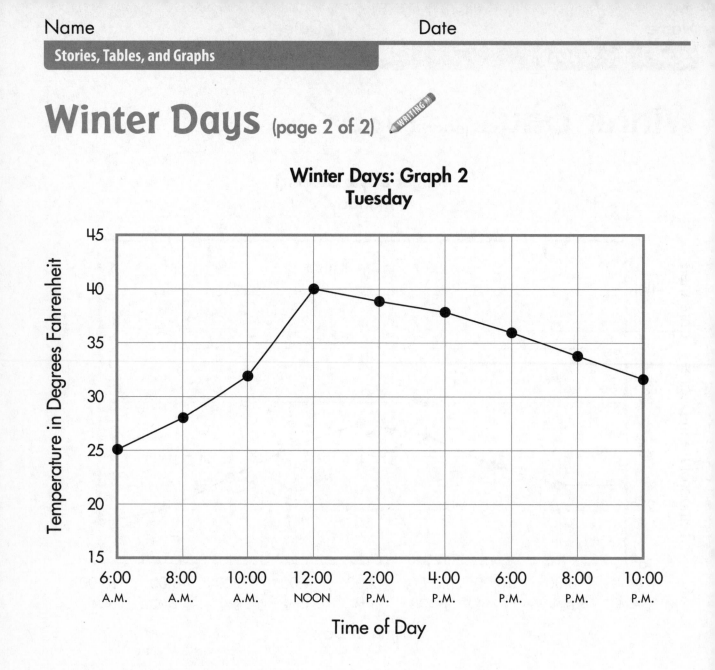

Winter Days: Graph 2
Tuesday

Write your story below.

Factor Pairs

For each number below, list as many factor pairs as you can.

NOTE Students practice multiplication combinations ("facts") by finding pairs of factors for a given product.

1. Example: 16
 	
      2×8
 	
      4×4
	2. 18

3. 24	**4.** 12
5. 20	**6.** 36

More Story Problems

Write an equation. Solve the problem.
Show your work.

NOTE Students solve story problems about multiplication and division.

SMH 39–41, 47–48

1. Beatriz is going to make 9 goodie bags to give out at her birthday party. She wants to put 8 cookies in each bag. How many cookies does she need?

2. Ms. Ko's class was counting around the class by 60s. What number did the 9th person say?

3. Oscar figured out that it is 14 weeks until his birthday. How many days until Oscar's birthday? (Remember, a week is 7 days.)

4. Spiders have 8 legs. I counted 72 legs on one web. How many spiders were there?

Temperature Graphs (page 1 of 2)

NOTE Students practice reading temperatures on a graph and describing the temperature change over the course of the day.

SMH 70, 71–72

Temperature: Graph 1

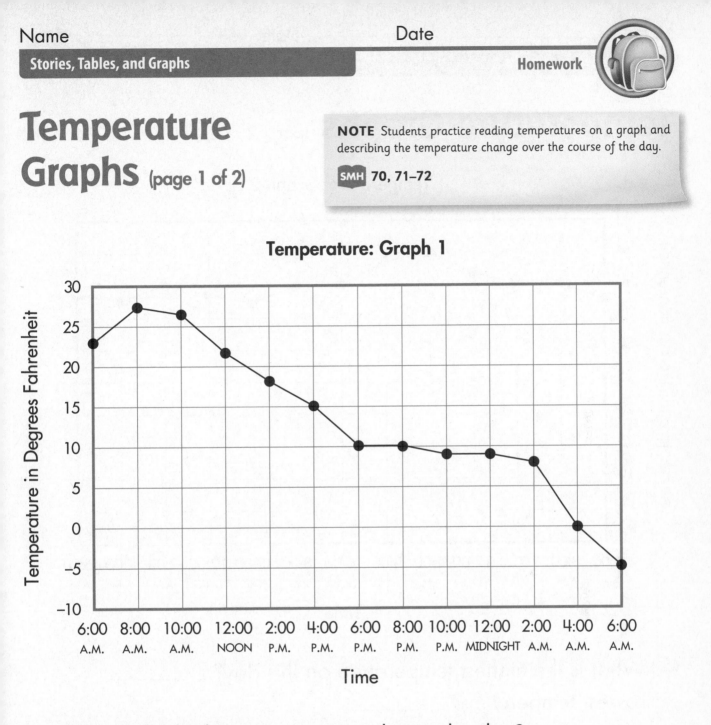

1. What is the highest temperature during the day? _____
   Lowest temperature? _____

2. Describe the temperature change on this day.
   Use the words "increasing," "decreasing," or
   "stayed the same."

3. Where and when might a day with these
   temperatures happen?

Temperature Graphs (page 2 of 2)

Temperature: Graph 2

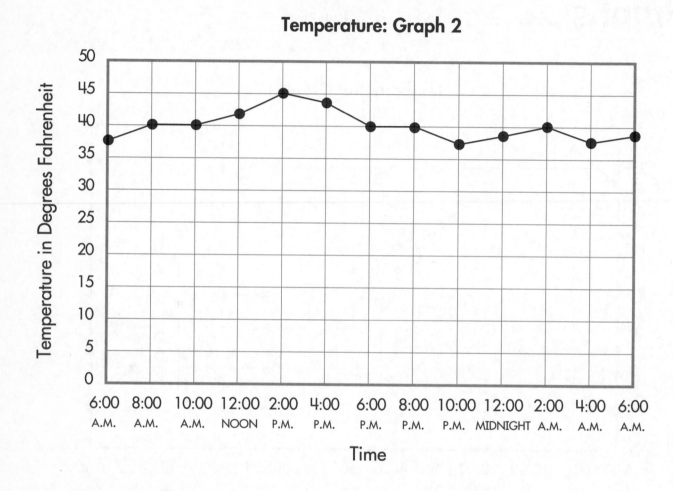

4. What is the highest temperature on this day? _____
Lowest temperature? _____

5. Describe the temperature change on this day.
Use the words "increasing," "decreasing," or
"stayed the same."

6. Where and when might a day with these
temperatures happen?

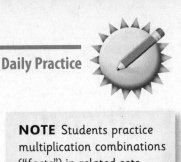

Related Multiplication Problems

NOTE Students practice multiplication combinations ("facts") in related sets.

SMH 44, 49–51

Solve the following sets of related multiplication problems.

How would you use one problem to solve the next one?

1.

$3 \times 4 =$ _____

$6 \times 4 =$ _____

2.

$7 \times 3 =$ _____

$7 \times 6 =$ _____

3.

$6 \times 3 =$ _____

$9 \times 3 =$ _____

$12 \times 3 =$ _____

4.

$5 \times 4 =$ _____

$5 \times 8 =$ _____

5.

$11 \times 2 =$ _____

$11 \times 4 =$ _____

6.

$2 \times 8 =$ _____

$3 \times 8 =$ _____

$4 \times 8 =$ _____

7.

$2 \times 9 =$ _____

$4 \times 9 =$ _____

8.

$3 \times 5 =$ _____

$3 \times 10 =$ _____

9.

$2 \times 6 =$ _____

$4 \times 6 =$ _____

$6 \times 6 =$ _____

Related Multiplication Facts

Solve the following sets of related multiplication problems.

How would you use one problem to solve the next one?

NOTE Students practice multiplication combinations ("facts") in related sets.

SMH 44, 49–51

1.

$4 \times 4 =$ _____

$8 \times 4 =$ _____

2.

$7 \times 3 =$ _____

$7 \times 6 =$ _____

3.

$3 \times 6 =$ _____

$4 \times 6 =$ _____

$6 \times 6 =$ _____

4.

$7 \times 2 =$ _____

$7 \times 4 =$ _____

5.

$3 \times 9 =$ _____

$6 \times 9 =$ _____

6.

$8 \times 2 =$ _____

$8 \times 4 =$ _____

$8 \times 6 =$ _____

7.

$2 \times 6 =$ _____

$2 \times 12 =$ _____

8.

$3 \times 8 =$ _____

$6 \times 8 =$ _____

9.

$11 \times 3 =$ _____

$11 \times 4 =$ _____

$11 \times 8 =$ _____

Cube Patterns:
Red, Blue, Green

Build a train of 12 cubes with these colors,
in this order:

red, blue, green, red, blue, green, red, blue, green,
red, blue, green

1. What is the unit of this pattern? _____

2. How many cubes are in the unit? _____

3. If this pattern keeps repeating the same colors:

   a. What is the color of the 13th cube? _____

   b. What is the color of the 18th cube? _____

   c. What is the color of the 20th cube? _____

   d. What is the color of the 25th cube? _____

   e. What is the color of the 33rd cube? _____

4. How did you figure out the color of the
33rd cube?

Multiplication Picture Problems

NOTE Students practice solving multiplication problems.

SMH 40–41

For each problem, draw a picture to represent the problem and then solve the problem.

1. $9 \times 3 = $ _____

2. $4 \times 7 = $ _____

3. $6 \times 5 = $ _____

Solving Multiplication Problems

NOTE Students practice solving multiplication problems.

SMH 40–41

Solve the problems below. For story problems, write a multiplication equation for each problem and show how you solved it.

1. $6 \times 7 =$ _____

2. Markers come in sets of 8. Mr. Thompson has 5 sets in his classroom. How many markers does he have in all?

3. Folders come in packs of 12. Mr. Thompson orders 3 packs. How many folders does he order?

4.
$$\begin{array}{r} 9 \\ \times\ 4 \\ \hline \end{array}$$

Rounding to Tens and Hundreds

NOTE Students round whole numbers to the nearest ten and hundred.

SMH 6, 10–11

For each problem, write the number in expanded form and then round to the nearest ten and hundred.

1. 432

Expanded form: _____

What is 432 rounded to the nearest ten? _____

What is 432 rounded to the nearest hundred? _____

2. 903

Expanded form: _____

What is 903 rounded to the nearest ten? _____

What is 903 rounded to the nearest hundred? _____

3. 289

Expanded form: _____

What is 289 rounded to the nearest ten? _____

What is 289 rounded to the nearest hundred? _____

4. 777

Expanded form: _____

What is 777 rounded to the nearest ten? _____

What is 777 rounded to the nearest hundred? _____

Where Are the Greens? (page 1 of 2) ✏️ WRITING

red	blue	green	red	blue	green	red	blue	green	red	blue	green
1	2	3			?			?			?

The number 3 is matched with the 1st green cube.

1. What number is matched with the 2nd green cube? _____

2. What number is matched with the 3rd green cube? _____

3. What number would be matched with the 6th green cube? _____

4. What number would be matched with the 10th green cube? _____

5. Talk to your partner about how you found out what number would be matched with the 10th green cube. Then write how you figured it out.

Where Are the Greens? (page 2 of 2)

6. What are the numbers for the first
10 green cubes?

1st green _____   6th green _____

2nd green _____   7th green _____

3rd green _____   8th green _____

4th green _____   9th green _____

5th green _____   10th green _____

7. What are you noticing about the numbers
that are matched with the green cubes?
Why does it work that way?

Where Are the Blues? (page 1 of 2)

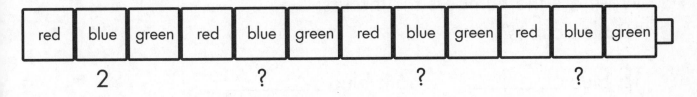

red	blue	green	red	blue	green	red	blue	green	red	blue	green
	2			?			?			?	

The number 2 is matched with the 1st blue cube.

1. What number is matched with the 2nd blue cube? _____

2. What number is matched with the 3rd blue cube? _____

3. What number would be matched with the 6th blue cube? _____

4. What number would be matched with the 10th blue cube? _____

5. Talk to your partner about how you found out what number would be matched with the 10th blue cube. Then write down how you figured it out.

Stories, Tables, and Graphs

Where Are the Blues? (page 2 of 2)

6. What are the numbers for the first 10 blue cubes?

1st blue _____   6th blue _____

2nd blue _____   7th blue _____

3rd blue _____   8th blue _____

4th blue _____   9th blue _____

5th blue _____   10th blue _____

7. What are you noticing about the numbers that are matched with the blue cubes? Why does it work that way?

8. The 13th blue cube in the pattern matches with 38. What number matches with the 14th blue cube? _____

How do you know?

Where Are the Reds? (page 1 of 2)

red	blue	green	red	blue	green	red	blue	green	red	blue	green
1			?			?			?		

The number 1 is matched with the 1st red cube.

1. What number is matched with the 2nd red cube? _____

2. What number is matched with the 3rd red cube? _____

3. What number would be matched with the 6th red cube? _____

4. What number would be matched with the 10th red cube? _____

5. Talk to your partner about how you found out what number would be matched with the 10th red cube. Then write down how you figured it out.

Where Are the Reds? (page 2 of 2)

6. What are the numbers for the first
10 red cubes?

1st red _____   6th red _____

2nd red _____   7th red _____

3rd red _____   8th red _____

4th red _____   9th red _____

5th red _____   10th red _____

7. What are you noticing about the numbers that are
matched with the red cubes? Why does it work
that way?

8. The 12th red cube in the pattern matches with 34.
What number matches with the 13th red cube? _____

How do you know?

Stories, Tables, and Graphs

NOTE Students practice multiplication by solving story problems.

SMH 40–41

Things That Come in Groups

Solve the story problems below. Write a multiplication equation for each problem and show how you solved it.

Spiders have 8 legs.

1. How many legs do 3 spiders have? _____

Equation: $3 \times 8 =$ _____

2. How many legs do 4 spiders have? _____

Equation: _____

3. How many legs do 5 spiders have? _____

Equation: _____

What Color Is It? (page 1 of 2) ✏️WRITING

Here is a train with the following 12 cubes:

red	blue	green	red	blue	green	red	blue	green	red	blue	green

1. If this pattern keeps repeating:

   a. What color is the 53rd cube? _____

   Find a way to figure this out without counting by ones.

   b. How did you figure this out?

What Color Is It? (page 2 of 2)

red	blue	green	red	blue	green	red	blue	green	red	blue	green

2. If this pattern keeps repeating:

    a. What color is the 100th cube? _____

       Find a way to figure this out without counting
       by ones.

    b. How did you figure this out?

School Supplies

Solve the following story problems
and be sure to show your work.

NOTE Students practice solving multiplication problems in story problem contexts.

SMH 40–41

1. A box of glue sticks has 12 sticks in it.

How many glue sticks are in 3 boxes?

2. A package of crayons has 8 crayons in it.

How many crayons are in 5 packages?

3. A bag of erasers has 9 erasers in it.

How many erasers are in 4 bags?

A Repeating Pattern

A cube train has this repeating pattern:

NOTE Students look at the repeating pattern to determine the color of cubes associated with particular numbers.

SMH 73–74

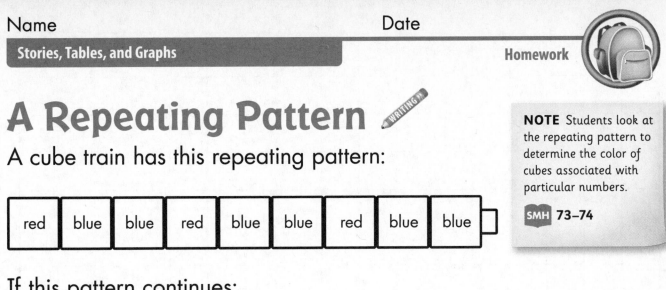

| red | blue | blue | red | blue | blue | red | blue | blue |

If this pattern continues:

1. What color is the 45th cube? _____
How do you know?

2. What color is the 61st cube? _____
How do you know?

42 Unit 6

Franick's Marbles

Franick had 30 Magic Marbles left from the year before. She was then given 3 Magic Marbles on the first night, 3 more Magic Marbles on the second night, 3 more Magic Marbles on the third night, and so on.

Make a diagram, table, or picture that shows how many Magic Marbles Franick has after 30 nights.

Bolar's Marbles

Bolar had no Magic Marbles left from the year before. He was then given 5 Magic Marbles on the first night, 5 more Magic Marbles on the second night, 5 more Magic Marbles on the third night, and so on.

Make a diagram, table, or picture that shows how many Magic Marbles Bolar has after 30 nights.

Zupin's Marbles

Zupin had 60 Magic Marbles left from the year before. She was then given 2 Magic Marbles on the first night, 2 more Magic Marbles on the second night, 2 more Magic Marbles on the third night, and so on.

Make a diagram, table, or picture that shows how many Magic Marbles Zupin has after 30 nights.

In the Garden

Solve the following story problems and be sure to show your work.

NOTE Students practice solving multiplication problems in story problem contexts.

SMH 40–41

1. Kenji finds 8 ladybugs in his garden. Each ladybug has 4 spots on it. How many spots are there on all the ladybugs?

2. Ines wants to plant 12 tomato plants in her garden. She will plant them in equal rows. One way that Ines can arrange the tomato plants is 1 row of 12 plants. What are other possible arrangements? Draw and label as many arrangements as you can think of.

3. Cristobal has 3 sunflowers in his garden. He saves 12 seeds from each sunflower for his garden next year. How many seeds does he save altogether?

How Many Days?

Solve the story problems below. Write a multiplication equation for each problem and show how you solved it.

NOTE Students practice multiplication by solving story problems.

SMH 40–41

There are 7 days in a week.

1. How many days are in 3 weeks? _____

Example: Equation: $3 \times 7 =$ _____

2. How many days are in 5 weeks? _____

Equation: _____

3. How many days are in 7 weeks? _____

Equation: _____

Area and Perimeter

NOTE Students find the area and perimeter of rectangles.

SMH 114

1. Each rectangle has an area of 40 square
units. Find the perimeter of each rectangle.

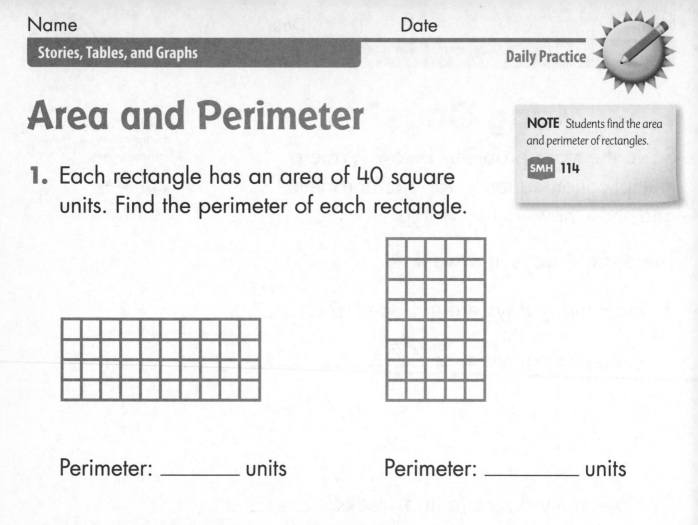

Perimeter: _____ units   Perimeter: _____ units

2. Each rectangle has a perimeter of 30 units.
Find the area of each rectangle.

Area: _____ square units   Area: _____ square units

Comparing Tovar and Zupin (page 1 of 3)

Tovar had 20 Magic Marbles left from the year before. He was given 2 Magic Marbles each night for 30 nights.

Zupin had 60 Magic Marbles left from the year before. She was given 2 Magic Marbles on each night for 30 nights.

Fill in the table for Tovar and Zupin. Then answer the questions on pages 50–51.

Day	Tovar	Zupin
Beginning	20	60
5		
10		
15		
20		
25		
30		

Comparing Tovar and Zupin (page 2 of 3)

1. Compare Tovar and Zupin as the month goes by. Describe what happens and why it happens.

2. How did you find the number of marbles for Tovar on Day 10?

3. How did you find the number of marbles for Tovar on Day 20?

Comparing Tovar and Zupin (page 3 of 3)

4. Write a rule (or a set of directions) for how to figure out how many marbles Tovar has on **any** day. The directions should tell how to figure out Tovar's marbles on any day—Day 3, Day 5, Day 10, Day 12, Day 29, or any other day.

Counting Around the Class

NOTE Students find the multiples of a given number and solve multiplication problems.

SMH 42

1. Mr. Brown's class counted by 4s. The 1st person said 4, the 2nd said 8, and the 3rd said 12. How many people counted to get to 36? How do you know?

2. Ms. Wilson's class counted by 6s. The 1st person said 6, the 2nd said 12, and the 3rd said 18.

  a. What number did the 6th person say? How do you know?

  b. What number did the 12th person say? How do you know?

3. Ms. Ross's class counted by 5s. The 1st person said 5, the 2nd said 10, and the 3rd said 15.

  a. How many people counted to get to 100? How do you know?

  b. When Ms. Ross's class was counting by 5s, did anyone say the number 72? How do you know?

© Pearson Education 3

Comparing Tovar, Winger, and Jorad (page 1 of 3)

Tovar had 20 Magic Marbles left from the year before. He was then given 2 Magic Marbles each night for 30 nights.

Winger had 20 Magic Marbles left from the year before. She was then given 4 Magic Marbles on each night for 30 nights.

Jorad had 45 Magic Marbles left from the year before. She was then given 3 Magic Marbles on each night for 30 nights.

Fill in the table for Tovar and Winger. The table shows how many marbles they have after every 5 nights. (Do **not** fill in Jorad's yet.)

Day	Tovar	Winger	Jorad
Beginning	20	20	45
5			
10			
15			
20			
25			
30			

Comparing Tovar, Winger, and Jorad (page 2 of 3)

1. How did you find the number of marbles on Day 10 for Winger?

2. How did you find the number of marbles on Day 20 for Winger?

3. Write a rule (or a set of directions) for how to figure out how many marbles Winger has on **any** day.

Comparing Tovar, Winger, and Jorad (page 3 of 3)

4. Compare Tovar and Winger. What happens as the month goes by? Describe what happens and why it happens.

5. Fill in the table for Jorad. How did you find the number of marbles on Day 10 for Jorad?

6. How did you find the number of marbles on Day 20 for Jorad?

Leg Riddles

Birds have 2 legs.
Dogs have 4 legs.
Ladybugs have 6 legs.

There are 36 legs in the house. All the legs belong to birds, dogs, and ladybugs. How many of each creature—birds, dogs, and ladybugs—could be in the house?

(There are many possible answers. How many can you find?)

NOTE Students solve a multiplication problem in a story context.

Birds	Dogs	Ladybugs

Magic Marbles

Choose one of the pages that you did not complete at the beginning of this Investigation.

NOTE Students make a representation of a Rhomarian person's marble accumulation and solve related story problems.

SMH 75–80

Page 43, *Franick's Marbles*
Page 44, *Bolar's Marbles*
Page 45, *Zupin's Marbles*

Make a diagram, table, or picture according to the directions on that page. Then answer these questions:

1. Circle the person you chose: FRANICK   BOLAR   ZUPIN

2. If this person received the same number of marbles for 10 more nights, how many marbles would the person have? Show how you figured this out.

3. If this person then spent 23 marbles on snacks and 67 marbles on a special game, how many marbles are left? Show how you figured this out.

Unit 6

Stories, Tables, and Graphs

Graphs for Tovar and Winger (page 1 of 2)

Tovar and Winger

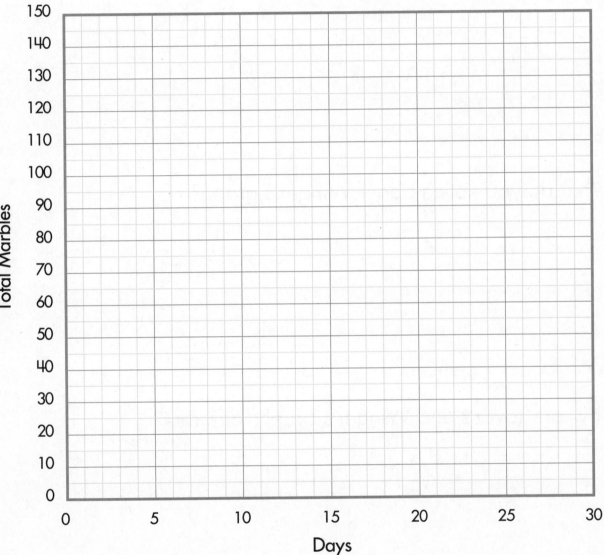

Total Marbles

Days

Graphs for Tovar and Winger (page 2 of 2) ✏️WRITING

1. What do you notice about Tovar's graph?

2. What do you notice about Winger's graph?

3. How are Tovar's and Winger's graphs different?

Why are they different?

Table and Graph for Tovar and Gowen (page 1 of 3)

Tovar had 20 Magic Marbles left from the year before. He was then given 2 Magic Marbles each night for 30 nights.

Gowen had no Magic Marbles left from the year before. He was then given 3 Magic Marbles on each night for 30 nights.

Fill in the table for Tovar and Gowen. The table shows how many marbles they have after every 5 nights.

Day	Tovar	Gowen
Beginning		
5		
10		
15		
20		
25		
30		

Table and Graph for Tovar and Gowen (page 2 of 3)

Tovar and Gowen

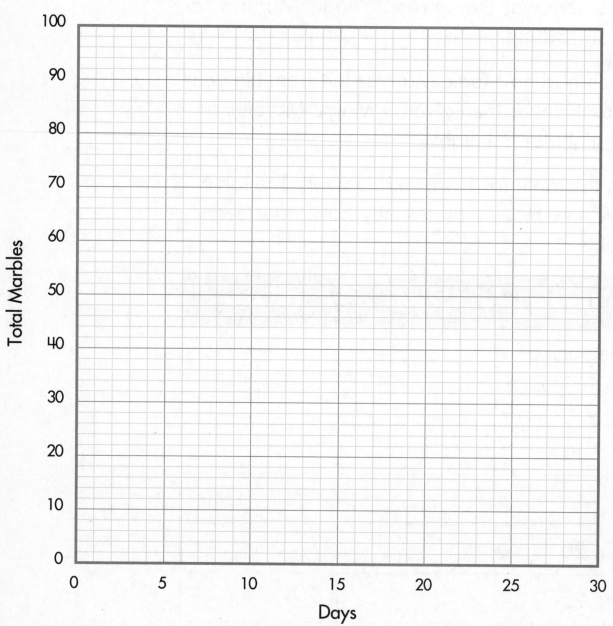

Table and Graph for Tovar and Gowen (page 3 of 3)

1. How did you find the number of marbles on Day 20 for Gowen?

2. Write a way to find the number of marbles for Gowen for **any** day.

3. How are Tovar's and Gowen's graphs different?

Why are they different?

What's the Total?

Write the dimensions of each array.
Then write the total number of squares.

NOTE Students practice
multiplication, using arrays.

SMH 45–46

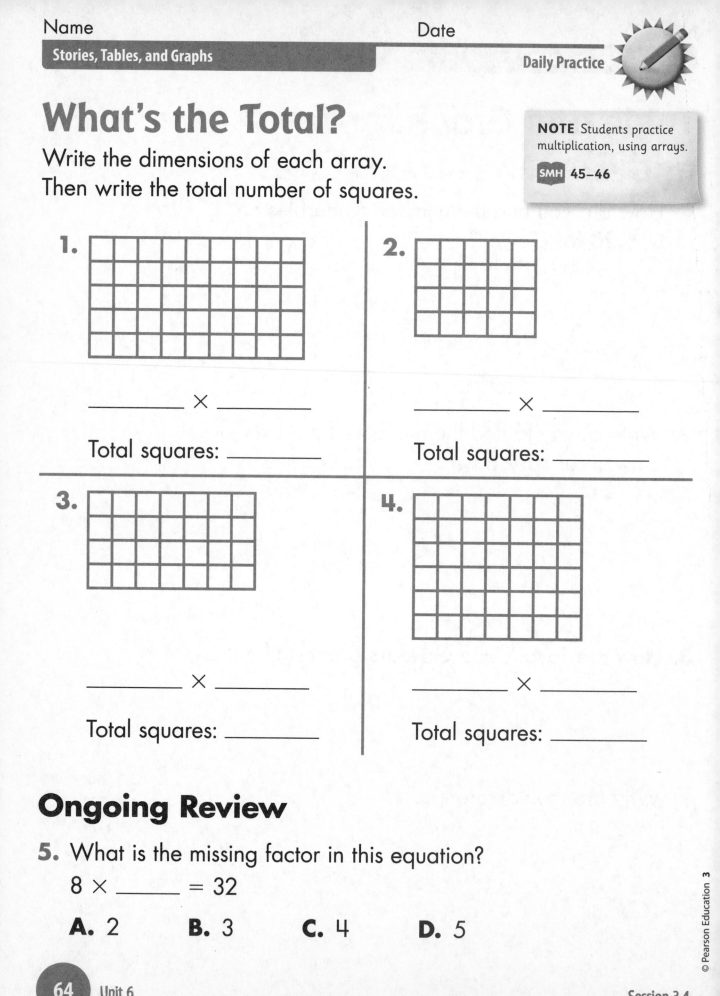

1.

_____ × _____

Total squares: _____

2.

_____ × _____

Total squares: _____

3.

_____ × _____

Total squares: _____

4.

_____ × _____

Total squares: _____

Ongoing Review

5. What is the missing factor in this equation?

$8 \times$ _____ $= 32$

A. 2   **B.** 3   **C.** 4   **D.** 5

Table and Graph for Tovar and Lazik (page 1 of 3)

Tovar had 20 Magic Marbles left from the year before. He was then given 2 Magic Marbles each night for 30 nights.

Lazik had 12 Magic Marbles left from the year before. He was then given 2 Magic Marbles on each night for 30 nights.

Fill in the table for Tovar and Lazik. The table shows how many marbles they have after every 5 nights.

Day	Tovar	Lazik
Beginning		
5		
10		
15		
20		
25		
30		

Table and Graph for Tovar and Lazik (page 2 of 3)

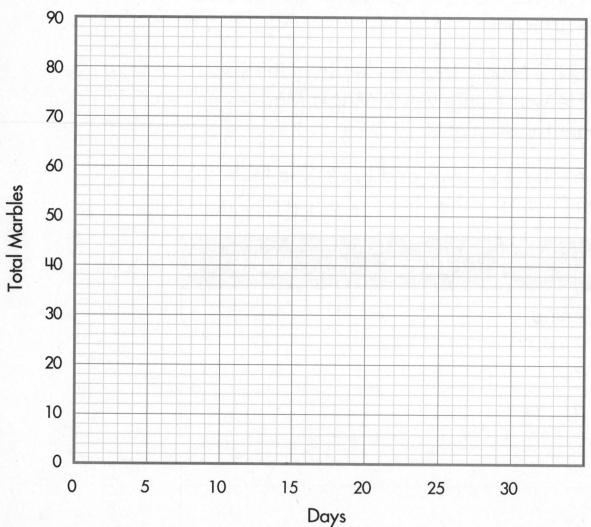

Tovar and Lazik

Table and Graph for Tovar and Lazik (page 3 of 3)

1. How did you find the number of marbles on Day 20 for Lazik?

2. Write a way to find the number of marbles for Lazik for **any** day.

3. Compare Tovar's and Lazik's graphs. What do you notice? What would happen if Tovar and Lazik kept getting the same number of marbles for 10 more nights?

Multiply or Divide?

Solve the story problems. Write whether you used multiplication or division to solve each problem.

NOTE Students solve story problems and decide whether they used multiplication or division.

SMH **39, 40–41, 47, 48**

1. Pentagons have 5 sides. How many sides do 9 pentagons have?

Did you multiply or divide? _____

2. Benjamin borrowed 15 books from the library. If he reads 3 books a day, in how many days will he finish reading all the books?

Did you multiply or divide? _____

3. There are 49 chairs in the room. They need to be set up in rows of 7. How many rows can be made?

Did you multiply or divide? _____

Ongoing Review

4. Which expression does **not** equal 36?

A. 2×17 **B.** 3×12 **C.** 4×9 **D.** 6×6

How Many Each Day?

NOTE Students fill in a table to show constant change and solve a problem.

1. Becky and her brother Kenji are saving pennies. Every week they put 25 pennies in their jar.

Here is a table of how much they have saved. Fill in the rest of the table. Notice that the table skips some weeks.

Week	Total Amount
Week 1	$0.25
Week 2	$0.50
Week 3	$0.75
Week 4	
Week 5	
Week 10	
Week 15	

2. Becky and Kenji saved $6.00. Then they spent $1.50 on a book and $3.75 on a present for their grandmother. How much money did they have left?

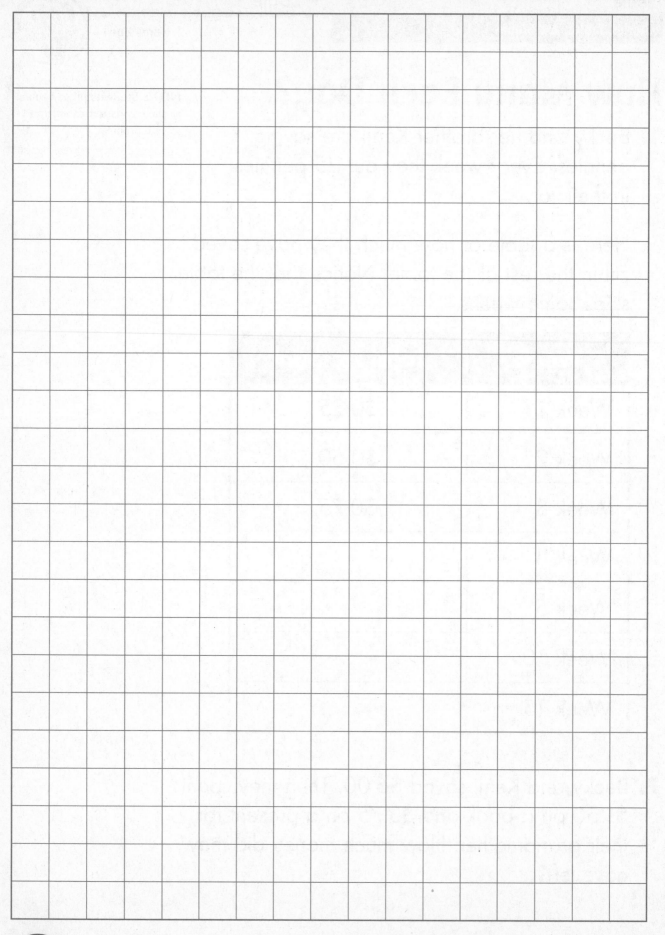

Division Problems

Solve each problem. Show your work.

NOTE Students solve division problems.

SMH 47, 48

1. $50 \div 5 =$ _____

2. $48 \div 6 =$ _____

3. $7\overline{)35}$

Ongoing Review

4. Which number is **not** a multiple of 3?

A. 3   **B.** 12   **C.** 18   **D.** 28

A Bake Sale

NOTE Students solve multiplication and division problems in story contexts.

SMH 40–41, 47, 48

Write an equation for each story problem.
Solve each one and show how you solved it.

1. Zhang made 48 muffins for the bake sale.
   He can fit 8 muffins in a box. How many
   boxes does he need for all of his muffins?

2. Gina baked 4 sheets of cookies. On each sheet
   were 12 cookies. How many cookies did
   she bake?

3. Casawn baked 3 cakes. He sliced each cake
   into 9 pieces. How many pieces of cake
   are there?

4. Jane baked 36 dinner rolls. She put 6 rolls in
   each bag. How many bags did she make?

Children's Library

NOTE Students construct a
graph in a real-world context.

SMH 70, 71–72

Make a graph of the number of patrons
visiting the children's room at your local library
on a Saturday. Consider the weather, special
programs and children's typical weekend
routines (naps, lessons, chores).

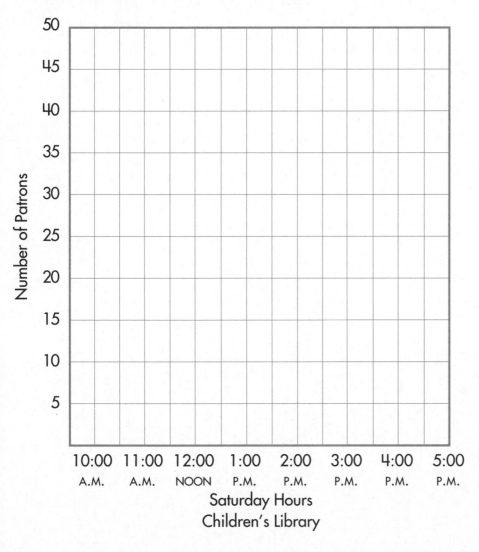

Saturday Hours
Children's Library

On a separate piece of paper, write the story of
your graph. Explain when people were entering and
exiting the library at the fastest rate and why.

Ikenaga 2 Jos Leys

"A relatively simple formula can generate immensely complex images." – **Jos Leys**

IN NUMBER, DATA, AND SPACE®

Finding Fair Shares

Investigation 3

Sharing One Brownie (page 1 of 2)

Cut up large brownie rectangles and glue the pieces below. Show how you would make fair shares.

1. 2 people share a brownie. Each person gets _____.

2. 4 people share a brownie. Each person gets _____.

3. 8 people share a brownie. Each person gets _____.

Sharing One Brownie (page 2 of 2)

4. 3 people share a brownie. Each person gets _____.

5. 6 people share a brownie. Each person gets _____.

Factor Pairs

For each number below, list as many factor pairs as you can.

NOTE Students practice multiplication combinations ("facts") by finding pairs of factors for a given product.

1. Example: 18

     __2__ × __9__

     __3__ × __6__

     _____ × _____

2.   12

     _____ × _____

     _____ × _____

     _____ × _____

3.   36

     _____ × _____

     _____ × _____

     _____ × _____

     _____ × _____

4.   16

     _____ × _____

     _____ × _____

     _____ × _____

5.   40

     _____ × _____

     _____ × _____

     _____ × _____

6.   24

     _____ × _____

     _____ × _____

     _____ × _____

     _____ × _____

Things That Come in Groups

Solve the story problems below. Write a multiplication equation for each problem and show how you solved it.

NOTE Students practice multiplication by solving story problems.

SMH 40–41

A package of popsicles has 6 popsicles.

1. How many popsicles are in 2 packages? _____

Example: Equation: _____ $2 \times 6 =$ _____

2. How many popsicles are in 4 packages? _____

Equation: _____

3. How many popsicles are in 8 packages? _____

Equation: _____

Finding Halves

Draw a line to create $\frac{1}{2}$ of each picture.
Label each half you create.

NOTE Students are learning that half of an area is 1 of 2 equal pieces.

SMH **56, 57, 58–59**

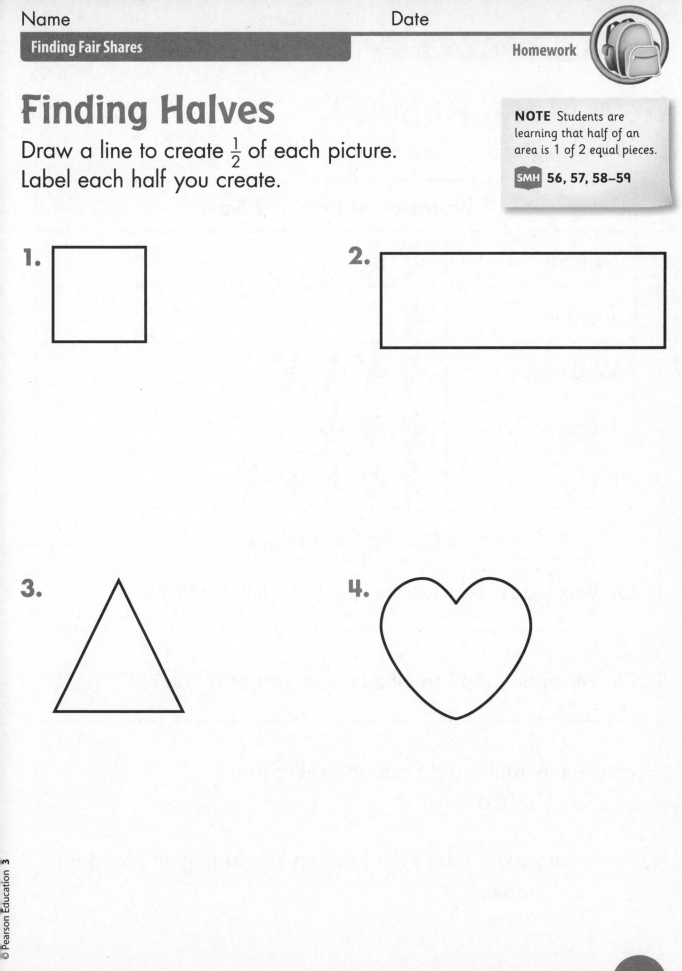

1.

2.

3.

4.

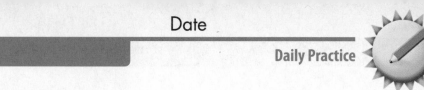

How Many Robins?

Use the pictograph to answer the problems.

NOTE Students interpret a pictograph.

Number of Robins I Saw	
Monday	🐾 🐾
Tuesday	🐾
Wednesday	🐾 🐾 🐾 🐾
Thursday	🐾 🐾 🐾
Friday	🐾 🐾 🐾 🐾 🐾

Each 🐾 = 3 robins

1. On which day did I see the greatest number of robins?

_____

2. On which day did I see the fewest number of robins?

_____

3. How many robins did I see on Wednesday?
_____ robins

4. How many more robins did I see on Thursday than Monday?
_____ robins

Finding Thirds

Draw lines to create $\frac{1}{3}$ of each picture.
Label each third you create.

NOTE Students are learning that $\frac{1}{3}$ of an area is 1 of 3 equal pieces.

SMH 56, 57, 58–59

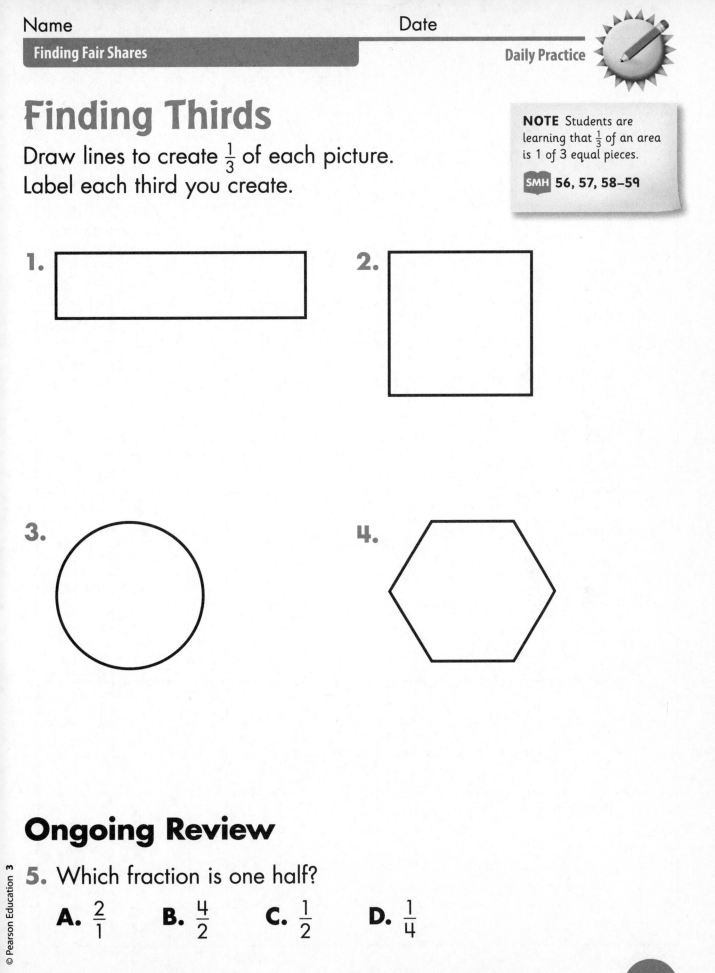

1.

2.

3.

4.

Ongoing Review

5. Which fraction is one half?

   A. $\frac{2}{1}$ **B.** $\frac{4}{2}$ **C.** $\frac{1}{2}$ **D.** $\frac{1}{4}$

Halves, Fourths, and Eighths on Number Lines

1. Divide the zero-to-one number line in half.
Label each half.

0 ———————————————————— 1

2. Divide the zero-to-one number line into fourths.
Label each fourth.

0 ———————————————————— 1

3. Divide the zero-to-one number line into eighths.
Label each eighth.

0 ———————————————————— 1

On the Farm

Solve each problem. Show your work.

NOTE Students solve problems by multiplying 1-digit numbers.

SMH 39–41

1. A farmer feeds the horses on his farm 9 bales of hay every day. How many bales does the farmer feed the horses in 1 week?

2. There are 9 chickens in the chicken coop. Each chicken laid 9 eggs. How many eggs did the chickens lay?

3. There are 9 cows on the farm. They each produced 6 gallons of milk. How much milk did the cows produce?

4. There are 7 spiders in the barn. Each spider has 8 legs. How many legs do the spiders have altogether?

Representing and Comparing Thirds and Sixths

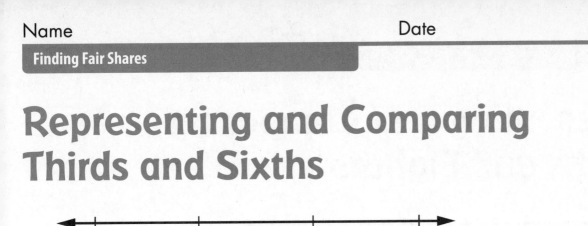

1. Label the thirds on the number line. Divide the number line into sixths and label the sixths.

2. Ant A walked $\frac{1}{3}$ the distance from 0 to 1. Ant B walked $\frac{2}{3}$ the distance from 0 to 1. Show how far each ant walked on the number line. Use >, <, or = to compare the fractions.

   $\frac{1}{3}$ ☐ $\frac{2}{3}$

3. Ant C walked $\frac{1}{3}$ the distance from 0 to 1. Ant D walked $\frac{1}{6}$ the distance from 0 to 1. Show how far each ant walked on the number line. Use >, <, or = to compare the fractions.

   $\frac{1}{3}$ ☐ $\frac{1}{6}$

4. Ant E walked $\frac{1}{3}$ the distance from 0 to 1. Ant F walked $\frac{3}{6}$ the distance from 0 to 1. Show how far each ant walked on the number line. Use >, <, or = to compare the fractions.

   $\frac{1}{3}$ ☐ $\frac{3}{6}$

Representing and Comparing Fourths and Eighths

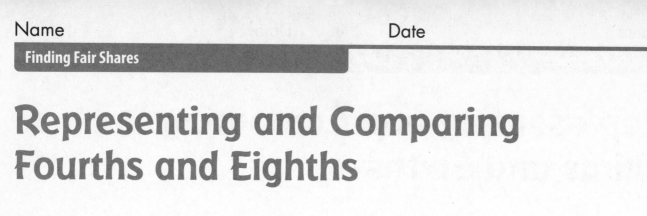

1. Label the fourths on the number line. Divide the number line into eighths and label the eighths.

2. Ant A walked $\frac{1}{4}$ the distance from 0 to 1. Ant B walked $\frac{2}{4}$ the distance from 0 to 1. Show how far each ant walked on the number line. Use >, <, or = to compare the fractions.

   $\frac{1}{4}$ ☐ $\frac{2}{4}$

3. Ant C walked $\frac{3}{8}$ the distance from 0 to 1. Ant D walked $\frac{1}{4}$ the distance from 0 to 1. Show how far each ant walked on the number line. Use >, <, or = to compare the fractions.

   $\frac{3}{8}$ ☐ $\frac{1}{4}$

4. Ant E walked $\frac{3}{4}$ the distance from 0 to 1. Ant F walked $\frac{6}{8}$ the distance from 0 to 1. Show how far each ant walked on the number line. Use >, <, or = to compare the fractions.

   $\frac{3}{4}$ ☐ $\frac{6}{8}$

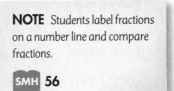

Comparing Fractions on a Number Line

NOTE Students label fractions on a number line and compare fractions.

SMH 56

1. Fill in the missing fractions on the number line.

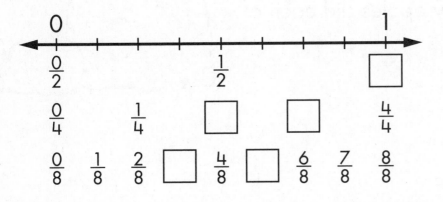

Write >, <, or = in each box to compare the fractions.

2. $\frac{2}{8}$ ☐ $\frac{1}{2}$

3. $\frac{3}{4}$ ☐ $\frac{7}{8}$

4. $\frac{3}{4}$ ☐ $\frac{5}{8}$

5. $\frac{1}{4}$ ☐ $\frac{1}{8}$

6. $\frac{6}{8}$ ☐ $\frac{3}{4}$

7. $\frac{2}{2}$ ☐ $\frac{7}{8}$

Sharing 12 Things

Solve each of these problems and show how you figured out your answers.

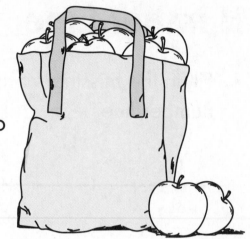

1. Oscar picked 12 apples. He gave $\frac{1}{3}$ of the apples to Gil and $\frac{1}{3}$ of the apples to Becky. How many apples did each of them get?

2. Pilar picked 12 apples. She gave $\frac{1}{4}$ of the apples to Dwayne, $\frac{1}{4}$ of the apples to Murphy, and $\frac{1}{4}$ of the apples to Kelley. How many apples did each of them get?

3. Chiang picked 12 apples. She gave $\frac{1}{6}$ of the apples to each of her 5 friends. How many apples did each friend get?

Multiplication Combinations of 2s, 4s, and 8s

NOTE Students practice multiplication combinations ("facts"). They look for patterns in the 2s, 4s, and 8s combinations.

SMH 49–51

1. Solve these problems.

$1 \times 2 =$

$2 \times 2 =$ $1 \times 4 =$

$3 \times 2 =$

$4 \times 2 =$ $2 \times 4 =$ $1 \times 8 =$

$5 \times 2 =$

$6 \times 2 =$ $3 \times 4 =$

$7 \times 2 =$

$8 \times 2 =$ $4 \times 4 =$ $2 \times 8 =$

$9 \times 2 =$

$10 \times 2 =$ $5 \times 4 =$

$11 \times 2 =$

$12 \times 2 =$ $6 \times 4 =$ $3 \times 8 =$

2. What patterns do you notice?

3. Ask someone at home to help you practice the multiplication combinations that you are working on.

What Fraction Is Shaded?

NOTE Students determine what fraction of the whole rectangle is shaded.

SMH 57, 58–59

Look at each rectangle below. Label the fraction that is shaded.

1.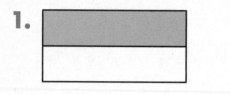

_____

2.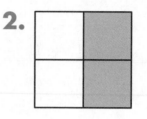

_____

3.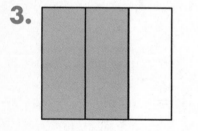

_____

4.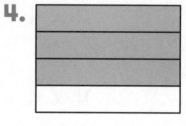

_____

5.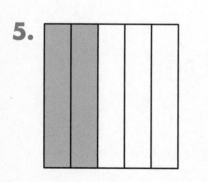

_____

Sharing Several Brownies

_____ brownies shared by _____ people

number of brownies   number of people

Draw a picture to show your solution or
explain in words how you solved the problem.

How many brownies does each person get? _____

Guess the Rule with Number Pairs

NOTE Students look for multiplication relationships between numbers in a table.

Can you figure out the rule for each table below? For each table, fill in the missing numbers and write the rule. Make sure that the rule works for all of the numbers in each table.

1.

⊠	△
3	15
6	30
2	10
4	____
10	____
____	35

What is the rule? _____

2.

⊠	△
4	32
2	16
5	40
3	____
6	____
____	8

What is the rule? _____

3.

⊠	△
4	24
2	12
5	30
3	____
6	____
____	42

What is the rule? _____

4.

⊠	△
9	3
21	7
33	11
12	____
30	____
____	9

What is the rule? _____

Are These Equal?

Answer these questions. Show your work.

NOTE Students use drawings or stories to show whether these fractions are equivalent.

SMH 63, 64

1. Does $\frac{1}{2} = \frac{2}{4}$? _____

Show how you know:

2. Does $\frac{1}{2} + \frac{1}{2} = \frac{2}{4} + \frac{2}{4}$? _____

Show how you know:

3. Does $\frac{1}{8} + \frac{1}{8} = \frac{1}{4}$? _____

Show how you know:

14 Unit 7

Sharing Many Things (page 1 of 2)

Solve these problems and show your solutions.

1. There are 6 brownies on a plate. Four people share them equally. How many brownies does each person get?

2. There are 3 apples in a bag. Two people share them equally. How many apples does each person get?

3. How much is $\frac{1}{4}$ of 8 pies?

Finding Fair Shares

Sharing Many Things (page 2 of 2)

4. How much is $\frac{2}{3}$ of 9 marbles?

5. I have $\frac{1}{3}$ of $15.00. How many dollars do I have?

6. How much is $\frac{3}{4}$ of 32 color tiles?

Identifying and Naming Fractions

NOTE Students identify and name fractions of rectangles.

SMH **58–59**

Name the fraction that is shaded.

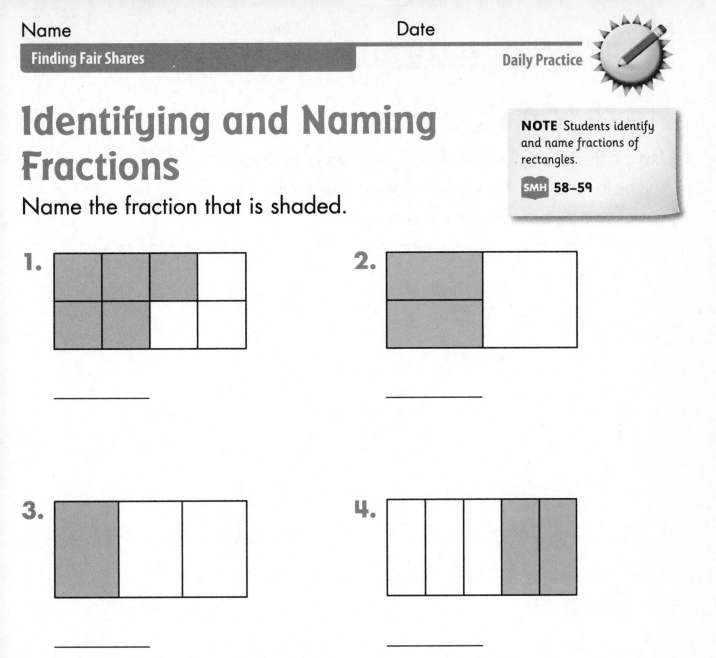

1. _____

2. _____

3. _____

4. _____

Ongoing Review

5. Is this true or false? $\frac{1}{4} + \frac{1}{2} = 1$

   A. true   **B.** false

Hexagon Cookies

Use pattern blocks. Show all the ways to make
1 whole cookie. Have you found them all?
Are any of your designs the same?

Multiplication Picture Problems

NOTE Students practice solving multiplication problems.

SMH **40–41**

For each problem, draw a picture to represent the problem and then solve the problem.

1. $8 \times 3 =$ _____

2. $6 \times 6 =$ _____

3. $7 \times 4 =$ _____

How Many Legs?

Birds have 2 legs.
Dogs have 4 legs.
Ladybugs have 6 legs.

NOTE Students solve multiplication and division problems in story problem contexts.

SMH **40–41, 48**

1. There are 48 legs and they all belong to dogs. How many dogs are there?

2. There are 48 legs and they all belong to ladybugs. How many ladybugs are there?

3. There are 3 ladybugs, 7 dogs, and 11 birds in the house. How many legs are there altogether?

Smallest to Largest ✏️

For each set of rectangles below, label the shaded part as a fraction of the rectangle. Then write the fractions in order from smallest to largest.

NOTE Students practice putting unit fractions in order from smallest to largest.

SMH 58–59

Set 1

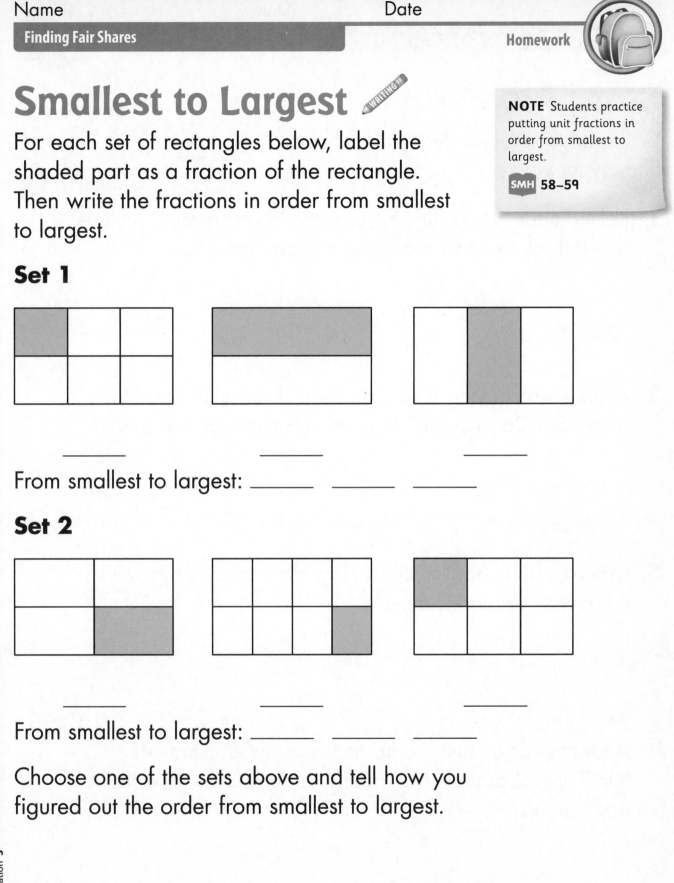

_____   _____   _____

From smallest to largest: _____ _____ _____

Set 2

_____   _____   _____

From smallest to largest: _____ _____ _____

Choose one of the sets above and tell how you figured out the order from smallest to largest.

Story Problems

Write an equation. Solve each problem.
Show your work.

NOTE Students use division to solve story problems.

SMH 39, 47

1. Kelley made 81 muffins for a party. She can put 9 muffins on each plate. How many plates does she need?

2. A store was having a sale on shirts. Each shirt cost $9. Jung has $36 to spend. How many shirts can she buy?

3. Cameron runs 8 miles every day. How many days will it take him to run 72 miles?

4. A teacher at a music camp needs to put 63 students into 7 equal groups. How many students should be in each group?

Many Ways to Make a Share

Think of sharing brownies or hexagon cookies.
Write all the fractions you know that work.

1. Ways to make 1 whole	**2.** Ways to make $\frac{1}{3}$
3. Ways to make $\frac{1}{4}$	**4.** Ways to make $\frac{1}{2}$
5. Ways to make $\frac{3}{4}$	**6.** Ways to make $\frac{2}{3}$
7. Challenge: Ways to make $\frac{5}{6}$	**8. Challenge:** Ways to make $\frac{5}{8}$

Fractions of a Group

Solve these problems and show
your solutions.

NOTE Students solve problems
about sharing objects equally.

SMH 56, 60

1. How much is $\frac{3}{5}$ of $10?

2. There are 12 computers in the lab. $\frac{3}{4}$ are being
used by students. How many computers are
available for others to use?

3. I have 6 erasers and gave $\frac{1}{3}$ to my friend. How
many erasers did I give her?

Ongoing Review

4. Oscar had 9 pencils and gave $\frac{1}{3}$ to his sister.
How many pencils did he have left?

A. 2   **B.** 3   **C.** 5   **D.** 6

Triangle Paper

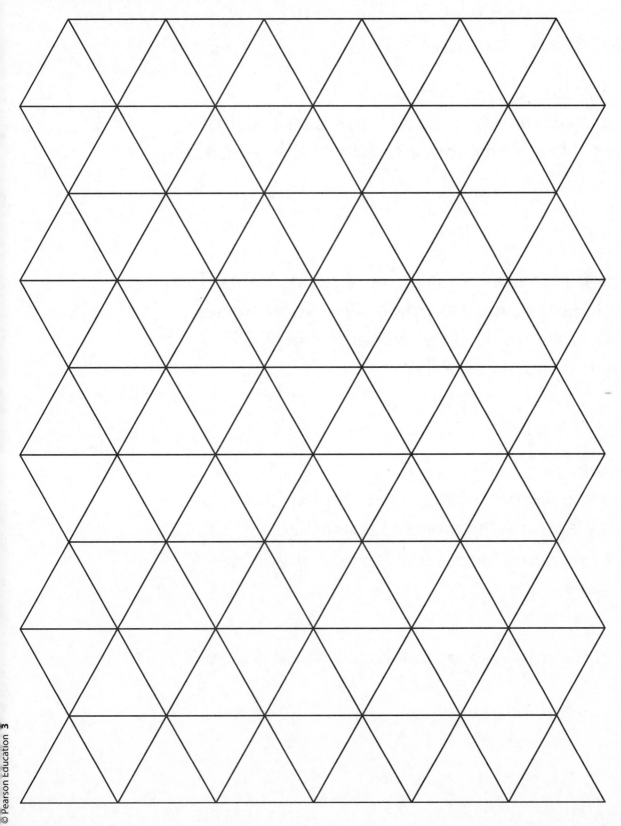

Feeding Animals

Solve the following story problems and be sure to show your work.

NOTE Students practice solving multiplication and division problems in story problem contexts.

SMH 40–41, 48

1. At one stable, horses are fed carrot sticks each morning. Each horse eats 6 carrot sticks. How many carrot sticks will 4 horses eat?

2. Horses also like to eat apple slices as treats. The stable keeper has 48 apple slices for 4 horses. How many apple slices will each horse get if they are shared equally?

3. Fuzzy is the pet rabbit in Ms. Tham's classroom. Fuzzy eats 3 lettuce leaves each day.

a. How many leaves will Fuzzy eat in 6 days?

b. How many leaves will Fuzzy eat in 9 days?

Equal Shares

Answer each question below, and show how you figured it out.

NOTE Students use what they have been learning about fractions as equal parts to answer questions about making equal shares.

SMH 57

1. How can 4 people share this corn bread equally? What would each person's share be?

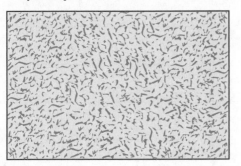

2. How can 5 people share this corn bread equally? What would each person's share be?

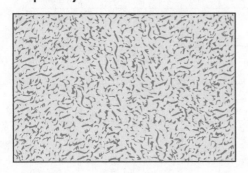

3. How can 10 people share this corn bread equally? What would each person's share be?

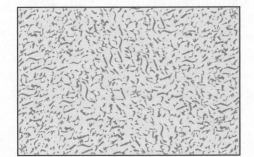

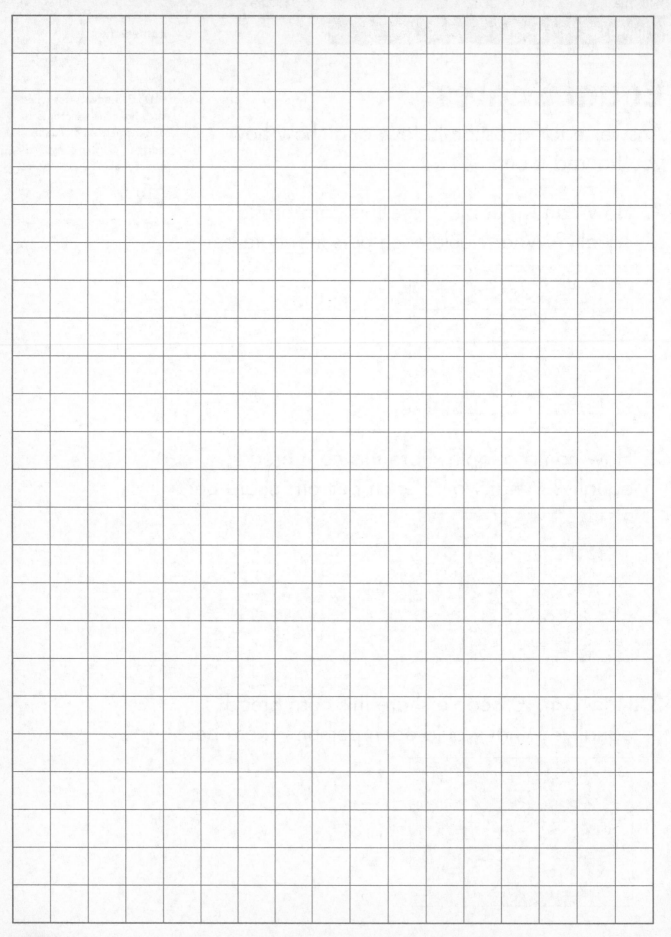

Other Things to Share

How would you share each of the following? Make equal shares if possible. If equal shares are not possible, decide what you would do. Show your thinking for each.

1. 9 brownies shared among 4 people

2. 9 balloons shared among 4 people

3. 9 dollars shared among 4 people

4. Solve this problem on a calculator: 9 ÷ 4

Sharing Dollars

Solve the following problems. Show how you solved each.

1. Suppose that 4 friends share $1.00 equally. How much money will each one get?

2. How much would each person get if 4 friends shared $2.00 equally?

3. How much would each person get if 8 people shared $2.00 equally?

4. How much would each person get if 4 people shared $5.00 equally?

Missing Factors

Fill in the missing factors in these problems.

NOTE Students practice multiplication combinations ("facts") in related sets.

1.

$6 \times \underline{\hspace{1cm}} = 24$

$6 \times \underline{\hspace{1cm}} = 36$

2.

$5 \times \underline{\hspace{1cm}} = 35$

$5 \times \underline{\hspace{1cm}} = 45$

3.

$\underline{\hspace{1cm}} \times 12 = 36$

$\underline{\hspace{1cm}} \times 12 = 48$

4.

$9 \times \underline{\hspace{1cm}} = 27$

$9 \times \underline{\hspace{1cm}} = 36$

5.

$\underline{\hspace{1cm}} \times 7 = 21$

$\underline{\hspace{1cm}} \times 7 = 42$

6.

$3 \times \underline{\hspace{1cm}} = 24$

$3 \times \underline{\hspace{1cm}} = 30$

7.

$\underline{\hspace{1cm}} \times 8 = 32$

$\underline{\hspace{1cm}} \times 8 = 40$

$\underline{\hspace{1cm}} \times 8 = 48$

8.

$3 \times \underline{\hspace{1cm}} = 9$

$5 \times \underline{\hspace{1cm}} = 25$

$7 \times \underline{\hspace{1cm}} = 49$

9.

$\underline{\hspace{1cm}} \times 4 = 28$

$\underline{\hspace{1cm}} \times 4 = 36$

$\underline{\hspace{1cm}} \times 4 = 44$

Many Ways to Make a Whole

NOTE Students practice naming fractions and combining them to make one whole.

SMH 58–59, 64

For each hexagon below, write the name of the fraction on each piece. Then write an equation to show what fractions make the whole.

1.

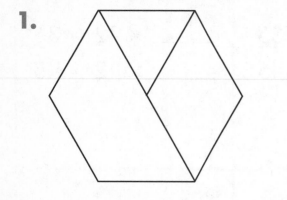

Equation: _____

2.

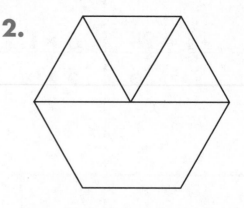

Equation: _____

3.

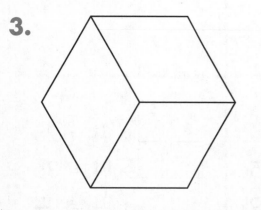

Equation: _____

Finding Fair Shares

Sharing With and Without a Calculator (page 1 of 2)

Solve each of the problems below. First solve the problem without using a calculator and show how you figured it out. Then solve it with a calculator.

1. When 2 people share $3.00 equally, what is each person's share?

One person's share: _____

Calculator answer: _____

2. When 4 people share $3.00 equally, what is each person's share?

One person's share: _____

Calculator answer: _____

Sharing With and Without a Calculator (page 2 of 2)

3. When 8 people share $6.00 equally, what is each person's share?

One person's share: _____
Calculator answer: _____

4. When 2 people share 5 brownies equally, what is each person's share?

One person's share: _____
Calculator answer: _____

My Own Sharing Problems ✏️WRITING

1. Make up a problem about equal shares so that each person gets one half of something. Show the problem and the solution.

For example: If 6 people share 3 apples, each person will get $\frac{1}{2}$ of an apple.

2. Make up a problem about equal shares so that each person gets one fourth of something.

3. Make up a problem about equal shares so that each person gets three fourths of something.

Counting Around the Class

NOTE Students find the multiples of a given number and solve multiplication problems.

SMH 42

1. Ms. Jorge's class counted by 3s. The first person said 3, the second said 6, and the third said 9. How many people counted to get to 36? How do you know?

2. Mr. Snell's class counted by 8s. The first person said 8, the second said 16, and the third said 24.

a. What number did the 6th person say? How do you know?

b. What number did the 12th person say? How do you know?

3. Ms. O'Leary's class counted by 10s. The first person said 10, the second said 20, and the third said 30. There are 24 students in Ms. O'Leary's class. What number did the last person say?

Finding Fair Shares   Homework

More Equal Shares

Answer each question below, and
show how you figured it out.

NOTE Students use what they have been
learning about fractions as equal parts to
answer questions about sharing a pizza.

SMH 57

1. How can 3 people share this
pizza equally? What would each
person's share be?

2. How can 6 people share this
pizza equally? What would each
person's share be?

3. How can 12 people share this
pizza equally? What would each
person's share be?

What's the Area?

Find the area of the rectangle. Show your work.

NOTE Students find the area of rectangles.

SMH 114

1.

Area: _____ square units

Draw a picture and find the area. Show your work.

2. Kim is planting a garden. Her garden is 3 feet wide by 6 feet long. What is the area of Kim's garden?

Area: _____ square feet

NOTE Students find ways to divide a group of objects equally.

SMH 60

Different Ways to Share

Solve each problem. Draw pictures to help you explain your answer.

1. 2 people share 5 granola bars equally. How many granola bars does each person get?

2. 6 people share 8 waffles equally. How many waffles does each person get?

3. If 4 people share $2.00 equally, how much does each person get?

Ongoing Review

4. 6 people share 4 sandwiches equally. How much does each person get?

A. $\frac{1}{2}$ **B.** $\frac{1}{4}$ **C.** $\frac{2}{3}$ **D.** $\frac{3}{2}$

Turkey Sandwiches

Nick is helping his mother make
sandwiches for a school outing. He
has a loaf of bread, sliced turkey,
and cheese.

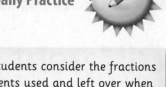

NOTE Students consider the fractions
of ingredients used and left over when
making sandwiches.

SMH 56, 57, 58–59, 60, 61–62, 63

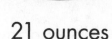

24 ounces   21 ounces   8 ounces

1. To make one sandwich, Nick uses two slices of
   bread, which equal two ounces. What fraction
   of the loaf of bread does he use to make one
   sandwich?

2. Nick will use 3 ounces of sliced turkey for each
   sandwich. What fraction of the sliced turkey will
   Nick use to make one sandwich?

3. If Nick uses 1 ounce of cheese for each
   sandwich, what fraction of the cheese will he use
   for one sandwich?

4. How many sandwiches can Nick make if he
   uses 2 slices of bread, 3 ounces of turkey, and
   1 ounce of cheese for each sandwich? What
   will he run out of first? Explain how you know.

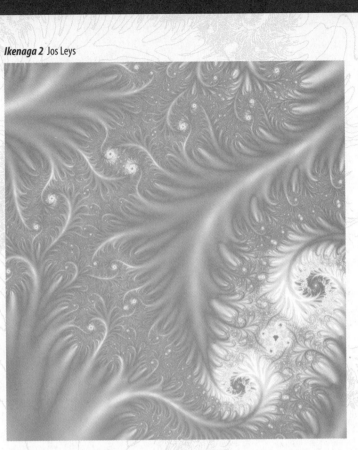

Ikenaga 2 Jos Leys

"A relatively simple formula can generate immensely complex images." – Jos Leys

Student Activity Book

How Many Hundreds? How Many Miles?

UNIT 8

Investigations

IN NUMBER, DATA, AND SPACE®

How Many Hundreds?
How Many Miles?

100 Grids

Paper Clip Problems (page 1 of 3)

Solve these problems. Show your solutions.
Remember, each box contains 100 paper clips.

1. Mrs. Lopez had 3 boxes of paper clips. How many paper clips did she have? She gave 20 clips to another teacher. How many clips does she have left?

2. a. Joel and his cousin bought 4 boxes of paper clips. How many paper clips did they have?

b. They used 45 paper clips for a school project. How many paper clips do they have now?

Paper Clip Problems (page 2 of 3)

3. Toni and her sister had 500 paper clips. They found 15 more in their mom's desk. They used 65 clips to make a chain. How many paper clips did they have left?

4. a. There were 200 paper clips on the shelf in Mr. Vega's classroom. He bought 5 more boxes and put them on the shelf. How many clips were on the shelf then?

b. Later, Mr. Vega took 28 clips. How many paper clips are left on the shelf?

Paper Clip Problems (page 3 of 3)

5. a. There were 11 boxes of paper clips in the third-grade closet. The students from Ms. River's class used 53 clips. The students from Ms. Washington's class used one whole box. How many paper clips were left in the closet?

b. Later, the students in Mr. Chang's class used 47 paper clips. How many clips are in the closet now? How many boxes are left?

6. a. Heather's mother is an artist. She bought 800 paper clips and used 39 clips to make a wire sculpture. How many paper clips were left?

b. Later, Heather's mother used 71 more clips for her sculpture. Now how many clips are left?

Identifying and Naming Fractions 1

Name the fraction or a mixed number for the shaded part.

NOTE Students identify and name fractions of rectangles.

SMH 58–59, 61–62

1.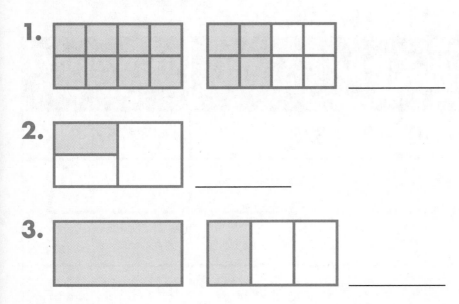

_____

2.

_____

3.

_____

Shade in the fraction or mixed number on the rectangles.

4. $\frac{3}{6}$

5. $2\frac{2}{3}$

Capture from 300 to 600 Recording Sheet

As an equation, record your starting number, the Plus and Minus Cards you used, and your ending number for each move. Then, find how many spaces you moved in all.

Equation	How many spaces?
Example: $316 + 50 + 10 - 3 = 373$	57
1.	
2.	
3.	
4.	
5.	
6.	
7.	
8.	
9.	
10.	

Boxes of Crayons

Solve these problems. Show your solutions.
Each box of crayons contains 100 crayons.

> **NOTE** Students solve problems that involve combining and then subtracting from groups of 100.
>
> **SMH** 20–24, 32–35

1. **a.** The art teacher had 400 crayons in his classroom. He bought 3 more boxes. How many crayons does he have?

   b. At the end of the day, 34 crayons were broken. How many whole crayons does the art teacher have left?

2. Emily and Marshall each have 2 boxes of crayons. Emily gave 58 crayons to her younger sister.

   a. How many crayons does Emily have left?

   b. How many crayons does Marshall have?

   c. How many crayons do they have all together?

Ongoing Review

3. Which expression is less than 400?

   A. 400 + 20 − 5   **C.** 550 − 200 + 80

   B. 420 − 30 + 5   **D.** 200 + 100 + 150

Practicing with Multiplication Cards (page 1 of 2)

NOTE Students practice multiplication combinations they do not know. Ask your child to explain how the clues help.

SMH 49–51

1. Look at each Multiplication Card.

2. Say the answer to the problem as quickly as you can. If you get the answer right away, put the card in a pile of combinations that you "just know" and set this pile aside. Otherwise, put the card in a pile of combinations that you are still "working on."

3. For each card in your "working on" pile, think of an easy multiplication combination that you already know to help you remember this one. Write it on the line that says "Start with _____."

   Example: "For 6×7, I know that $7 \times 7 = 49$, so it must be one 7 less—that's 42."

   6×7
   7×6
   Start with: $7 \times 7 = 49$

4. Go through all of the cards in your "working on" pile at least 3 times, using your "start with" combinations to help you find the answers.

5. Keep practicing until you have no more cards in your "working on" pile. Practice at school and at home with a family member.

© Pearson Education 3

Practicing with Multiplication Cards (page 2 of 2)

1. Which multiplication combinations are you practicing?

2. Write two multiplication combinations that are hard for you, and explain what helps you remember them.

Multiplication combination: _____

What helps me:

Multiplication combination: _____

What helps me:

3. How did you practice your multiplication combinations? Who helped you?

Name _____   Date _____

How Many Hundreds? How Many Miles?   **Daily Practice**

More Story Problems

Write an equation. Solve the problem.
Show your work.

NOTE Students solve story problems.

SMH 39

1. a. Kim is packing cookies into bags. She packs 8 cookies into each of 8 bags. How many cookies does she pack?

b. What if Kim wanted to fill 9 bags with 9 cookies each? How many cookies would she need?

2. Mr. Reid's class was counting around the class by 80s. What number did the 7th person say?

3. It is 13 weeks until Keith's birthday. How many days is it until Keith's birthday? (Remember, a week is 7 days.)

Related Subtraction Problems

As you work on these problems, think about how they are related and how some of the problems help you solve others.

Set 1 $100 - 90 = $ _____ $300 - 90 = $ _____ $330 - 90 = $ _____ $430 - 90 = $ _____	**Set 2** $100 - 93 = $ _____ $300 - 93 = $ _____ $500 - 93 = $ _____ $520 - 93 = $ _____
Set 3 $\begin{array}{cccc} 200 & 300 & 500 & 500 \\ -150 & -150 & -150 & -250 \end{array}$	**Set 4** $100 - 85 = $ _____ $115 - 85 = $ _____ $215 - 85 = $ _____ $215 - 185 = $ _____
Set 5 $\begin{array}{cccc} 300 & 300 & 500 & 540 \\ -\ 75 & -175 & -175 & -175 \end{array}$	**Set 6** $200 - 60 = $ _____ $300 - 60 = $ _____ $200 - 55 = $ _____ $300 - 55 = $ _____

Choose one problem set. On another sheet of paper, explain how you used each problem in the set to solve the next problem.

Identifying and Naming Fractions 2

NOTE Students identify and show fractions.

SMH 58–59, 61–62

Name the fraction or a mixed number for the shaded part.

1. 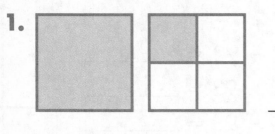 _____

2. 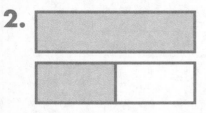 _____

Draw a diagram to show each fraction.

3. $\frac{2}{3}$

4. $\frac{2}{2}$

5. $\frac{3}{2}$

How Many Students?

For each problem, write an equation, solve the problem, and show your solution.

NOTE Students practice solving addition and subtraction problems in story contexts.

SMH 20–24, 32–35

1. South City School has 427 girls and 353 boys. How many students does the school have altogether?

2. Riverside School had 517 students last year. This year, 60 students moved away before school started. How many students does the school have now?

3. Westburg School has 284 students altogether. There are 136 girls. How many boys are there in the school?

4. Ocean View School had 641 students last year. This year, there are 168 more students. How many students does the school have now?

More Related Subtraction Problems

Solve the first problem in each set and show your solution. Then solve the next two problems to see how some problems help you solve others.

Set 1

First solve:

93 − 67 = _____

Now solve these:

193 − 67 = _____

293 − 67 = _____

Set 2

First solve:

84 − 28 = _____

Now solve these:

184 − 28 = _____

384 − 28 = _____

Set 3

First solve: 126
               − 65

Now solve these:

226   226
− 65   −165

Set 4

First solve: 130
               − 75

Now solve these:

330   330
− 75   −175

More Paper Clip Problems

Solve these problems. Show your solutions.
Remember, each box contains 100 paper clips.

1. There were 6 boxes of paper clips in the office
of Springdale School. On Monday, the secretary
used 62 paper clips. How many clips were left?

2. Ms. Valentine had 900 paper clips. Her students
used 262 clips to make a display for Family
Math Night. How many paper clips were left?

3. a. There were 15 boxes of paper clips in the
Rosewood Company supply room. On
Monday, someone took 35 paper clips from
one box. How many paper clips were left in
the supply room?

b. On Tuesday, someone took 25 more clips
from that box. How many paper clips were in
the supply room then?

Making Estimates

First, estimate the answer to each problem.
Then, solve the problem and show your solution.
Each box of crayons contains 100 crayons.

> **NOTE** Students first estimate and then solve addition and subtraction problems.
>
> **SMH** 20–24, 32–35

1. Jordan had 4 boxes of crayons. He gave 67 crayons to Erika. How many crayons does he have left?

Estimate: _____

Solution:

2. Rachel has 173 crayons. Her mother gives her a new box and she finds 18 more in her desk drawer. How many crayons does Rachel have?

Estimate: _____

Solution:

3. There were 517 crayons in a bucket. Laura took 69 crayons home. How many crayons were left in the bucket?

Estimate: _____

Solution:

Ongoing Review

4. What is the greatest number of dimes you need to make $4.72?

A. 7   **B.** 40   **C.** 47   **D.** 72

Many Ways to Make a Whole

In the shapes below, identify each piece with a fraction. Then write an equation to show what fractions make the whole.

NOTE Students identify fractions that add up to one.

SMH 64

Example.

Equation: $\dfrac{1}{2} + \dfrac{1}{2} = 1$

Try it.

1.

Equation: _____ = 1

2.

Equation: _____ = 1

3.

Equation: _____ = 1

Subtraction Practice

Solve these problems. Show your solutions.
You may draw a number line to help explain
your thinking.

NOTE Students practice
solving subtraction problems
with 2- and 3-digit numbers.

SMH 32–35

1. $\begin{array}{r} 370 \\ -\ 91 \\ \hline \end{array}$

2. $277 - 62 =$ _____

3. $456 - 228 =$ _____

4. $346 - 297 =$ _____

Name   Date

How Many Hundreds? How Many Miles?   **Daily Practice**

More Comparing Fractions

NOTE Students label fractions on a number line and compare fractions.

SMH 56

1. Fill in the missing fractions on the number line.

Write $>$, $<$, or $=$ in each box to compare the fractions.

2. $\frac{2}{6} \square \frac{2}{6}$

3. $\frac{5}{6} \square \frac{1}{3}$

4. $\frac{1}{6} \square \frac{2}{3}$

5. $\frac{3}{3} \square \frac{6}{6}$

6. $\frac{0}{3} \square \frac{4}{6}$

7. $\frac{2}{6} \square \frac{1}{3}$

Name _____ Date _____

How Many Hundreds? How Many Miles?   Daily Practice

Practice with Related Subtraction Problems 1

NOTE Students continue to practice solving related subtraction problems.

SMH 32–35

As you work, think about how the problems in each set are related and how some of the problems help you solve others.

Set 1

100 − 35 = _____

200 − 35 = _____

380 − 35 = _____

380 − 135 = _____

Set 2

100 − 67 = _____

300 − 67 = _____

600 − 67 = _____

640 − 67 = _____

Set 3

$$\begin{array}{cccc} 500 & 600 & 700 & 750 \\ -215 & -215 & -215 & -215 \\ \hline \end{array}$$

Set 4

100 − 95 = _____

300 − 95 = _____

500 − 95 = _____

583 − 95 = _____

Ongoing Review

443 − 20 + 100 − 15 = _____

A. 415   **B.** 418   **C.** 508   **D.** 515

Addition Starter Problems (page 1 of 3)

In each set, solve all three starter problems.
Then solve the final problem. Show your solution.
Use one of the starter problems to help you.

Set 1

$100 + 600 = $ _____ $150 + 650 = $ _____ $152 + 600 = $ _____

Final problem: **$152 + 683 = $** _____

Show your solution.

Set 2

$400 + 200 = $ _____ $429 + 200 = $ _____ $430 + 200 = $ _____

Final problem: **$429 + 266 = $** _____

Show your solution.

Addition Starter Problems (page 2 of 3)

In each set, solve all three starter problems.
Then solve the final problem. Show your solution.
Use one of the starter problems to help you.

Set 3

$30 + 90 =$ _____ $835 + 100 =$ _____ $97 + 3 =$ _____

Final problem: $835 + 97 =$ _____

Show your solution.

Set 4

$700 + 346 =$ _____ $700 + 300 =$ _____ $709 + 340 =$ _____

Final problem: $709 + 346 =$ _____

Show your solution.

Addition Starter Problems (page 3 of 3)

In each set, solve all three starter problems.
Then solve the final problem. Show your solution.
Use one of the starter problems to help you.

Set 5

500 + 300 = _____   584 + 300 = _____   378 + 2 = _____

Final problem: **584 + 378** = _____

Show your solution.

Set 6

600 + 400 = _____   630 + 470 = _____   488 + 12 = _____

Final problem: **636 + 488** = _____

Show your solution.

More Ways to Make a Whole

In the shapes below, identify each piece with a fraction. Then write an equation to show what fractions make the whole.

NOTE Students continue to identify fractions that add up to one.

SMH 64

Example.

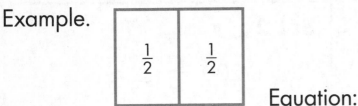

Equation: $\dfrac{1}{2} + \dfrac{1}{2} = 1$

Try it.

1.

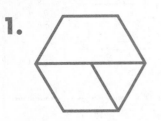

Equation: _____ = 1

2.

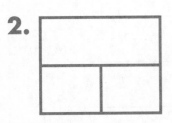

Equation: _____ = 1

3.

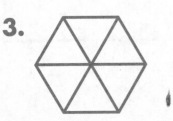

Equation: _____ = 1

Addition and Subtraction: Related Problems 1

As you work, think about how the problems in each set are related and how some of the problems help you solve others.

NOTE Students use what they know from solving one problem to help them solve related addition and subtraction problems.

SMH 20–24, 32–35

Set 1	Set 2
250 − 60 = _____	130 + 200 = _____
250 − 65 = _____	130 + 190 = _____
250 − 67 = _____	130 + 180 = _____
255 − 67 = _____	132 + 180 = _____

Set 3

$$\begin{array}{cccc} 70 & 170 & 370 & 370 \\ +90 & +\ 90 & +\ 90 & +290 \end{array}$$

Set 4

420 − 20 = _____

415 − 20 = _____

415 − 120 = _____

415 − 220 = _____

Solving Addition Problems (page 1 of 2)

Solve each problem and show your solution.
For each story problem, solve the problem and
write an equation to go with it.

1. 425 + 288 = _____

2. 623
      +249
      _____

3. Ms. Shaw had 5 boxes of paper clips in her
   classroom closet and another 74 clips on
   her desk. She bought 3 more boxes and found
   28 more clips in her desk drawer. How many
   paper clips does she have now?

Solving Addition Problems (page 2 of 2)

Solve each problem and show your solution. For each story problem, solve the problem and write an equation to go with it.

4. 758
     + 76
     ————

5. 930 + 377 = _____

6. Hannah and her sister both collect pennies. Hannah has 561 pennies and her sister has 459 pennies. If they put all their pennies together, how many will they have? How much is that in dollars and cents?

Name _____   Date _____

How Many Hundreds? How Many Miles?   Daily Practice

NOTE Students solve a variety of possible "first steps" before solving a final addition problem.

SMH 20–24

More Addition Starter Problems

In each set, solve all three starter problems. Then solve the final problem. Show your solution. Use one of the starter problems to help you.

Set 1

$200 + 500 =$ _____ $233 + 500 =$ _____ $595 + 5 =$ _____

Final problem: $233 + 595 =$ _____

Show your solution.

Set 2

$200 + 700 =$ _____ $280 + 700 =$ _____ $286 + 700 =$ _____

Final problem: $286 + 707 =$ _____

Show your solution.

Ongoing Review

If you have 1,005 bottle caps, how many piles of 100 could you have?

A. 100   **B.** 10   **C.** 5   **D.** 1

Adding More Than Two Numbers (page 1 of 2)

For each problem, first estimate about how many hundreds the answer will have. Then solve the problem and show your solution.

1. 343 + 487 + 55 = _____

About how many hundreds? _____

Solution:

2. 145 + 628 + 37 = _____

About how many hundreds? _____

Solution:

3. 245 + 386 + 465 = _____

About how many hundreds? _____

Solution:

Adding More Than Two Numbers (page 2 of 2)

For each problem, first estimate about how many hundreds the answer will have. Then solve the problem and show your solution.

4. 801 + 27 + 446 = _____

About how many hundreds? _____

Solution:

5. 78 + 296 + 813 = _____

About how many hundreds? _____

Solution:

6. 190 + 791 + 359 = _____

About how many hundreds? _____

Solution:

More Addition Problems

Solve each problem and show your solution.

1. 451 + 546 = _____	**2.** 316 + 490 = _____
3. 298 + 548 = _____	**4.** 135 + 821 = _____
5. 276 + 765 = _____	**6.** 386 + 331 = _____
7. 502 + 799 = _____	**8.** 738 + 834 = _____

Combining Collections: How Many Altogether?

Choose three matches you made in *Collections Match*. Make addition problems about combining the two collections in each match. Solve each problem and show your solution.

1. Category of collections: _____

   Problem: _____ + _____ = _____

2. Category of collections: _____

   Problem: _____ + _____ = _____

3. Category of collections: _____

   Problem: _____ + _____ = _____

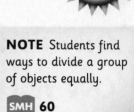

How Can We Share?

Solve each problem. Draw pictures to help you explain your answer.

NOTE Students find ways to divide a group of objects equally.

SMH 60

1. How can 6 people share 8 hot dogs?

2. How can 5 people share 10 pencils?

3. How can 6 people share $3.00?

4. How can 6 people share 3 granola bars?

Ongoing Review

5. Which expression is more than 1,000?

A. 833 + 150

C. 556 + 424

B. 899 + 119

D. 378 + 602

Two Ways to Solve a Problem

Solve each problem in two ways, using each of the first steps below. Show your solutions.

NOTE Students develop efficiency and flexibility in their computation skills by solving addition problems in more than one way.

SMH 20–24

---

1. 378 + 381 =

Start by solving 378 + 300.	Start by solving 300 + 300.

---

2. 566 + 284 =

Start by solving 500 + 200.	Start by solving 284 + 16.

Name   Date

How Many Hundreds? How Many Miles?   Daily Practice

What's the Area?

NOTE Students find the area of rectangles.

SMH 114

1. Use the dimensions given to find the area of the rectangle.

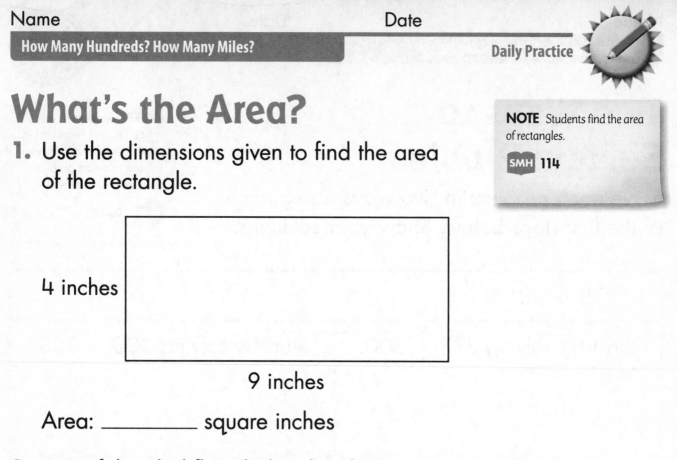

4 inches

9 inches

Area: _____ square inches

2. Part of the tiled floor below has been covered with a rug. Determine how many tiles are in the entire rectangle and explain how you found your answer.

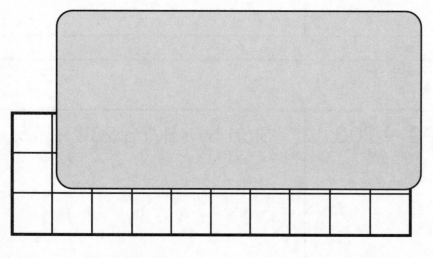

 _____ tiles

Name _____   Date _____

How Many Hundreds? How Many Miles?   Daily Practice

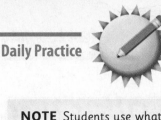

Addition and Subtraction: Related Problems 2

> **NOTE** Students use what they know from solving one problem to help them solve related addition and subtraction problems.
>
> **SMH** 20–24, 32–35

1. Solve each set of related problems.

Set 1	**Set 2**
400 + 200 = _____	500 − 50 = _____
401 + 201 = _____	500 − 60 = _____
399 + 198 = _____	500 − 62 = _____

Set 3

$$
\begin{array}{r} 300 \\ 300 \\ +300 \\ \hline \end{array}
\qquad
\begin{array}{r} 298 \\ 297 \\ +301 \\ \hline \end{array}
\qquad
\begin{array}{r} 310 \\ 290 \\ +295 \\ \hline \end{array}
$$

Set 4

$$
\begin{array}{r} 1{,}000 \\ -\ \ 50 \\ \hline \end{array}
\qquad
\begin{array}{r} 900 \\ -\ 50 \\ \hline \end{array}
\qquad
\begin{array}{r} 702 \\ -\ 50 \\ \hline \end{array}
$$

2. Pick one problem set. Explain how you used some of the problems in the set to solve others.

_____

_____

_____

_____

Collections Compare Recording Sheet

Three times during the game, stop and record the numbers listed on both of your cards and on both of your partner's cards. Find the sum of both pairs of cards. Show your solutions. Then answer the questions about who has more and how many more.

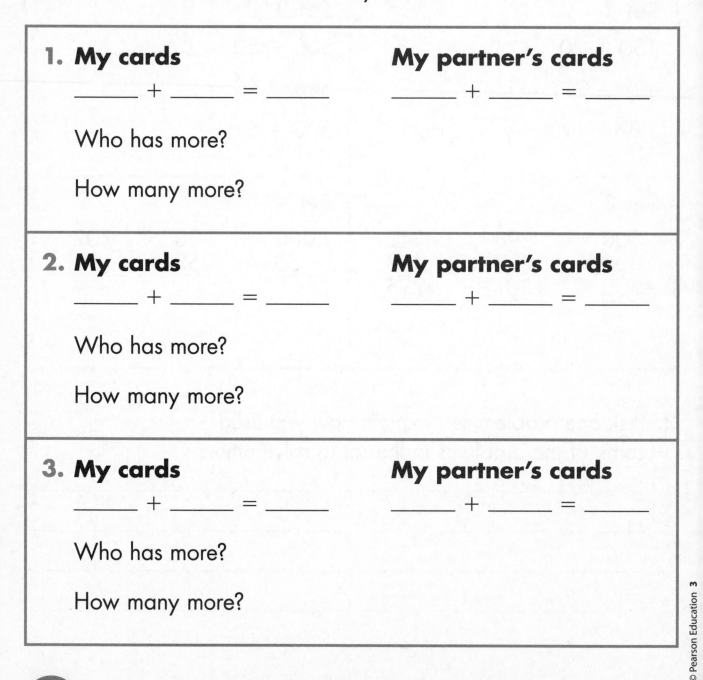

1. My cards

_____ + _____ = _____

Who has more?

How many more?

My partner's cards

_____ + _____ = _____

2. My cards

_____ + _____ = _____

Who has more?

How many more?

My partner's cards

_____ + _____ = _____

3. My cards

_____ + _____ = _____

Who has more?

How many more?

My partner's cards

_____ + _____ = _____

Fraction Story Problems

Solve these problems and show your solutions.

NOTE Students practice finding fractions of a group.

SMH 60

1. What is $\frac{1}{2}$ of 22 bananas?

2. I was given $\frac{2}{3}$ of $21.00. How many dollars did I get?

3. There are 12 empty juice bottles. You drank 8 bottles of juice. I drank the rest. What fraction did I drink?

Ongoing Review

4. What is $\frac{3}{4}$ of 24?

   A. 20   **B.** 18   **C.** 16   **D.** 12

Addition Practice

Solve each problem and show your solution.

NOTE Students practice solving addition problems with 3-digit numbers.

SMH 20–24

1. 447 + 328 = _____

2. 251 + 779 = _____

3. 388 + 344 = _____

4. 623 + 459 = _____

The Oregon Trail (page 1 of 2)

Solve these problems about a journey by covered wagon. Use this map to help you. Show your solutions for each problem.

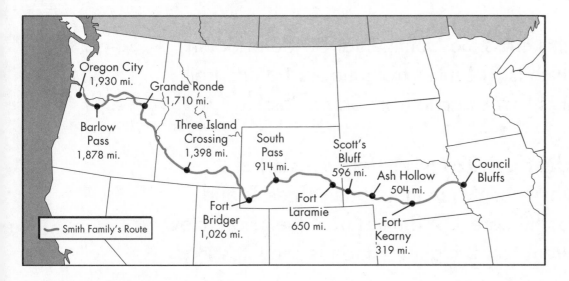

1. It's 1847, and the Smith family sets out from Council Bluffs, Iowa. In the first two weeks, they travel 319 miles to Fort Kearny. At the end of the first month, they cross the Platte River at Ash Hollow. They have traveled 504 miles since their trip began. How far did they travel from Fort Kearny to Ash Hollow?

2. After leaving Ash Hollow, the Smiths arrive at Scott's Bluff. They rest for several days. Scott's Bluff is 596 miles from the start of the trail. How far did they travel from Ash Hollow to Scott's Bluff?

The Oregon Trail (page 2 of 2)

3. When the family arrives at Fort Laramie, they are 650 miles from the start of the trail. How far did they travel from Scott's Bluff to Fort Laramie?

4. The Smiths cross the Continental Divide at South Pass, which is 914 miles from the start of the trail. How far is Fort Laramie from South Pass?

5. Fort Bridger is 1,026 miles from the start of the Smiths' trip. When they reach Three Island Crossing, they are 1,398 miles from their start. How far is it from Fort Bridger to Three Island Crossing?

6. Before reaching Barlow Pass, the family rests at Grande Ronde. They are 1,710 miles from the beginning of the trail. How far did they travel from Three Island Crossing to Grande Ronde?

7. At Barlow Pass, the Smiths' horses are tired. They have walked 1,878 miles on this trip! How far is it from Grande Ronde to Barlow Pass?

8. Finally, the Smiths arrive in Oregon City. They have traveled 1,930 miles altogether. How many miles was the last leg of their journey, from the Barlow Pass to Oregon City?

Name _____   Date _____

How Many Hundreds? How Many Miles?   Daily Practice

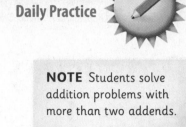

Practice with Adding More Than Two Numbers

NOTE Students solve addition problems with more than two addends.

SMH 25

For each problem, first estimate about how many hundreds the answer will have. Then solve the problem and show your solution.

1. $312 + 588 + 375 =$ _____

About how many hundreds? _____

Solution:

2. $667 + 385 + 298 =$ _____

About how many hundreds? _____

Solution:

3. $79 + 385 + 412 =$ _____

About how many hundreds? _____

Solution:

Ongoing Review

4. Which expression is more than 1,000?

A. $358 + 512 + 98$ **C.** $668 + 55 + 459$

B. $299 + 510 + 127$ **D.** $125 + 225 + 450$

Practicing Subtraction Facts 1

NOTE Students are reviewing the subtraction "facts." Ask your child to explain how the clues help with these subtraction problems.

 31

1. Which subtraction facts are you practicing?

2. Write two subtraction facts that are hard for you, and explain what helps you remember them.

Subtraction fact: _____

What helps me:

Subtraction fact: _____

What helps me:

3. How did you practice your subtraction facts? Who helped you?

Write and Solve a Subtraction Problem 1 ✏️WRITING

1. Write a story problem to go with this problem.

$352 - 168 =$ _____

2. Solve the problem and show your solution.

Name _____ Date _____

How Many Hundreds? How Many Miles?   **Daily Practice**

More Fraction Story Problems

NOTE Students practice finding fractional parts of a whole.

SMH **56, 58–59**

Solve these problems and show your solutions.

1. One pizza has 8 slices. Deanna ate 2 slices. What fraction of the pizza did she eat?

2. What is $\frac{1}{3}$ of $6.00?

3. There are 6 cups of milk in the pitcher. Carlo drinks 2 cups of the milk. What fraction of the milk is left in the pitcher?

Ongoing Review

4. Which expression is less than 1,000?

   A. 378 + 612   **C.** 668 + 445

   B. 505 + 515   **D.** 499 + 599

Practicing Subtraction Facts 2

NOTE Students are still reviewing the subtraction "facts." Ask your child to explain how the clues help with these subtraction problems.

SMH 31

1. Which subtraction facts are you practicing?

2. Write two subtraction facts that are hard for you, and explain what helps you remember them.

Subtraction fact: _____
What helps me:

Subtraction fact: _____
What helps me:

3. How did you practice your subtraction facts? Who helped you?

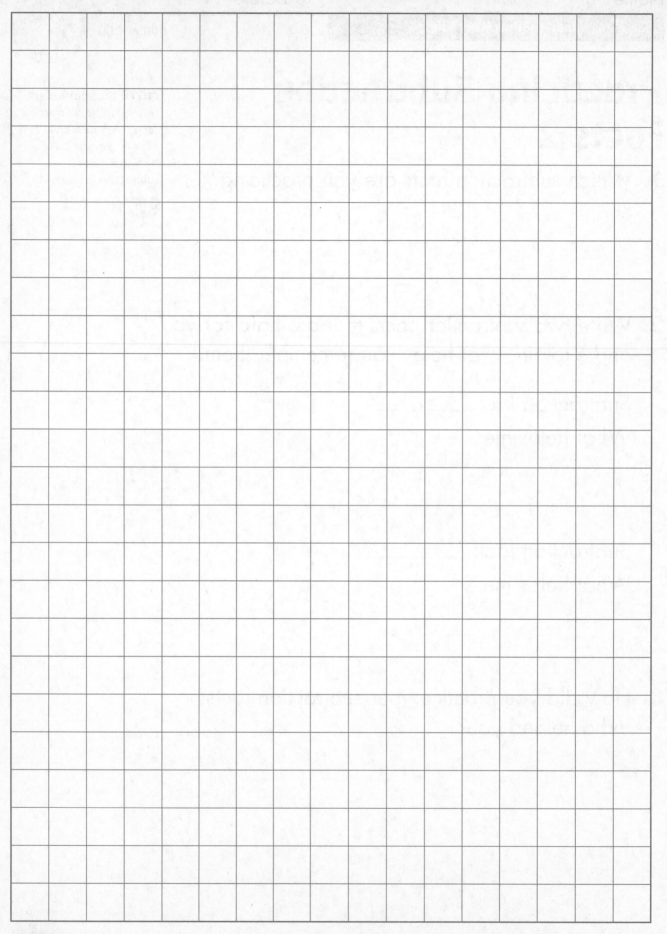

How Much Change? (page 1 of 2)

Answer these questions. You may use play money to help you.

1. At the grocery store, you spend $1.49.

   a. How much change will you get if you pay with two one-dollar bills ($2.00)? _____

   b. How much change will you get if you pay with a five-dollar bill ($5.00)? _____

   c. How much change will you get if you pay with a ten-dollar bill ($10.00)? _____

2. At the trading card store, you spend $3.78.

   a. How much change will you get if you pay with four one-dollar bills ($4.00)? _____

   b. How much change will you get if you pay with a five-dollar bill ($5.00)? _____

   c. How much change will you get if you pay with a ten-dollar bill ($10.00)? _____

How Much Change? (page 2 of 2)

3. At the snack bar, you spend $4.25.

a. How much change will you get if you pay
with a five-dollar bill ($5.00)? _____

b. How much change will you get if you pay
with a ten-dollar bill ($10.00)? _____

c. How much change will you get if you pay
with a twenty-dollar bill ($20.00)? _____

Earning and Spending

Solve these problems. Show your solutions.

1. Marisa earned $7.75 babysitting for her cousin. She spent $5.98 on a birthday present for her best friend. How much money did she have left?

2. Josh earned $8.10 collecting and returning bottles for recycling. He spent $2.85 at the arcade. How much money did he have left?

3. Zhang earned $6.25 walking the dog for his neighbors. He spent $4.27 on a new comic book. How much money did he have left?

4. Julia earned $9.50 doing chores for her grandfather. She spent $6.90 at the movies. How much money did she have left?

Write and Solve a Subtraction Problem 2

NOTE Students write a subtraction story problem and find the solution.

SMH 26–28, 32–35

1. Write a story problem to go with this problem.

426 − 238 = _____

2. Solve the problem and show your solution.

Ongoing Review

3. 500 − 301 = _____

A. 298   **B.** 201   **C.** 198   **D.** 199

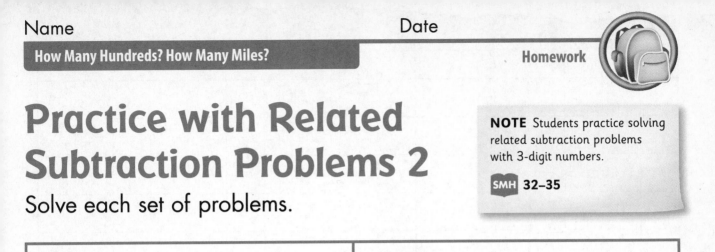

Practice with Related Subtraction Problems 2

NOTE Students practice solving related subtraction problems with 3-digit numbers.

SMH 32–35

Solve each set of problems.

Set 1

300 − 75 = _____

300 − 175 = _____

300 − 178 = _____

Set 2

600 − 350 = _____

605 − 350 = _____

615 − 350 = _____

Set 3

800 − 600 = _____

820 − 600 = _____

820 − 610 = _____

Set 4

516 − 200 = _____

516 − 210 = _____

516 − 220 = _____

54 Unit 8

Name _____   Date _____

How Many Hundreds? How Many Miles?   **Daily Practice**

Sharing Money

Solve the following problems and
show your solutions.

> **NOTE** Students solve problems that
> involve sharing money. They practice
> writing decimals in each answer.
>
> **SMH** 48, 65

1. Four friends sold lemonade and made
   $5.00. If they share the money equally,
   how much does each friend receive?

2. Five friends sold lemonade and made $6.00. If
   they share the money equally, how much does
   each friend receive?

3. Six friends sold lemonade and made $3.00. If
   they share the money equally, how much does
   each friend receive?

Ongoing Review

4. Jenna spends $1.79 at the store. How much
   change does she get from a 5-dollar bill?

   A. $3.12   **B.** $3.21   **C.** $4.21   **D.** $4.31

Solving Subtraction Problems (page 1 of 2)

Solve each problem. Show your solutions.

1. Some of the students at Riverside School walk to school. All of the other students take the bus. There are 404 students in the school. 166 of them take the bus. How many walk to school?

2. On Monday, 339 children had the school lunch. On Tuesday, 252 children had the school lunch. How many more children had the school lunch on Monday than on Tuesday?

3. The Ortiz family traveled to the Washington Zoo, which is 264 miles away from their home. When they stopped for lunch, they had gone 117 miles. How many more miles did they have to travel after lunch?

4. The Asian History Museum had 324 Japanese stamps. They sold all the samurai stamps to a collector. Now the museum has 291 stamps in its collection. How many stamps did the museum sell?

Solving Subtraction Problems (page 2 of 2)

Solve each problem. Show your solutions.

5. 436 − 219 = _____

6. 315 − 288 = _____

7. 527 − 174 = _____

8. 764 − 248 = _____

Coupon Savings

These coupons are from
a newspaper ad.

NOTE Students find combinations of
numbers that equal given amounts.

SMH 25

1. Find and list coupons with savings that
add up to $3.00.

2. Find and list three coupons with savings
that add up to $1.50.

3. Will the savings on cereal, yogurt, and eggs
be more or less than $2.00? Explain.

Ongoing Review

4. Which expression equals 159?

A. 10 + 58 + 100

C. 200 − 41

B. 118 + 30 + 1

D. 250 − 100 − 50

© Pearson Education 3

Problems About Money

Solve these problems. Show your solutions.

NOTE Students practice solving addition and subtraction problems in the context of money.

SMH **20–24, 32–35**

1. Eve had $4.75 in her piggy bank. She earned $2.50 babysitting. How much money does Eve have now?

2. $3.28 + $7.46 = _____

3. Marcus had $5.98 in his wallet. He bought a notebook for $2.68. How much money does Marcus have now?

4. $6.00 − $1.49 = _____

Book Orders (page 1 of 2)

Title	Price	Title	Price
Monster Jokes	$1.99	Silly Kid Jokes	$3.42
10 Projects with Wood	$1.73	10 Projects with Paper	$2.54
Mystery of Owl Island	$2.50	Mystery of the Silver Wolf	$3.35
Going West	$4.28	About America	$4.46
Time Machine	$3.15	Upside-Down Town	$4.25

If you have $10.00, which books can you buy?
Find combinations of at least three different books
that cost close to $10.00 in all. Then find how much
money you have left. Write equations to show your
solutions.

Book Order 1 List titles and prices.

_____ _____

_____ _____

How much did you spend? _____ How much is left? _____
Equations:

Book Order 2 List titles and prices.

_____ _____

_____ _____

How much did you spend? _____ How much is left? _____
Equations:

Book Orders (page 2 of 2)

Title	Price	Title	Price
Monster Jokes	$1.99	Silly Kid Jokes	$3.42
10 Projects with Wood	$1.73	10 Projects with Paper	$2.54
Mystery of Owl Island	$2.50	Mystery of the Silver Wolf	$3.35
Going West	$4.28	About America	$4.46
Time Machine	$3.15	Upside-Down Town	$4.25

Find other combinations of at least three different books that cost close to $10.00 in all. For one order, find a combination of at least four books.

Book Order 3   List titles and prices.

_____   _____

_____   _____

How much did you spend? _____   How much is left? _____
Equations:

Book Order 4   List titles and prices.

_____   _____

_____   _____

How much did you spend? _____   How much is left? _____
Equations:

Two-Step Money Problems (page 1 of 2)

Solve these problems. Show your solutions.

1. Lakesha had $4.75 in her piggy bank. She spent $3.29 on a present for her sister. Then she earned $2.00 sweeping the front steps for a neighbor. How much money does Lakesha have now?

2. Greg had $8.15 in his wallet. He spent $5.87 on a sandwich. Then his friend paid him back $7.50 that he owed him. How much money does Greg have now?

Two-Step Money Problems (page 2 of 2)

3. Mike earned $12.20 babysitting. He went to the card store and spent $6.49. Then he went to the science store and spent $4.80. How much money does Mike have now?

4. Cammy had $9.36 that she saved in pennies. She earned $6.40 doing chores for her grandfather. Then she spent $8.68 on a new book. How much money does Cammy have now?

Name _____ Date _____

How Many Hundreds? How Many Miles?   Daily Practice

Who Gets More?

NOTE Students solve two sharing problems and compare the answers.

SMH 60

1. Today the students in Mr. Wong's room have blueberry muffins to share. Each group gets 8 muffins to share equally.

Group A: 6 students share 8 muffins.

Group B: 5 students share 8 muffins.

Which students get the larger share, Group A or Group B?

Tell how you decided. Use words and drawings to help you explain.

Ongoing Review

2. Four people each get $1\frac{1}{4}$ sandwiches. How many sandwiches are there in all?

A. 4   **B.** 5   **C.** 6   **D.** 8

How Many Altogether?

NOTE Students make estimates and then solve addition problems with more than two addends.

SMH 20–24, 25

1. How many students altogether go to these three schools?

Elm Street School 567 students	Valley School 275 students	Oak Park School 404 students

About how many hundreds in all? Estimate. _____

How did you decide on your estimate?

_____

_____

Add the numbers to find the exact total. _____

2. How much money will Sophie spend for these school supplies?

Notebook $2.99	Pen $1.79	Markers $3.95

About how many dollars in all? Estimate. _____

How did you decide on your estimate?

_____

_____

Add the numbers to find the exact total. _____

Count Your Change

Complete this chart.

NOTE Students solve subtraction problems in the context of money.

SMH **32–35**

Item Bought	Cost of Item	Amount Given to Clerk	Amount of Change
1. Ruler	$0.47	$1.00	
2. Sandwich	$3.18	$5.00	
3. Seeds	$1.55		$0.45
4. Socks	$2.74		$2.26
5. Shampoo		$1.00	$0.11
6. Taffy apple		$5.00	$4.10
7. Stickers	$1.16	$10.00	
8. Magazine		$10.00	$6.35

Ongoing Review

9. How much greater is 147 than 85?

A. 43   **B.** 51   **C.** 53   **D.** 62

Plan a Meal (page 1 of 2)

Doctors say you should eat meat or beans, grains, fruits, and vegetables, and drink milk every day. It is suggested that a third grader eat between 600 and 800 calories for dinner.

NOTE Students solve real-world problems involving the math content of this unit.

SMH 20–24

Grains | Vegetables | Fruits | Sweets | Milk | Meat & Beans

Food	Calories	Food	Calories
Peanut butter and jelly sandwich	440	Small salad with dressing	166
Grilled cheese sandwich	436	Green beans	20
Hamburger with bun	275	Peas	55
Slice of cheese pizza	290	Corn on the cob	123
Taco	210	Broccoli	27
1 orange or apple	85	Tomato soup	161
1 banana	109	Vegetable soup	145
Apple juice	120	Low-fat milk	122

Plan a Meal (page 2 of 2)

1. Use the food chart to plan a meal. Try to make the total number of calories as close to 800 as you can.

   a. Write an equation to show the total calories.

   b. How close to 800 calories did you get?

2. Plan a different meal with close to 800 calories.

   a. Write an equation to show the total calories.

   b. How close to 800 calories did you get?

Ikenaga 2 Jos Leys

"A relatively simple formula can generate immensely complex images." – **Jos Leys**

Investigations
IN NUMBER, DATA, AND SPACE®

Solids and Boxes

How Much Change? (page 1 of 2)

Answer the following questions. You may use
play money to help you.

NOTE Students
solve subtraction
problems using the
context of money.

SMH 32–35

1. At the grocery store, you spend $1.79.

   a. How much is your change if you
   pay with two 1-dollar bills ($2.00)?   _____

   b. How much is your change if you
   pay with a 5-dollar bill ($5.00)?   _____

   c. How much is your change if you
   pay with a 10-dollar bill ($10.00)?   _____

2. At the trading card store, you spend $3.24.

   a. How much is your change if you
   pay with four 1-dollar bills ($4.00)?   _____

   b. How much is your change if you
   pay with a 5-dollar bill ($5.00)?   _____

   c. How much is your change if you
   pay with a 10-dollar bill ($10.00)?   _____

How Much Change? (page 2 of 2)

3. At the snack bar, you spend $4.48.

a. How much is your change if you
pay with a 5-dollar bill ($5.00)?   _____

b. How much is your change if you
pay with a 10-dollar bill ($10.00)?   _____

c. How much is your change if you
pay with a 20-dollar bill ($20.00)?   _____

Identifying Geometric Shapes in the Real World (page 1 of 3)

NOTE Students find geometric shapes around the house and in newspapers and magazines.

SMH 125–126

Geometric Shapes

Real-World Objects

cube

_____

_____

_____

_____

cylinder

_____

_____

_____

hexagonal prism

_____

_____

_____

sphere

_____

_____

_____

Identifying Geometric Shapes in the Real World (page 2 of 3)

Geometric Shapes   Real-World Objects

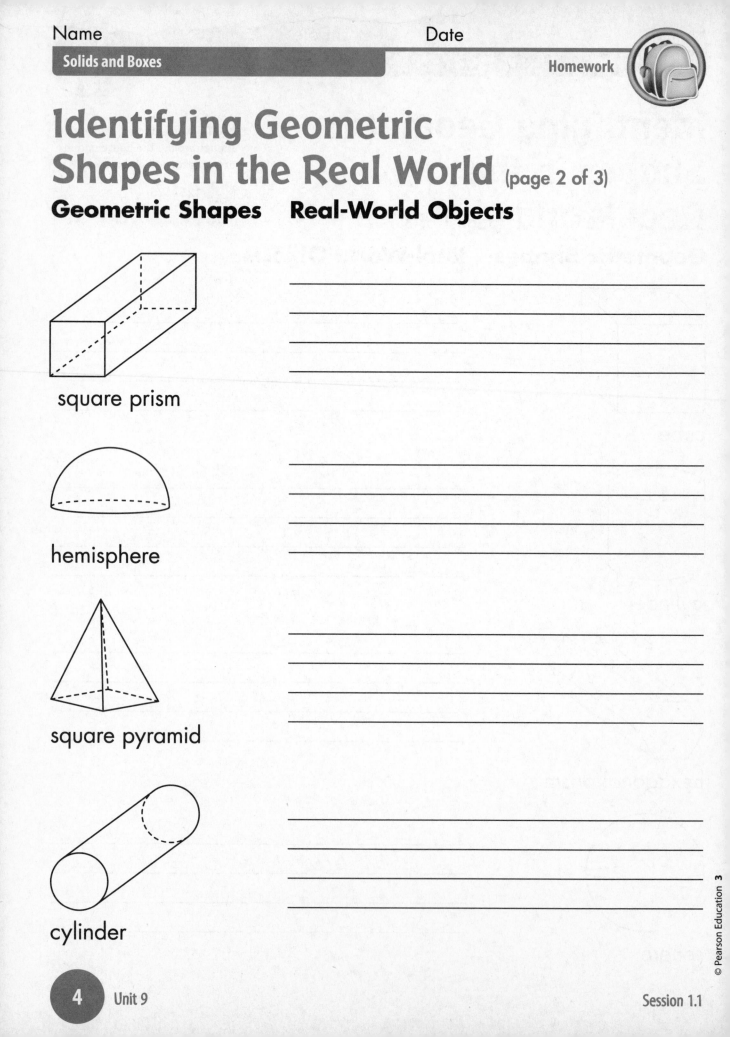

square prism

_____

_____

_____

_____

hemisphere

_____

_____

_____

_____

square pyramid

_____

_____

_____

_____

cylinder

_____

_____

_____

_____

Identifying Geometric Shapes in the Real World (page 3 of 3)

Geometric Shapes   Real-World Objects

octagonal prism

_____
_____
_____
_____

cone

_____
_____
_____
_____

triangular prism

_____
_____
_____
_____

rectangular prism

_____
_____
_____
_____

Which One Does Not Belong?

Circle the shape that does **not** belong.
Then explain how you made your choice.

NOTE Students explain which shape is different from the others.

SMH 125–126, 129–130

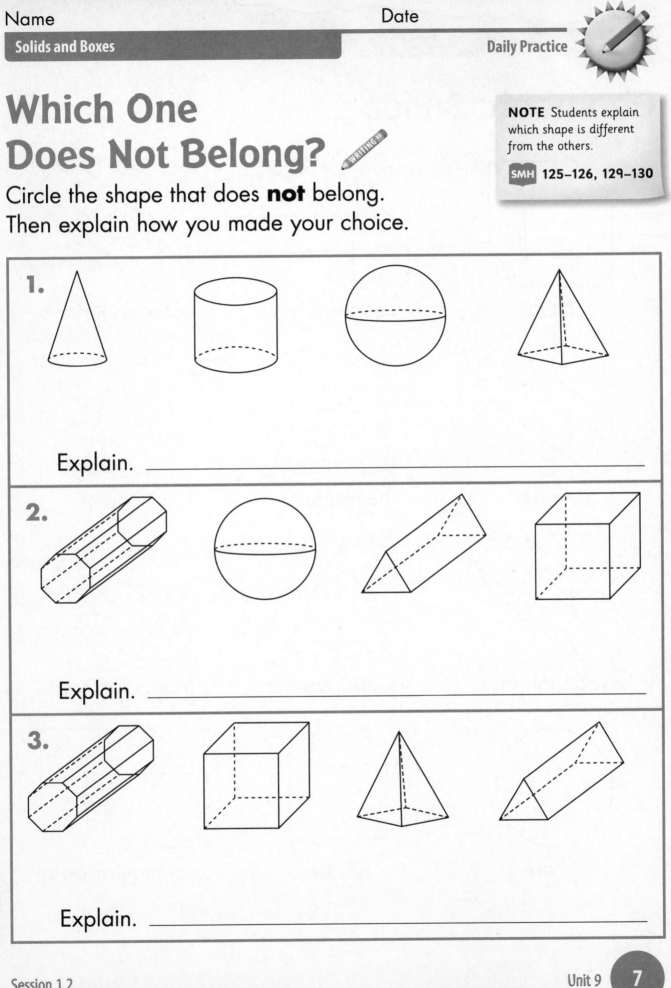

1.

Explain. _____

2.

Explain. _____

3.

Explain. _____

Geometric Solids

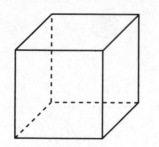
cube

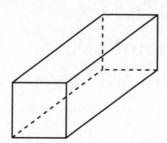
square prism

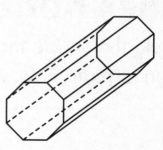
octagonal prism

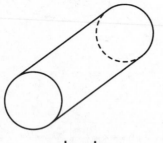
cylinder

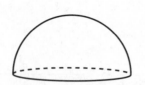
hemisphere

cone

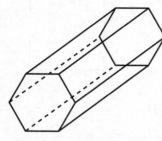
hexagonal prism

square pyramid

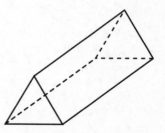
triangular prism

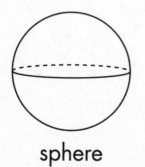
sphere

cylinder

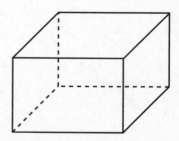
rectangular prism

Our Collections (page 1 of 2)

For each problem, write an equation that represents the problem, solve the problem, and show your solution.

NOTE Students solve addition and subtraction problems in a story problem context.

SMH 20–24, 32–35

1. Deondra collects coins. She had 385 coins in her collection. On her birthday her uncle gave her 125 more coins to add to her collection. How many coins does Deondra have now?

2. Oscar collects comic books. He has 462 superhero comic books and 394 cartoon comic books. How many comic books does he have altogether?

Our Collections (page 2 of 2)

3. Nancy collects toy cars. She had 429 in her collection. She sold 180 of them to a friend. How many toy cars does Nancy have left?

4. Adam collects flag stickers. He had 534 in his collection. He gave 172 of them away to the history teacher. How many flag stickers does Adam have left?

Solving Addition Problems

NOTE Students solve addition problems with 3-digit numbers.

SMH 20–24

Solve each problem and show your solution. For the story problem, write an equation to go with the problem.

1. 821 + 594 =

2.   419
      +784

3. The softball team hit 385 balls during batting practice on Monday, 349 balls on Wednesday, and 415 balls on Friday. How many balls did they hit during the week?

12 Unit 9

Building Polyhedra

1. Build a polyhedron that has exactly 6 square faces.

2. Build a polyhedron that has exactly 1 square face and 4 triangular faces.

3. Build a polyhedron that has exactly 3 rectangular faces and 2 triangular faces.

4. Build a polyhedron that has exactly 8 corners and 6 faces.

5. Build a polyhedron that has exactly 5 corners and 5 faces.

6. How many differently shaped polyhedra can you make that have exactly 12 edges?

Optional

Make a polyhedron that has exactly 6 edges and 4 triangular faces.

Addition Starter Problems

Solve each problem two ways, using the first steps listed below. Show your work clearly.

NOTE Students practice solving addition problems. They work on efficiency and flexibility by solving the same problem in two different ways.

SMH 20–24

1. $157 + 664 =$ _____

Start by solving 100 + 600.	Start by solving 150 + 650.

2. $719 + 384 =$ _____

Start by solving 700 + 384.	Start by solving 19 + 81.

© Pearson Education 3

Solve Two Ways

Solve this problem in two different ways. Be sure to record the equations and representations that show how you got your answer.

NOTE Students practice solving addition problems. They work on efficiency and flexibility by solving the same problem in two different ways.

SMH 20–24

674 + 395 = _____

Here is the first way I solved it:

Here is the second way I solved it:

Related Problem Sets

Solve the following sets of related problems. How would you use one problem to solve the next one?

NOTE Students solve addition and subtraction problems in related sets.

1.		
400 $-\ 75$	400 -175	400 -178

2. $400 - 200 =$ _____

$400 - 220 =$ _____

$420 - 220 =$ _____

3. $300 - 150 =$ _____

$300 - 152 =$ _____

$301 - 152 =$ _____

$302 - 153 =$ _____

4. $174 - 44 =$ _____

$174 - 144 =$ _____

$274 - 144 =$ _____

$274 - 154 =$ _____

5. $700 +$ _____ $= 1,000$

$650 +$ _____ $= 1,000$

$647 +$ _____ $= 1,000$

$644 +$ _____ $= 1,000$

6.		
300 300 $+300$	300 299 $+299$	301 299 $+300$

Addition Practice

Solve each problem and show your solution.

NOTE Students solve addition problems with 3-digit numbers.

SMH 20–24

1. 774 + _____ = 1,309

2. 197 + 934 = _____

3. 238 + 662 = _____

4. _____ + 419 = 1,005

Representing and Comparing Fractions

NOTE Students label fractions on a number line and compare fractions.

SMH 56

1. Divide the zero-to-one number line in eighths. Label each eighth.

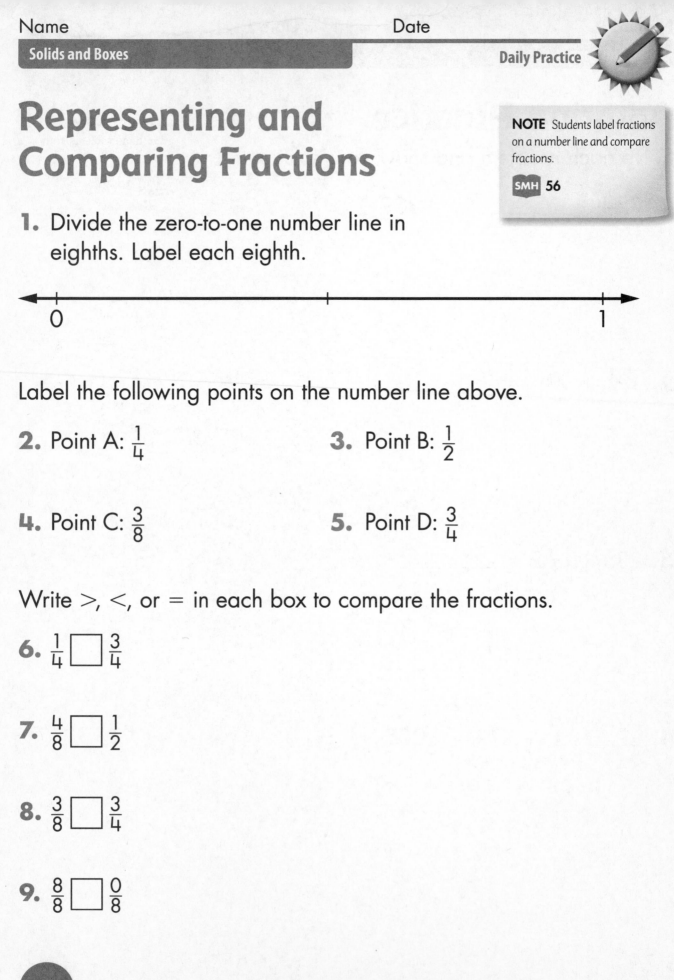

0   1

Label the following points on the number line above.

2. Point A: $\frac{1}{4}$

3. Point B: $\frac{1}{2}$

4. Point C: $\frac{3}{8}$

5. Point D: $\frac{3}{4}$

Write >, <, or = in each box to compare the fractions.

6. $\frac{1}{4}$ ☐ $\frac{3}{4}$

7. $\frac{4}{8}$ ☐ $\frac{1}{2}$

8. $\frac{3}{8}$ ☐ $\frac{3}{4}$

9. $\frac{8}{8}$ ☐ $\frac{0}{8}$

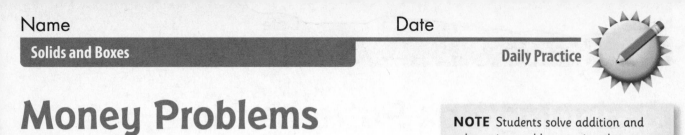

Money Problems

Solve the following problems and show your solutions.

NOTE Students solve addition and subtraction problems, using the context of money.

SMH 20–24, 32–35

1. $5.67 + $4.98 = _____

2. $7.43 + $3.87 = _____

3. $6.80 − $2.95 = _____

4. $8.25 − $5.27 = _____

Designing Box Patterns for Triangular Pyramids

Use triangle paper to make patterns for a triangular pyramid. Your pyramid can be any size.

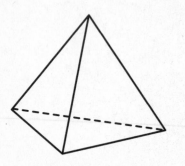

All of its sides should look like the triangle below.

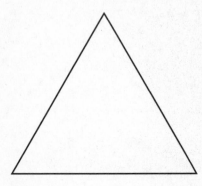

Find as many patterns as you can.

How Many Hundreds? How Many Altogether?

NOTE Students estimate and solve addition problems.

SMH 20–24, 25

Number of stamps in 3 collections	About how many altogether?	Add the numbers to find the exact total.
Adam's collection: 161 stamps Chiang's collection: 214 stamps Murphy's collection: 52 stamps	300 or 400 or 500? How did you decide?	

Cost of 3 items at the grocery store	About how many dollars altogether?	Add the numbers to find the exact total.
Juice: $1.91 Milk: $2.41 Crackers: $1.77	$4.00 or $5.00 or $6.00? How did you decide?	

Subtraction Story Problems

NOTE Students solve subtraction problems with 3-digit numbers.

SMH 32–35

Solve each problem and show your solution.

1. A medium pizza costs $9.49 and a small pizza costs $7.85. How much more is a medium pizza than a small pizza?

2. Barney had 605 postcards in his collection. He gave 136 postcards to his younger sister so that she could start her own collection. How many postcards does Barney have now?

3. Mr. Gillespie's class goal was to collect 1,350 signatures for the petition. So far the class has collected 968 signatures. How many more signatures do they need to meet their goal?

Comparing Solids

Use the solids to answer
each question.

NOTE Students compare solids by finding the
number of faces, corners, and edges of each.

SMH 127–128

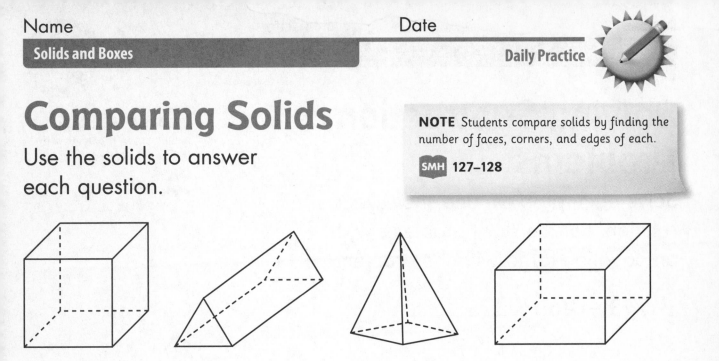

1. Which figures have exactly 6 faces?

2. Which figure has exactly 2 triangular faces?

3. Which figure has exactly 5 corners and
8 edges?

4. Look at the triangular prism. Tell how many
faces, edges, and corners it has.

Faces _____   Edges _____   Corners _____

Ongoing Review

5. Which numbers do **not** make 128?

   A. 100 + 20 + 8   **C.** 50 + 50 + 8

   B. 99 + 21 + 8   **D.** 80 + 40 + 8

Solving Subtraction Problems

NOTE Students solve subtraction problems with 3-digit numbers.

SMH 32–35

Solve each problem and show your solution. For the story problem, write an equation to go with the problem.

1. 713 − 461 = _____

2. $8.43 − $5.95 = _____

3. Pete, a western lowland gorilla, weighs 411 pounds. Nina, his mate, weighs 263 pounds. How much heavier is Pete than Nina?

Straw Structures ✏️ WRITING

Gwen built these polyhedra with straws.

NOTE Students write about shape similarities and differences.

SMH 127–128, 129–130

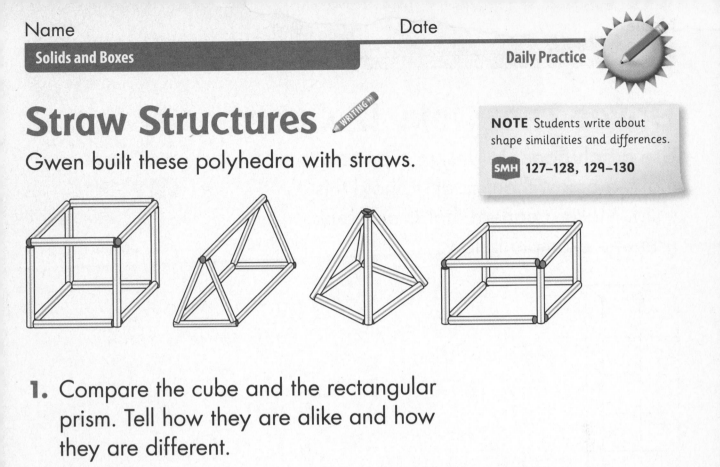

1. Compare the cube and the rectangular prism. Tell how they are alike and how they are different.

_____

_____

_____

2. Compare the triangular prism and the square pyramid. Tell how they are alike and how they are different.

_____

_____

_____

Ongoing Review

3. 25¢ + 10¢ + 5¢ + 1¢ + 1¢ = _____

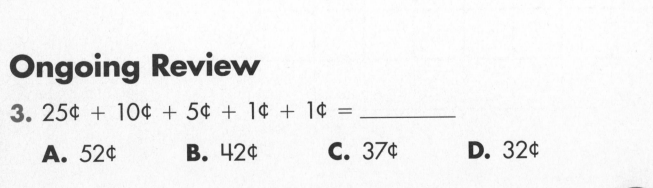

A. 52¢   **B.** 42¢   **C.** 37¢   **D.** 32¢

Boxes That Hold 12 Cubes

Use graph paper to design a pattern to make a box without a top to hold this solid. Make a pattern that is different from the example below.

NOTE Students make an open box to hold the 12-cube solid pictured below.

SMH 132–133

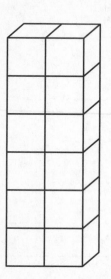

You should be able to cut out the pattern you design and fold it into a box that will hold this solid.

Here is an example:

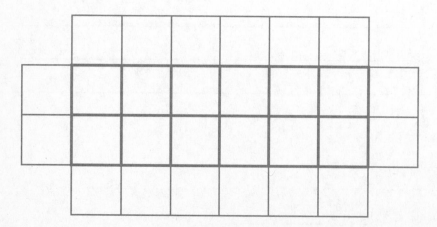

How Many More?

Solve the following problems and show your solutions on the number lines provided.

NOTE Students find the missing numbers to make correct addition equations.

SMH 20–24, 32–35

1. $612 +$ _____ $= 850$

2. $371 +$ _____ $= 795$

3. $508 +$ _____ $= 725$

4. $461 +$ _____ $= 835$

Subtraction Practice

Solve each problem and
show your solution.

NOTE Students solve
subtraction problems with
3-digit numbers.

SMH 32–35

1. 975 − 626 = _____

2. 584 − 391 = _____

3. 608 − 215 = _____

4. 535 − 265 = _____

Riddles About Boxes

Find the answers to the riddles below. Make sure that your work shows how you solved each one.

1. I am building a box that holds a 12-cube solid. The bottom layer has 4 cubes in it. How many layers will I have in my box?

2. I am building a box that has 3 layers. Each layer has 8 cubes in it. How many cubes will my box hold?

3. Elena built a box to hold 30 cubes. Her box has 5 layers. How many cubes are in each layer?

4. Oscar built a box to hold 48 cubes. Each layer holds 8 cubes. How many layers are in his box?

Box Patterns

Each of the six patterns below could be cut out and taped together to make a box without a top.

How many cubes would fit in each box?

NOTE Students use 2-dimensional drawings of box patterns to determine how many cubes each pattern will hold after it has been cut out and folded into a 3-dimensional box.

SMH 132–133

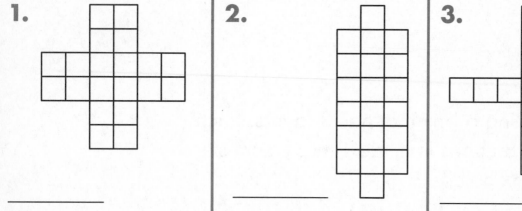

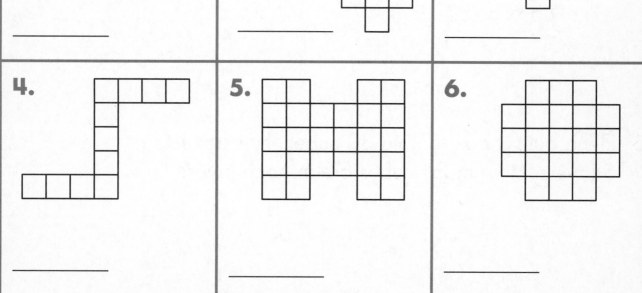

Ongoing Review

7. Which number, when combined with 49, makes 100?

A. 48   **B.** 50   **C.** 51   **D.** 61

More Riddles About Boxes

NOTE Students think about the structure of rectangular prisms while reviewing the multiplication and division work they did earlier in the year.

SMH 132–133

Find the answers to the riddles below. Make sure that your work shows how you solved each one.

1. I am building a box to hold a 24-cube solid. My box will be 4 layers high. How many cubes will be in each layer? Explain how you know.

2. Gil built a box to hold a 32-cube solid. There are 8 cubes in each layer. How many layers does his box contain? Explain how you got your answer.

3. I am building a box that has 4 layers. Each layer has 12 cubes in it. How many cubes will my box hold?

More Area and Perimeter

NOTE Students find the area and perimeter of rectangles.

SMH 110–111, 114–115

1. Each rectangle has an area of 36 square units. Find the perimeter of each rectangle.

Perimeter: _____ units   Perimeter: _____ units

2. Each rectangle has a perimeter of 24 units. Find the area of each rectangle.

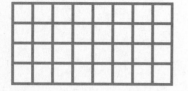

Area: _____ square units   Area: _____ square units

2 and 3 Dimensions (page 1 of 2)

NOTE Students visualize and compare 2-dimensional and 3-dimensional objects.

SMH 125–126, 127–128

A globe and a map are both representations of the world. How are they different?

If you wrap a map around the globe, will it fit? Explain your thinking.

2 and 3 Dimensions (page 2 of 2)

Here is a different 2-dimensional representation of the world globe. If you wrap this map around the globe, will it fit? Explain your thinking.

Can you think of another 2-dimensional representation of the world globe? Draw it here.

Units for Measuring Liquid Volume

Write whether you would use liters or milliliters to measure each object.

1. Fish tank

2. Juice box

_____

_____

Circle the measurement that is more likely.

3. Drinking glass

250 milliliters or 250 liters

4. Bathtub

115 milliliters or 115 liters

5. Pot of soup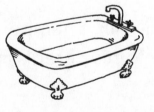

6 milliliters or 6 liters

6. Teaspoon

5 milliliters or 5 liters

Story Problems About Liquid Volume

Solve each problem. Show your work. Be sure to include the units in your answer.

1. A juice carton has 600 milliliters of juice in it. Philip poured 250 milliliters of juice into a glass. How much juice is left in the carton?

2. One morning, a gas station sold 590 liters of regular gas and 370 liters of super gas. How much gas did the gas station sell that morning?

3. Dwayne drank 200 milliliters of milk. Then he poured 150 milliliters of milk onto his cereal. How much milk did Dwayne use?

4. A water tank had 180 liters of water in it. After it rained overnight, there were 205 liters of water in it. How much water was added to the tank?

NOTE Students choose
appropriate units of liquid volume.

Liquid Volume

Write whether you would use liters or milliliters
to measure each object.

1. Ladle

2. Pail

3. Washer

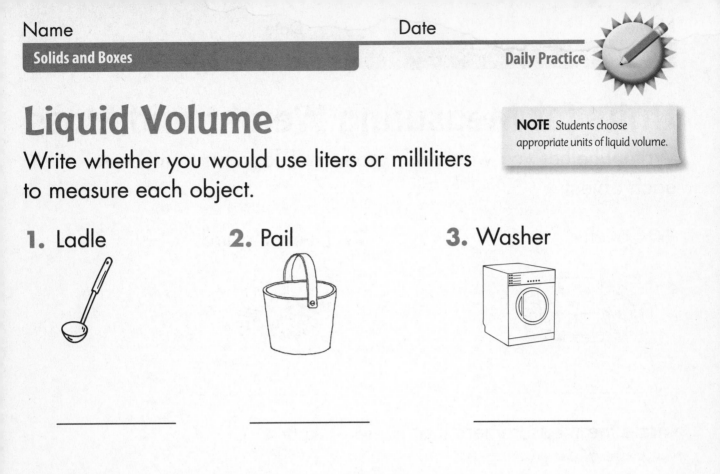

_____   _____   _____

Circle the measurement that is more likely.

4. Milk jug

4 milliliters or 4 liters

5. Eye dropper

5 milliliters or 5 liters

6. Wading pool

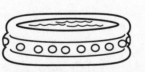

120 milliliters or 120 liters

Units for Measuring Weight and Mass

Write whether you would use grams or kilograms to measure each object.

1. Couch

2. Hummingbird

_____

_____

Circle the measurement that is more likely.

3. Glasses

60 grams or 6 kilograms

4. Watermelon

800 grams or 8 kilograms

5. Bag of oranges

20 grams or 2 kilograms

6. Apple

180 grams or 18 kilograms

Story Problems About Weight and Mass

Solve each problem. Show your work. Be sure to include the units in your answer.

1. Chiang used 250 grams of flour to make waffles. Later, she used 130 grams of flour to make muffins. How much flour did she use?

2. Kenji had a 25-kilogram box of blue tiles and a 15-kilogram box of gray tiles. How many kilograms of tiles did he have?

3. Murphy had 500 grams of peanuts. He ate 150 grams of the peanuts. How much does he have left?

4. A grocer is putting 15 kilograms of onions into 5 bags. If each bag weighs the same, how much does 1 bag weigh?

Weight and Mass

Write whether you would use grams or kilograms to measure each object.

NOTE Students choose appropriate measurement units.

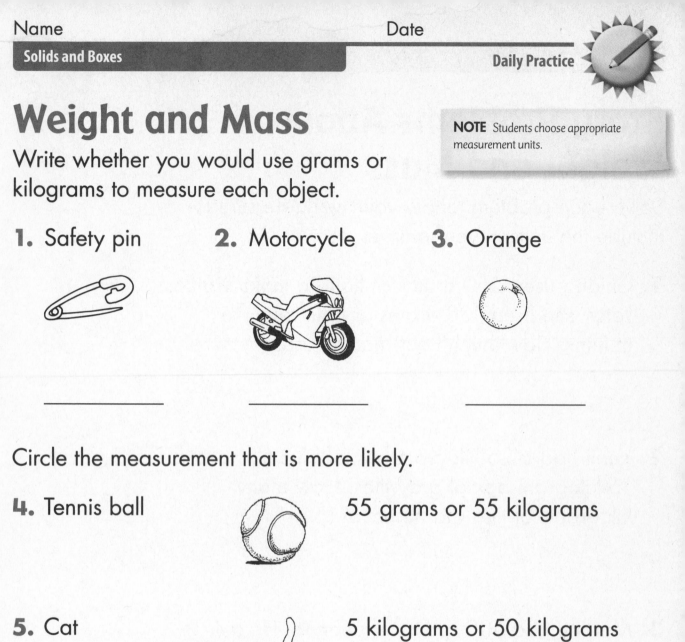

1. Safety pin

2. Motorcycle

3. Orange

_____   _____   _____

Circle the measurement that is more likely.

4. Tennis ball   55 grams or 55 kilograms

5. Cat   5 kilograms or 50 kilograms

6. Bunch of grapes      1 gram or 1 kilogram

Measurement Story Problems

Solve each problem. Show your work. Be sure to
include the units in your answer.

1. Bridget bought 2 cans of soup. Each can
was marked 305 grams. How many grams of
soup did she buy?

2. A baby elephant weighed 130 kilograms at the
start of May. At the end of May, it weighed
182 kilograms. How many kilograms did the
elephant gain during May?

3. Kim bought 950 milliliters of orange juice and
600 milliliters of pineapple juice. How many
milliliters of juice did she buy?

4. A bakery had 4 bins of flour. There were
6 kilograms of flour in each bin. How much
flour did the bakery have?

Liquid Volume and Weight and Mass

Write the volume of liquid in each measuring cylinder shown.

NOTE Students find the liquid volume of measuring cylinders and choose appropriate units of liquid volume and weight and mass.

1.

100 mL
90
80
70
60
50
40
30
20
10
0

_____

2.

100 mL
90
80
70
60
50
40
30
20
10
0

_____

Tell what unit of liquid volume you would use to measure the liquid in each container. Write *milliliter* or *liter*.

3. Pitcher

_____

4. Cup

_____

Tell what unit of weight and mass you would use to measure each object. Write *gram* or *kilogram*.

5. Feather

_____

6. Car

_____